ALCO VIOLENCE, FEASTS AND FAIRS:

LEISURE PURSUITS IN BRUTON, SOMERSETSHIRE c.1500-c1900.

P. W. Randell

Pen Press

First published in Great Britain

All paper used in the printing of this book has been made from wood grown in managed, sustainable forests.

ISBN13: 978-1-78003-343-3

Printed and bound in the UK
Pen Press is an imprint of
Indepenpress Publishing Limited
25 Eastern Place
Brighton
BN2 1GJ

A catalogue record of this book is available from the British Library

Cover design by Jacqueline Abromeit

Contents

Books by the same Author:

Stones We Cannot Eat: Poverty, the Poor Law, Philanthropy and Self Help in Bruton, Somerset, c1500-c1900.
Pen Press, 2009.

Life in a Rural Workhouse: Wincanton Workhouse, Somerset, 1834-1900.
Pen Press. 2010.

Crime, Law and Order in a Somersetshire Market Town: Bruton, c1500-c1900.
Pen Press, 2011.

Introduction.

It is truly amazing how much the rural world changed in the four hundred years covered by this book. Customs, traditions and leisure pursuits which were already centuries old by 1500 either disappeared or were significantly altered, frequently by the Victorian middle class. A desire for refinement, gentility and a pronounced work ethic sounded the death knell of activities which had helped to sustain the mass of the ordinary people through the trials and tribulations of their precarious existence.

In order to set the scene at the end of the medieval world the first chapter examines the occasions and festivities which punctuated the rural calendar. All were associated with either the Christian Church or the natural agricultural year. A few, such as Christmas and Easter, are still with us but the majority of the days highlighted no longer have the same significance.

These celebrations involved all members of the community, no matter what their social rank. Bruton was in fact very fortunate, as the second chapter demonstrates, that various factors required to exploit and develop these activities were present: the Church, landed families, a large agricultural base, some industrial employment and, in the Victorian period, a strong middle class.

Within Bruton itself there were four major influences which brought all members of the community together: the Church, both as an institution and also as a physical presence, fairs, feasts, and markets. These are explored in chapter three and it soon becomes clear that while the Church tended to be formal, apart from Church ales, the other three were all treated as significant festive occasions to be enjoyed by all the population. Here they socialized, traded, gossiped, ate and drank, the last two sometimes to excess.

While these were the occasions which brought all the population of Bruton together, it is clear that even by 1500 there were differences in attitude. The remaining chapters therefore examine the leisure pursuits of the various classes and the way in which they gradually, although not necessarily intentionally, moved apart. By the end of the eighteenth century the wealthy were aiming for greater refinement in their lives and as such abandoned their support or patronage for many of the traditional, more violent rural pastimes, hunting excepted of course.

The Victorian middle class as well as emulating their social superiors, had their own pronounced views on what constituted appropriate entertainment. They certainly appear to have dominated Bruton and it is possibly very unfortunate that they believed that everyone else of a lower social status should adhere to their values and ideas as well. In imposing these values, aided by a strong Non-Conformist element in the town, they changed the traditional violent, alcohol-dominated popular culture out of all recognition.

While many of the activities in previous centuries may seem barbaric and alien to the present day, it is important to stress that they must be viewed in the context of their time and not from the perspective of a later period.

The use of leisure time and the type of entertainment available in Bruton in 1900 was radically different from that of four hundred years before. A way of life had been transformed and much of it lost forever.

1. Setting the Scene: General.

In the countryside throughout the medieval period and beyond, two elements came together to create and maintain the festive year: one was the natural agricultural cycle and the other the customs and celebrations of the Christian Church, at first Roman Catholic and later Protestant. All levels in society were involved in the festivities which surrounded these events, but they were particularly welcomed by the great mass of the labouring population. For them everyday life was hard, unrelenting toil, punctuated by periodic famine and illnesses which they did not understand. For most of them life was uncertain and hazardous with few chances to plan for the future and therefore they embraced anything which relieved their burden with marked enthusiasm. As one historian has commented, "hence experience or opportunity is grabbed as occasion arises, with little thought of the consequences."

It is in fact remarkable just how many significant festivals there were throughout the year, even leaving aside the fact that in the Catholic calendar virtually every day was a particular saint's day. On the other hand, some of the celebrations were very localized and therefore not all the labouring population experienced them. In addition the same activities did not occur in all the villages and market towns that celebrated a particular festival. As Bruton was dominated by a monastery for some four hundred years, it is a reasonable assumption that Catholic festivities played a major role in everyday life, even though practically no specific evidence has survived.

Midwinter had traditionally been a time for feasting amongst the wealthy after four weeks of fasting from Advent Sunday and in some areas labourers were freed from working upon the lord of the manor's estate on the twelve days of Christmas. In return tenants were required to bring a gift to their lord, usually in the form of produce and a Survey of Bruton in 1669 revealed that Lord Fitzharding could expect at least fifty-four capons at Christmas, and one more on New Year's Day. Increasingly, however, local landowners and other wealthier members of the community started to feed the poor and make other gestures at this time of the year, although at this earlier period Christmas Day itself was not a public holiday. One Tudor poet, Thomas Tusser, expressed the sentiment:

Good husband and housewife, now chiefly be glad
Things handsome to have, as they ought to be had,
They both do provide against Christmas do come,
To welcome their neighbour, good cheer to have some
Good bread and good drink, a good fire in the hall,
Brawn pudding and souse, and good mustard withal.
Beef, mutton, and pork, shred pies of the best,
Pig, veal, goose, and capon, and turkey well dressed;
Cheese, apples, and nuts, jolly carols to hear,
As then in the country is counted good cheer.

This celebration became a tradition which continued throughout the eighteenth and nineteenth centuries, for example, in 1770 Revd. James Woodforde of Ansford recorded in his Diary that he had some poor parishioners to dinner on December 27th as usual and gave each of them 1s and a 6d loaf of bread. Feasting also occurred on 1st January and on Twelfth Night, 6th January, the latter after a church service. Entertainment could be provided for the wealthy at Christmastide, for example, the Accounts of the Ilchester family at Redlynch record that they gave 2s   6d on several occasions when they were in residence and visited by the Bruton Singers in the 1740s and 1750s. On 2nd January 1769 Revd. Woodforde noted that, "We had the fine Mummers this evening at Parsonage", and that on 27th December 1771 he gave the Ansford Mummers 1s. One of the commonest stories which the mummers performed centred on the legend of St. George and the dragon but invariably ended with appeals for money.

> Ladies and gentlemen,
> Our story is ended,
> Our money-box is recommended;
> Five or six shilling will not do us harm,
> Silver or copper, or gold if you can.

It was also customary to decorate the Church with greenery on Christmas Eve and for many candles to be lit then and on Christmas Day. Some areas also staged processions which could include a Lord of Misrule, and a wassail cup was taken from house to house to offer a drink and in return make a donation to parochial finances. The same seems to have been the purpose of groups which appeared in some parts of Somerset and Devon called Hogglers or Hognells but there is no evidence for their existence in Bruton.

The agricultural year traditionally started on the first Monday after Twelfth Night, usually called Plough Monday and this was often treated as a holiday for farm labourers, with various activities occurring, such as dragging a plough through the streets to raise money. Although pasture and meadowland dominated the Bruton area about 20% of the land was used for arable purposes in the late eighteenth century and so considerable labour was invested in ploughing there and hence some celebration was possible. It often went unrecorded as it was just taken for granted.

February 2nd was celebrated as Candlemas, the day of the Purification of the Virgin Mary and the recognition of Christ as the Messiah by

Simeon. Traditionally this day marked the end of winter and the day before was marked with a fast with just bread and water and so on the day itself there was a service in the parish church with many candles, followed by a communal feast.

For many communities Shrovetide was more important, a time to eat up all food such as meat, eggs and cheese before the fast of Lent. It seems to have developed as a time for misbehaviour, especially for the young and apprentices before the sombre days which were to come. Some areas staged huge football matches with dozens involved or cock-throwing but while there is no evidence for these in Bruton some disorder did occur and the period remained a constant problem for the Constable and tithingmen. For the Church it was a very solemn occasion, reminding the people of their mortality and sin. On Ash Wednesday a priest blessed ashes, sometimes derived from burning the dried palm leaves from Palm Sunday of the previous year to indicate continuity, sprinkled them with holy water and placed them on the heads of the people while reciting in Latin, "Remember, O Man, that thou art dust and to dust thou shalt return." At the same time for the Lenten period the rood and the images and statues of the saints, of which there were many in Bruton Church, were covered up so that the congregation would not be comforted for their sins.

Eastertide, and the build-up to it, was another time for celebration. Palm Sunday, the week before Easter Day, saw one of the longest church services of the year which included processions and the rood cloth drawn aside to reveal once again the image of Christ. Maundy Thursday, the Feast of the Last Supper, witnessed not only altars unveiled and washed but was the day when the King, bishops, abbots and priors washed the feet of the poor, presumably a function performed in Bruton. On Good Friday more services occurred with particular attention to the Easter Sepulchre and it is possible that the recess in the south wall of the chancel in Bruton Church originally contained one of these. Easter Day had more services and was the end of the fast of Lent. Traditionally it was the time when houses were cleaned and fresh rushes and flowers put down on the floors. In addition many fairs were held on Easter Monday and Tuesday as these were two holidays for labourers and servants.

It was also the time of year when in some parishes a parish official could expect to be rewarded for his efforts as the Revd James Woodforde found when he started his curacy at Babcary. "1764, 19 April, For some Cakes of my Clarke (Sam Hutchins) it being customary here for him to sell them at Passion Week to the Parish – I gave him   0   1   0", and on the following day, "For two more of my Clarkes Cakes   0   0   4."

St. George's Day on 23rd April was a day celebrated in some places such as Croscombe when a feast was held. This day had some significance in Bruton as it was the period when one of the three-day fairs was held and at some stage before the eighteenth century there was a chapel dedicated to St George in Patwell Street. No specific evidence relating to actual celebrations has survived but may be assumed to be those normally associated with fairs.

May Day was one of the principal holidays of Spring with houses decorated with greenery and flowers. In some places ritual dances were performed around a Maypole but information from Bruton is almost completely lacking, except that in the eighteenth century there was a May Pole Inn. The first day of May was the usual date for this celebration but in some areas May 29th was adopted, also known as Oak Apple Day, the anniversary of Charles II's birthday and his return to London at the Restoration in 1660. Bruton may well have adopted this latter day as it was staunchly Royalist under the influence of the Berkeley family. As early as 29th May 1660 a note was added in the Bruton Baptism Register, "The Mayden troop went to Crich Hill to solemnize his birthday." In addition it was very close to the Whitsun holiday which seems to have been celebrated in Bruton over a long period of time. It was an occasion when feasts were held, when excessive drinking occurred and even in the late nineteenth century when many of its excesses had been curbed, drunkenness remained a problem in the town with the Friendly Societies' Club days.

Between the last two festivals came Rogation Day when the priest led parishioners around the boundaries of the parish to bless the land and boundary markers, originally with the idea of protecting the village while the crops were growing. It was usually followed by a communal feast. Replies to the Society of Antiquaries in the mid-1750s reported, "Annual Preambulations on the Rogation Day", and the Churchwardens' Accounts for Bruton later in the century indicate that the boundaries were still visited but that the associated feast had disappeared.

Midsummer Day was celebrated in various areas with houses decorated with greenery and bonfires lit. At times it coincided with the Feast of Corpus Christi. The latter was in fact the day selected by the Free School for its main celebration of the year when a service was held, prizes were awarded and a large dinner or feast held. It continues to this day. At the same time came St Peter's Eve with torch-bearing processions. This day was particularly important for Redlynch and Shepton Montague as their chapel and church respectively were dedicated to St. Peter and from the early seventeenth century was the time of the former's annual three-day fair.

Lammas which marked the formal start of the harvest season, a season which often ended with the harvest feast when master and servants could sit down together in a rare act of social levelling. Harvest feasts could still be found in the Bruton area in the nineteenth century, although in a rather different form.

There were other important days, some of which were part of the cycle of life and death and as such were just taken for granted. In October came Martinmas when surplus animals were slaughtered and salted, a recognition that there were not sufficient fodder for all of them through the long winter months. On November 1st All Saints' Day was celebrated when extra candles were taken to church to remember the dead and the church bells were rung to give comfort to departed souls.

Fairs were important occasions for recreation with servants frequently being given a day or several days off. From 1532 Bruton held two major three-day fairs in April and September which not only brought in large numbers of visitors which increased prosperity for the town as a whole but also may have been used for hiring purposes. In addition Bruton was to stage a feast later in September and this too brought in people from the neighbourhood and it included a wide range of country sports and other activities.

What this brief survey indicates is that there was the possibility of celebrations, recreation and other leisure activities throughout the year. Any one in the community could take part for they were open to all and there was the real opportunity to excel in a particular area which could be important for individual prestige or for gaining some personal recognition. While there were those in authority who feared that some events could get out of hand with drunkenness, violence and sexual licence, many of the recreational activities could be viewed as important for social cohesiveness, as a means of overcoming the weariness and boredom of an otherwise monotonous and dreary existence. In addition the absence of so many of these celebrations by 1900 indicates how extensively the rural world had changed. Only by examining what took place in rural communities in the medieval period and just after can an understanding be achieved of just what and how much disappeared over a relatively short period of time. (1)

2. Setting the Scene: Specific.

To be able to exploit fully the festive calendar and the accompanying popular culture related to the natural agricultural cycle and the celebrations of the Christian Church, various factors needed to be present in a particular locality.

The first of these was a strong presence by the Church. Bruton developed as a small market town, predominantly on the northern side of the River Brue as the southern side was occupied by an Augustinian priory which was elevated to the status of an Abbey in 1510. The presence of the monastery ensured that the inhabitants of the town were likely to adhere to all the festivals and Holy Days of the Catholic Church throughout the medieval period. The monastery certainly had economic advantages for the residents as not only did it bring in pilgrims who added to the prosperity of the town but also encouraged craftsmen and traders to settle there to do business with the canons.

While a weekly market under the control of the monastery had existed in Bruton from Norman, and possibly even pre-Conquest times, the first Abbot, William Gilbert, was also instrumental in obtaining the two three-day fairs which were important in the recreational calendar of the population, as well as economically. His successor, Abbot John Ely was regarded as responsible for constructing the Market Cross, according to John Leland writing in 1542, although there is no other documentary evidence for this claim. In fact there may have been more community involvement than has been acknowledged, for example, when Robert Chyk made his Will in July 1542 he left 20s "to the pformanc and bylding of the newe Crosse." It would seem natural for leading inhabitants to be interested in such a project as all involved in trade and commerce in any way would benefit in the long run.

The Dissolution of Bruton Abbey in 1539 paved the way for the acquisition of the property in 1545 by Sir Maurice Berkeley, himself the stepson of the other major landowner in the area at Redlynch, Sir John Fitzjames. The presence of two landed estates in the immediate vicinity was the second important factor ensuring leisure activities as they, and particularly the Berkeley family, sponsored some of the events until at least the late eighteenth and early nineteenth centuries. At that stage the end of the Berkeley association with Bruton on the death of the last Lord Berkeley in 1773 and a change in attitude nationally, meant that such sponsoring declined and there was a distinct movement towards more refined pastimes, especially in the Victorian era.

The third factor was the presence in the population of a significant number of families for whom agriculture was a major activity. At the time of the 1669 Survey of the Manor when the population of the town was no more than 1,100, some sixty men and women held land in the fields of Bruton by copyhold and thirty-four by leasehold, although a small number were in each category. As historians estimate that the average family size at the period was 4.3, it meant that about 36% of the inhabitants were directly involved in agriculture through leasing, but this does not include any other men or women who were employed by them as labourers and servants on the land. In addition this Survey did not cover those who leased land in the parish of Bruton from other landowners such as Sir Stephen Fox at Redlynch or the Cottington family at Discove and Godminster. The Survey also indicated that many of those who leased tenements, especially on either side of the High Street, had a garden of up to half an acre attached, and so they too would have been very dependent upon the seasons of the year.

By the time of the Census of 1821 there was an increase in those involved in agriculture for while 31.9% of families were classed as engaged in that activity, this represented approximately 28% of the total population, a figure which was to decline to 24% a decade later. As the population of the town had doubled between 1669 and 1831 in real terms far more people were actually involved in agriculture in some way.

In addition Bruton developed as a centre for industry in the area, which was another important consideration as it meant that there were significantly improved employment prospects, especially for women and children. This in turn meant that some families were able to benefit from one or more extra incomes, usually by working in their own homes. While that was obviously beneficial for families the level of wages in both agriculture and industry was so low that the majority of families remained poor, with some occasionally sinking into poverty as a result of such occurrences as severe weather and depressions in trade, both of which led to unemployment.

From the medieval period the cloth industry had flourished in Bruton so that in 1542 Leland noted that the town was "much occupied with making of clothe." For generations it was dominated by families such as the Yerburys and then the Whiteheads. When the eighteenth century witnessed the decline of the woollen industry in the West Country, from the 1770s silk throwing developed in the town under the Ward family. In 1816 John Sharrer Ward estimated that he had about one hundred employees in his two finishing mills in the town and about 700 more in their own homes and seven years later that there could be up to 1,000, "the children often working at their own houses with their parents." Foreign competition hastened the decline of this industry and although the Census of 1861 revealed some 102 women and girls aged from nine to fifty-nine, of whom fifty-four were under twenty, were still employed, it along with various Directories, also showed the presence of many more small industries, such as horsehair seating, often related to agriculture.

Whatever the rural employment it involved hard, often monotonous labour and so any opportunity for a celebration or festival of any kind was a welcome relief. These were the men and women who wholeheartedly turned out into the streets, the market place or the churchyard to take advantage of something enjoyable and very different from their daily lives. It was often a time when they did not feel so constrained by the usual requirements of society.

As the population increased in the eighteenth century to peak at 2,232 in 1861, it certainly became much more diverse. In the mid 1790s the Universal British Directory listed some 103 tradesmen, craftsmen and artisans, many of whom would have served the appropriate apprenticeship and then went on to employ others. Kelly's Directory for 1875 listed 110 men and women involved in commercial activities, and in addition included a further forty-eight "Private Residents". While some of the latter were clearly of independent means such as Mrs Saxon at Berkeley Villa, others were clergymen, doctors, solicitors, Headmaster of the Free School, Master of the Hospital and some were wealthy businessmen such as William Clarke, George Longman and George Meaden.

These inhabitants increasingly constituted the middle class and were the final important factor required. As the landed classes gradually withdrew from sustained direct involvement with the masses and moved away from popular culture in a very pronounced change in manners, their place was taken by the middle classes who frequently imitated their lifestyle on a lesser scale, but sought throughout the nineteenth century to impose their perspective of recreational and leisure time upon the ordinary people. The nineteenth century therefore was to witness not only the development of new middle class recreational pursuits but also substantial changes in popular culture. (2)

3. Across the Divide: Church, Fairs, Feasts and Markets.

By about 1500 it would probably be correct to view the various levels in society already moving apart, often motivated by different objectives. There were however factors and occasions which brought them together.

a) The Church

The parish church, both as an institution and as a location, was important to all levels in society. Prior to the Reformation the Catholic concepts of purgatory and eternal damnation rested heavily upon the population. Visual representations in stained glass windows and wall paintings were designed to ensure that the illiterate masses were left in no doubt about the consequences if they undertook any actions or behaviour which those in authority deemed inappropriate. For the wealthy the fear of what might happen after death led them to grant property and give money to the Church in return for prayers and masses to be said for their souls.

Throughout the medieval period Bruton Priory received significant amounts of land and other gifts for that purpose. A series of Wills in the late fifteenth and early sixteenth centuries followed the same pattern, for example in 1471 Richard Dekyn, mercer, required his executors to pay five poor men "every friday by an hole yere next ensuing my decease 5d, to pray for my soule." In 1496 Eleanor Ede provided nine marks for "a chaplain to celebrate mass yearly for the souls of the said Thomas [*her husband*], Thomas Ede, chaplain, and William Ede, my sons, and hereafter for the soul of me the said

Eleanor." Simon Grene made the same arrangement in his Will in 1506 when he left £6 for a chaplain to "celebrate for my soul and my parents and benefactors' souls," for one year.

The Fitzjames family of Redlynch were particularly generous, for example in 1526 Isabel left £20 for her executors to "fynde oone of the chanons of the monastery of Bruton to singe at my late husbonds aulter daily within the said monastery praying for his Soule, my Soule and for all my good frendes Soules." Finally in 1539 Sir John Fitzjames required at his burial "15 masses of the Fyve Wondes of Our Lord, by fyftyn most honest and best disposed Priests" who were each to receive 2s for their labour and pains.

The Church and its monasteries were certainly in the forefront in sponsoring superstitions along with the veneration of relics and images, many of which of course would have given considerable comfort to the ordinary people. At the Dissolution in 1539 Bruton Abbey possessed its own relic, "our Ladyes girdell of Bruton, redde silke." Late medieval wills from the townspeople making gifts to the Parish Church made reference to a whole series of altars dedicated to various saints and to the presence of statues including St Katherine and Our Lady, to which cloth and jewellery were left. The destruction of all shrines, pictures, paintings and images which started in July 1547 and continued throughout 1548 in the reign of Edward VI, must have caused the related collapse of so many popular customs associated with the Church. In reality some of these were to be resumed by the Church in the decades which followed while others became much more secular folk activities.

For all levels in society the Church figured prominently at the time of major rites of passage: christening, marriage and death. The Parish Registers show that very large numbers within the community were involved, for example, between 1600 and 1699, even with the disruption caused by the Civil War in the 1640s, there were some 4,911 baptisms, 810 marriages and 4,003 burials. The baptisms and marriages seem to have been the same for the majority of the inhabitants but in death there was a noticeable difference as the overwhelming majority of parishioners were just named and interred in the churchyard, usually in an unmarked grave, whereas the wealthy and influential could expect other treatment. As early as 1417 Richard Bruton, Canon of Wells, had directed that his body should be buried in the chancel of the parish church; in 1496 Eleanor Ede wished to be buried "in the middle of the parish church of Bruton, before the image of the Crucifix near the tomb of the said Thomas Ede"; in 1517 Alice Brymmore specified that her body should be buried "before the Awter of or blissid ladie." Elizabeth Fitzjames directed in 1545 that she too should be buried "at Our Lady Aulter where my husband lieth buried."

In his Will in 1600 Sir Henry Berkeley stated that he wished "my body to be bureyd in my parishe Church at Bruton in the vawlt wch I made for my father, if it shall plese God that I depart this life ther, or wthin an hundred myles thereof." The latter was a not insignificant distance to move a body at that period. Later members of the Berkeley family could expect the same resting place as on 26th June 1688 for example the Parish Clerk recorded that, "The Rt Honorble Charles Lord Viscount ffitzharding was between 12 & one of the clock in the night after a sermon preached by Mr John Randall, then Minist: of Brewton, buried in the vault in the Chancell in a coffin of lead." The Churchwardens' Accounts indicate that throughout the eighteenth century there was an average of two burials a year within the parish church itself.

All levels of society were expected to attend Divine Service on Sundays on a regular basis. The evidence for the vast majority of the inhabitants of Bruton would suggest that they did so faithfully. There was always, however, a small minority who did not and they were presented, that is reported, usually by the Churchwardens, in front of the Church Courts which were held each time that there was a Visitation, either by the Bishop triennially or the Archdeacon annually, and which were particularly active from the middle of the sixteenth century for about a hundred years.

Various reasons were put forward to explain non-attendance such as illness or old age, for example in 1600 when Joanne Poole was presented as she did not attend it was added, "butt she is an old woman." For a few the Church was obviously of little importance such as Jacob Wookie and Elizabeth Lucocke who not only were living together unmarried but also were "not frequenting the Church to heare divine Service." The usual punishment was a small fine or excommunication, if the offence persisted. One reason for non-attendance was continued adherence to the Catholic faith, usually referred to as recusancy. Once again any level in society could be involved for example the records show a Bruton baker and a groom but it was particularly strong amongst various members of local landowning families such as the Fitzjames, Cottingtons, Bisletts and Byfleets. The punishment was invariably a large fine and excommunication.

All parishioners were required to receive Holy Communion once a year at Easter and again the evidence suggests that while the vast majority did so a small minority refused such as John Burrow of Shepton Montague in 1588, William Shepparde of Pitcombe in 1597 and a number in Bruton itself such as Thomas Card in 1594, Henry Wymer and Edward Pavy in 1600 and Alicia Wilton in 1629. By the eighteenth century in order to hold any office in national or local affairs it became essential to receive Holy Communion and obtain a Certificate to that effect. A number of these survive in the Quarter Sessions Records for Bruton men, such as Benjamin Thomas in 1747, Charles Moore, the Parish Clerk in 1750, the Honourable Charles Berkeley in 1754, Andrew Agnew, Lieutenant in the Sixty Sixth Regiment of Foot in 1762 and the Right Honourable John Lord Berkeley of Stratton in 1767.

The Church Courts intruded into the lives of a significant proportion of the parishioners at some stage as defendant, witness, accuser or suitor. As well as church attendance they dealt with other church issues such as the payment of church rates, behaviour in church, work and drinking on the Sabbath and the allocation of pews, an often fertile source of dispute in a hierarchical society where social status was important to some people. The Courts were also responsible for ensuring that the Minister conducted himself appropriately and that the parish maintained the fabric of the church and the churchyard. More importantly, the Courts regulated relationships and behaviour amongst parishioners, especially on issues of immorality where illicit sex, adultery and bastardy were primary concerns. They also increasingly undertook some administrative functions such as acting as a court of probate.

It is therefore abundantly clear that not only did the Church and its Courts help to maintain social stability, albeit in a very intrusive manner, but also played a significant role in helping to maintain the overall behaviour and cultural pattern of all levels in society. While there was not always equality of treatment by the Church, the values which were imposed remained a cornerstone of life in a rural community, accepted by rich and poor alike.

The Church, of course, was important for other reasons as well as its ceremonies, services and courts. Physically it was frequently central in location, although in Bruton it was on the southern edge of the community and in widespread rural parishes such as Pitcombe and Shepton Montague, it was at a considerable distance from some dwellings. Nevertheless in a small town such as Bruton it was a meeting place, a place to congregate and exchange news and gossip and a place to administer community business. Before the Reformation and possibly just after, it is likely that the Fraternity of Our Lady would assemble in the Church to hold their meetings. The Parish Vestry, which consisted of most of the principal ratepayers, used the Church for its regular meetings until it transferred to the new Poorhouse in Silver Street after 1734.

After 1601 the Overseers of the Poor used the North Porch as the distribution point for Outdoor Relief each Sunday, sitting on the cold stone seats which still exist on the east and west sides of the interior of the Porch. The poor were required to attend in person "In ye Church Porch Sundays after evening Prayers", at which time they had to be wearing their pauper's badge. "No person to have pay without coming to the Pay Table unless not able." In the early eighteenth century Richard Moore was paid 3s a year to bring the table into the porch "at paying the Poor." In addition the fathers of bastard children were instructed to make their payments there at a different time, for example, the Bastardy Order imposed on Maurice Stevens als Hooper in January 1625 for the support of the illegitimate son of Elizabeth Bugden required him to pay "the sume of viijd of lawfull Englishe money" each week to the Overseers in the Church porch "every Sunday after thend of morning prayer." It was also the place where other parish business could be transacted, such as signing Apprenticeship Indentures and sealing contracts.

For hundreds of years the churchyard, although by Canon Law declared to be ecclesiastical property, was used for various secular purposes. This was in fact relatively easy to accomplish as before the seventeenth century it was largely an uncluttered space with very few monuments. In the days before purpose-built places of entertainment this was an open area which would bring together all levels of society and many parishes record fairs, markets and games taking place there. Little evidence has survived for Bruton although the parish was responsible for maintaining this area. In September 1799 it was noted by the Overseers of the Poor that "the Churchyard has for time Immemorial been Inclosed and kept in decent order at the expense of the Parish......And that no Cattle of any Kind was ever permitted to Graze therein." Pitcombe Churchyard was probably used for church ales at some time in the early seventeenth century (see below) (3)

One often overlooked feature in the celebrations, customs and communal life of all the parish was the role of the church bells, which in Bruton seem to have been very prominent. The bells were part of the everyday life of all parishioners and on many occasions brought them together. In 1698 one French visitor to England noted that nationally, "Ringing of Bells is one of their great Delights, especially in the Country." Such was this enthusiasm that in some parts of the country such as Cornwall bell-ringing competitions were staged between villages. Throughout the medieval period much of the ringing was associated with the different festivals and special days of the Church.

Prior to the Reformation a common sound was the "Passing Bell" which was rung as a source of comfort to a person on the point of death. It was customary to toll nine strokes for a man, six for a woman and three for a child. In each case this was followed by one stroke for each year of his or her age. In addition a bell was rung immediately after death, known as the knell and there was further bell-ringing at the time of the burial. The latter did not meet with the approval of ardent Protestants so in November 1547 Edward VI issued revised orders, "that they likewise do abstein from such unmeasurable ringing for ded persones at the burials, and at the feast of All Sowles, and that hencefurthe they use to ringe oon bell at soch tyme as sicke persones lyeth in extreme daunger of death, that they which be haile may be put in remembraunce of their owne mortalitie." He did however add that when a body was brought to the church for burial "then to ring also moderatelie in the time of the obsequies thereof, and no longer."

The tradition of the Passing Bell and the knell seems to have continued in Bruton. In 1584 the executors of William Walter spent 22s on his funeral, which included "for rynginge his knill for making his grave for the meat and drinke for the neighbourres after they came home from the buryall." In November 1641 the funeral of Thomas Albin cost his widow, Tabitha, £1 10s 0d "for a coffin a shroud making the grave, ringing the knell for Dakes beere and other necessarie expences in and about the funerall." As well as ringing the bell the custom of some communal feast was clearly still present. All levels of society could expect the Passing Bell, even paupers and the Overseers' Accounts contain a record of many payments, for example, in October 1673 they paid 2s "ffor making Wm Allens grave and ringing the Bell", and in July 1804 it cost them 2s 6d "for Passing the Bell for Judith Frank."

Many of the customs of ringing the Church bells centred about the monarch. The Coronation of a new monarch was a time for the whole community to celebrate and as part of this the bells were rung, for example, the Churchwardens paid the ringers 10s on the

Coronation Day of William IV in September 1831 and then in April 1837 10s 6d "on Proclaiming Queen Victoria." The anniversary of Coronation Days were often celebrated throughout a monarch's reign so in the 1730s the Churchwardens were paying the ringers 7s each year "ffor Ringing the Kings Coronation Day." In the 1830s the ringers were receiving 10s each September for the same event.

Three years after Queen Victoria's Coronation came her wedding to Prince Albert and again the ringers were paid 10s "for ringing the day" and another 10s in November 1840 "on the birth of the Princess." The birth of the Prince of Wales a year later attracted a payment to the ringers of 14s and one guinea in January 1842 on his Christening. The anniversary of the monarch's birthday was traditionally kept in Bruton, in the case of Charles II for well over a century after his death. In the early eighteenth century 7s was spent each year "ffor Ringing the Kings Birth Day", in this case George I.

Finally came the death of a monarch and that too was the occasion for the bells to be rung, although on this solemn occasion they were either muffled or just tolling, for example the ringers were paid 10s in June 1831 "for ringing the Bells muffled on the death of ye late King." The following month they received just 2s "for toling the Bell on the Burial of George 4th." The execution of Charles I had made a profound impact on the nation and as late as 30th January 1773 the Churchwardens in Bruton were paying 1s 6d "For Tolling the Great Bell for the Martyrdom of King Charles." In 1781 however for some unspecified reason the Vestry decided to discontinue that day as a tolling day at the expense of the parish.

Another custom was to ring the bells to mark or celebrate national events, in some cases after a national decree but in others as a result of a local decision. Victories and peace figured throughout the period and so in April 1747 the Churchwardens spent 2s 6d "for ringing on the day that the Duke of Cumberland gained a complete Victory over the rebels at Culloden in Scotland on Ap 16 1746." In September 1855 they paid £1 1s 0d to the "Ringers on the taking of Sebastopol" during the Crimean War. Nearly half a century later in June 1902 "the ringers spread the news by merry peals" that the Second Boer War was over and peace proclaimed.

Probably the most widely celebrated political anniversary was that of the Gunpowder Plot of 1605 and it was one which the Churchwardens in Bruton were to maintain as their Accounts show that they were paying for ringing that day annually, such as 7s in 1735. Once again for an unspecified reason they decided to discontinue this practice at parish expense in 1781. It is therefore not possible to determine if ringing continued with finance coming from other sources.

One event which seems to have prompted a spontaneous reaction came in March 1831 with the passing of the Reform Bill through the House of Commons by one vote. According to one local newspaper a group of six or seven men staying at the Blue Ball Inn "suggested the propriety of an instant and consequently a midnight peal and subscribed a necessary sum for the remuneration of the ringers." The bell ringers were woken up and within half an hour "the bells were pouring forth as loud, merry and melodious a peal as ever resounded from the ancient and beautiful tower of that church."

The parish itself seems to have decided to mark, with the bells, issues which were important to people locally, even though the actual origin of the event may initially have been broader. Originally on Shrove Tuesday a bell had been rung to summon the parishioners to shriving, that is to go to church to confess, and so became known as the Pancake Bell. This custom died out in many areas but for some reason retained its popularity in Bruton. As late as 1906 it was recorded that "On Shrove Tuesday the pancake Bell was rung at Midday, a custom some hundreds of years old." It was not mentioned as happening in other parishes in the locality.

While bells rung upon St Mathias Eve, 14th February, may have been religious in origin, it was the attack upon the town in 1642, as recorded in the Parish Registers by "our rageing foes that Thursday night", later amended to "the Batcombeites", and "our deliverance Mathias Eve", that ensured it became a local custom [see Appendix 1]. The bells were rung on that evening for nearly one hundred years afterwards. Significantly the cost of the ringing, which was generally 6s, came out of the Constables' Accounts, emphasizing the defensive nature of the event.

In reality any local event could be marked by ringing the bells, even the most mundane, for example throughout the eighteenth century 2s was paid "for tolling the Bell at chooseing fresh Overseers." In the same period the Churchwardens paid 6d for tolling the bell when their annual accounts were passed and on any occasion when a Vestry Meeting was called. In October 1842 they paid 14s to "the Ringers on the reopening of the Church after the Repewing." By the early twentieth century as well as ringing twice on Sundays and on Easter Day, Whitsunday, Christmas Day and on Harvest and Patronal Festivals, the ringers could undertake private occasions such as weddings, Flower Shows, Friendly Society Festivals and Corpus Christi Day. By this time the ad hoc payments by the Churchwardens had ceased and in return for their church-related duties each ringer was paid twelve guineas a year while fees not exceeding 25s could be charged for private functions.

All the formal Accounts make it clear that the Bruton ringers were paid in cash for their efforts but that does not always seem to have been the case in some parishes as in January 1764 Revd. James Woodforde recorded in his Diary that when he started his Curacy at Babcary, "I was rung into the Parish by Mr John Bower's order, who gave the Ringers a pail of Cyder on purpose to ring me into the Parish." On the other hand, in 1901 Bruton's ringers were left in no doubt, "No Smoking, Drinking, or Bad Language to be allowed in the Belfry, under penalty of instant dismissal."

For centuries the bells provided a source of comfort and pleasure for many in the town. They were part of celebrations and customs both national and local; their peals must have been a welcome sound for those who were conditioned to constant labour as they could signal a period of relaxation, however short-lived. In fact the bells were such an integral part of town life that when they were not heard very much letters could appear in the local press, for example one in May 1858 which criticized the fact that the bells did not ring for the Blue Ball Friendly Society's Club day in that year, "There was one thing wanting to complete the joyful proceedings of the day, and that was a merry peal of bells." (4)

   b) Fairs.

The second communal event, which involved members from all levels of society, was the fair. These fairs were primarily for commercial purposes with the ones in Bruton mainly concerned with cattle but they were also important occasions for pleasure and recreation. As such they tended to attract not only local inhabitants but also people from much further a-field:

   How Pedlars Stalls with glitt'ring Toys are laid,
   The various Fairings of the Country Maid,

Long silken Laces hang upon the Twine,
And Rows of Pins and amber Bracelets shine…..
The Mountebank now treads the stage, and sells
His Pills, his Balsoms, and his Ague spells.

Fairs were also visited by strolling players and musicians, miscellaneous curiosities such as performing animals, giants and dwarfs along with fortune tellers and mountebanks (that is, quack doctors). In the eighteenth century such activities would suggest that beginnings of a highly commercialised leisure and entertainment industry. Many fairs were closely linked with the agricultural cycle so that late spring after sowing and the autumn after the summer harvest were the most popular times.

The fairs brought all the community together and not just the farmers and traders. When Revd. James Woodforde walked to Yarlington Fair on 27th August 1795 to attend the evening races he recorded that he found "a great deal Company and Many Carriages full of genteel People." On the other hand many labourers and servants went to fairs as they were often used as hiring fairs, although no evidence appears to have survived for that function in Bruton. Some of these fairs did cause concerns, such as the hiring fair at Axbridge on 25th March: "this fair is productive of much business for the country justices and their clerks, parish officers, and midwives, for many miles around." This implied immorality does not appear to have been so pronounced in Bruton as June, the appropriate time after September's fair saw very few baptisms and while January, after April's fair, along with February tended to be popular months for baptism, they were in keeping with several other months, for example, in the twenty years from 1750 to 1769 there were fifty-nine baptisms in January, seventy-four in February and sixty-six in March, with two, eight and seven respectively being classed as 'base', that is illegitimate. There may, however, be just a hint that the April celebrations followed by more in May could have had unfortunate consequences.

The two annual fairs in Bruton started as a result of the actions of the Abbey as on 11th April 1532 Abbot William Gilbert was granted a licence to hold "two yearly fairs of three day duration; viz on the eve, day, and morrow of the Feast of St George the Martyr, [*22nd-24th April*] and on the eve, day and morrow of the Feast of the Nativity of St Mary the Virgin." [*7th-9th September*] One year later the grant was extended to include a Court of Piepowder at each, namely that the Steward of the Abbey would have the right to administer justice to itinerant dealers and anyone else who was temporarily present in the town. In addition the Abbey was to be entitled to all tolls and customs as at St. Bartholomew's Fair in London.

Fairs were an important source of revenue for medieval monasteries. In Bruton all other shops would be closed on each of the six days covered, all goods had to be purchased at the stalls of the fair, and each one of these would pay a substantial ground rent. The monastery would station its officials at all the key points on the routes giving access to the fair and charge a toll on all merchandise and animals which were heading towards it. In the mid 1750s a toll of 2d per head was imposed on all such animals and paid to the Lord of the Manor.

The value of the Fairs to the Abbey may be judged by the amount of money it was prepared to spend to obtain them. On 22nd April 1532 Canon Richard Hart wrote a letter of thanks from Bruton to Lady Lisle, who with her husband had been instrumental in ensuring the licence was granted. He cited the contribution of Sir Richard

Weston, Thomas Cromwell and William Sulyard, all of who were anxious to please Lady Lisle. It is clear that a significant amount of money changed hands: "Mr Weston got my bill signed by the King, and had of me xx li for his labour. Mr Crumwell did read the bill to the King and gave it his good word, and he had v li, Mr Syllyard did speak to the King ij times, and helped it what he might, and he had x li. All these look for thanks of your ladyship, for they did more for my lord's sake and yours than for the money, and so they bid me tell your ladyship. Also Stowghton, Mr Weston's servant, took great pains in soliciting his master, and was always ready to help forth…..I gave him but xs and to his fellows I gave xs more."

Hart's letter does provide a fascinating glimpse on how the King's Court functioned and grants were obtained, in this instance at least £36 was distributed to ease the request through. The first fair must have been hastily arranged as the formal licence was only issued on 11th April, some eleven days before it took place. It was, nevertheless, according to Hart, a great success, "We have a great fair here, and much people resorteth to it." The timing of this Fair may indicate the high regard in which St George was held in the area. The September Fair was clearly arranged to coincide with the patronal festival of the Blessed Virgin, to whom both the Abbey and the Church were dedicated.

In the days immediately before, during and after the two Fairs the lanes and paths around Bruton must have been the scene of intense activity with the movement of scores of animals for sale and carts and mules bringing huge quantities of merchandise for a similar purpose. With it must have been a level of noise which would have shattered the relative peace of the countryside, from the various sounds of the animals such as the bleating of sheep to the cries of traders trying to attract custom to their standings, of entertainers wishing to gain an audience, of wandering street musicians and with the encouragement shouted by the supporters of the various entertainments on offer.

The Fairs were guaranteed to arouse excitement throughout the neighbourhood: a time to cast off the burden of the monotonous everyday toil experienced by so many of the population. In one of his poems John Clare captured the excitement and anticipation of fair day:

> Going to the Fair
> In every field larks twittered oer the grain
> As happy twas the fair so thought the swain
> Who hastened oer his labours to get free
> By times the pleasure of the fair to see.

Once at the fair all sorts of sights and entertainments would have greeted the swain. In addition to the typical stalls with their local produce which were common at the weekly market, there were others with biscuits and cakes moulded into figures or animals, largely made of flour and water, sticks of toffee, heaps of bulls'eyes and sugar candy. Some of the Victorian fairs included coconut shies and shooting galleries. It was a time to forget the daily toil, to meet friends and relatives from neighbouring villages and to enjoy the festivities and the usually unrestricted sale of alcohol.

Bruton's two fairs continued on their set days, with the possible exception of the Civil War and Commonweath, until 1752. In that year the calendar was altered to bring it into line with the European one and resulted in eleven days being missed out, that is September 3rd to 13th inclusive. This alteration required an amendment to Bruton Fair and so an advertisement appeared in a local newspaper on 17th August 1752:

"This is to Give Notice

That Brewton Fair which used to be kept the 8th of September will be (by reason of the Alteration of the Style) be on Tuesday the nineteenth of the same month."

The wording of this Notice may suggest that the Fair had already been reduced from three days to one day. It was to remain on September 19th until well into the nineteenth century when declining numbers in attendance necessitated changes.

The calendar change also affected the April Fair as in the following and subsequent years it was moved to 4th May. By 1815, however, it had reverted to 23rd April and remained there until at least 1888. Throughout all the period both fairs concentrated on the sale of all types of cattle, although they also included horses and pigs, for example on 19th September 1752 the Earl of Ilchester recorded the payment of £20 15s 0d "To 4 oxen bought at Bruton Fair." Various other forms of merchandise, often associated with pedlars, appeared regularly so that in this way it could appeal to the widest possible clientele. If anything the development of more local newspapers in the eighteenth century which contained advertizements and notices led to the greater popularisation of events such as fairs and markets.

The exact location of the Fairs would have been so commonplace to contemporaries that it was rarely written down. It is possible that like the weekly market, stalls spread from the Market Cross westwards along the High Street, but that would have made supervision fairly difficult. They are therefore much more likely to have been concentrated in one place near the Abbey and a reference in a Survey of 1754 may suggest a possible location. It records that in 1723 Anne Marshall was granted a lease for "A House and Orchard on the Plotts or Fair Place." A note added later remarked,

"Demolished by my Lord Berkeley in 1740."

The name 'Plotts' may well have been the origin of 'Plocks' later 'Plox' and one location may be suggested on some of the vacant land to the west of the Free School building now known as 'Old House'. This land remained undeveloped until the early twentieth century with the appearance of New House. It was also just outside of the precinct of the Abbey and was relatively flat unlike the land further to the west, especially beyond Three Ways, although eighteenth and nineteenth century maps indicate that this area was then known as Plocks. The site of the Fairs was unlikely to have been to the east of Old House, between it and Plox House, as a lease of 1713 refers to that area consisting of a garden belonging to Plox House and an orchard belonging to the Free School.

After the Reformation the Fairs passed to Sir Maurice Berkeley as Lord of the Manor in 1545 and he and subsequent Lords of the Manor were able to exploit the tolls for over two hundred and fifty years. When the Manor was surveyed for Sir John Brownlowe in 1713 the tolls of the two fairs together with the weekly markets was valued at £10 per year and were leased to John Cheeke for 4d or "A fat Capon on ye first of January." Such leases were to remain with the Cheeke family for over a hundred years as in the following year they passed to Thomas Cheeke, and in 1730 to Robert Cheeke. They were still leased by the Cheeke family c1816 when they were valued at £5 and a few years later were shown as being in the possession of Richard Biggs.

In the nineteenth century the recreational aspects of the Bruton Fairs seem to have declined sharply, probably as a result of the change in attitude towards popular culture and entertainments, and they became centred much more on the sale of cattle. Their success, however, was varied as in 1843 it was reported that the April Fair "on Monday last was well attended, business, however, was rather dull, excepting for heifers and calves, for which there was an extraordinary demand, which consequently realised high prices." Some improvement occurred by 1846 when it was reported that the fair "was well supported with every description of Stock, which met with a ready sale at good prices." The report however added somewhat ominously, "Pigs were rather on the decline."

By 1852 the fair "was very thinly attended, and but little stock was exhibited for sale, besides little business was done." Just over a decade later at the April 1864 Fair two Conservative candidates and the Liberal's agent did a considerable amount of electioneering "but the show of stock was small." In April 1873 a very low ebb had been reached with the presence of "a cow and calf and a few pigs." The reporter went on to remark that one gentleman was so disgusted "that he declared himself ashamed of the place and announced his intention of availing himself of the first train up or down." Another local newspaper commented, "We should think Bruton Fair will soon be numbered among the things of the past."

Both Fairs just seem to have faded away with the activities of the Bruton Agricultural Society playing a more prominent part instead, although a Royal Commission in 1888 listed them as taking place on 23rd April and 17th September of that year. The development of the railway network meant that mass-produced goods could be transported to shops quickly; cheap grain flooded into the country in the late 1870s with the opening up of the vast corn producing areas of the United States and Canada; beef was imported from South America and lamb, aided by refrigeration, and wool from Australia and New Zealand in the fast steam ships. Small provincial fairs and markets no longer seemed to have a place.

In the seventeenth century there may have been another Fair, although it was possibly short-lived, but it may have been more of a market and festival. Within the Overseers' Accounts for 1670-1 is the following agreement: "We do hereby Consent that the last overseers shall out of the money due on their acct pay to Mr Cheeke £40 towards the Procuring of the New Fayre & Market gained to this Towne as money paid to the undersherif." As 29th May was becoming an important time of celebration in Bruton this new fair was linked with that day. In an undated list of Fairs in his Account Book for the years 1679 to 1727 James Twyford included a Fair in Bruton on 29th May. Although there do not appear to be any further references to such an event, as so much money was spent obtaining it, the assumption must be that it did continue in some form or another. Twyford also listed another fair on 6th November which may be an early reference to the importance of the Guy Fawkes episode for the town.

As well as fairs in Bruton there were others in the neighbourhood, for example Yarlington Fair was still operating for the sale of cattle, horses and sheep in the eighteenth century, originally on 15th August, although eleven days later after 1752. This Fair survived until 1900 when an advertisement in a local newspaper gave notice that it was to be discontinued, a decision which did not meet with universal approval: "Thus was ignominiously brought to an end a fair which had been held for nearly 600 years, being granted by Edward II, to Simon de Montacute in 1315." Drinking was obviously an important aspect of this fair as it was reported in 1920 that, "Old inhabitants say that at Fair time any body in Yarlington could sell liquor."

Stavordale Fair took place on 5th August, possibly from the mid-fourteenth century with the foundation of the Priory but it seems to have started to decline in the sixteenth century, especially after 1556 when Wincanton received a Charter to stage two fairs a year and a market every Wednesday. It was, however, still in existence in 1793, held on Wincanton Common, when an advertisement mentioned "A ball the second evening. Ordinaries at the principal inns." By 1810 it had become much more of a pleasure fair with the commercial aspect being secondary.

Much closer was the fair held on the common at Redlynch which was well-established by 1617 when John Moore received the profits. It was mainly for the sale of oxen and sheep and held on 28th and 29th June which was the eve and day of St Peter the Apostle, to whom its chapel was dedicated. In 1669 for £20 and an annual rent of 4s Thomas Wilton leased "All that the Faire at Redlynch in a certaine place there called the ffaire place for two days (that is to say the Eve of St Peter the Apostle & the Feast of St Peter the Apostle) with all the liberties ffree Customes & profitts." In a Survey in September 1712 Thomas Scott was paying a rent of 2s per year "for Redlinch ffair."

A significant change occurred in this market in 1749 when John Cheek, junior, placed an advertisement in a local newspaper to inform readers that the Fair that year on 29th June would be at the Bear Inn in Dropping Lane, "for Sale of all Manner of Cattle and Merchandise: And this Year the Right Honourable Stephen Lord Ilchester's Steward will not demand any Manner of Toll. N.B. The Fair is removed from Redlinch Common to Dropping Lane as above." For more than twenty years extensive work had been undertaken on Redlynch House and the grounds and the whole of the park was walled in 1748-1750. These activities may be the main reason for the removal of the Fair from its traditional site. It also appears to have been reduced to just one day, possibly indicating a decrease in demand. The Fair however did continue into the nineteenth century as it appears in a General Directory published by the Somerset County Gazette in 1840 but had ceased by 1888.

Fairs allowed all members of the community, no matter what their status, to meet together in a much more relaxed atmosphere and to be free from the burdens of everyday life. In 1838 one observer commented, "Fairs are great sources of pleasure to all classes of country people.........all flock to the fair and find some business to be transacted, and a world of pleasure to be enjoyed." All could enjoy the festivities, although in some cases there were those who took their celebrations too far especially as whole days were involved with little to actually do and a somewhat drunken excess followed. There was always the fear amongst the wealthier in the community that large gatherings of people could create problems associated with disorder. It is somewhat ironic therefore that one of the most prominent cases of violence involved not the ordinary people but Sir Henry Berkeley of Bruton and the retainers of the Earl of Pembroke. In the 1590s there was a long drawn out dispute between these two men over a range of issues and in 1592 there was a significant fight at Stavordale Fair between more than thirty retainers of the two sides using a range of weapons which caused a number of injuries. Needless to say each side blamed the other.

So many goods on the stalls were of course too much of a temptation for some and so, for example, in April 1627 Dorothie Browne, who was the wife of a Devon 'Glasman', was accused by John Carey of stealing "a peece of Lynnen cloth of Eighte or Nyne yards or thereabuetes" from his Standing. Several traders on neighbouring stalls, such as butchers John Davis the Elder and his son Henry, witnessed the theft although the offender claimed that "Shee did carrye it noe farther than the said Carey gave her leave to doe." Items also disappeared from houses during fair-time as in April 1631 Mary Forte of Bruton gave evidence that she had seen Mary Jesse of Curry Rivel taking a loaf of brown bread from her husband's house.

One other unfortunate incident occurred in 1621. As Redlynch Fair was so popular it attracted many local inhabitants and hence their houses were empty. While Philip Pitman of Pitcombe was at the fair on St Peter's Day his house "was breaken upp and goods taken and carried awaie." The chief suspect was Edward Davidge, a husbandman from Hadspen, but he claimed that he was at the fair from 7 am until 7 pm. A witness, James Ames of Godminster, a labourer, however, recalled that he saw Davidge "with a woman in his companie comminge in a waie wch leads to Pitcombe" about two o'clock in the afternoon. The outcome was not recorded. (For an alleged episode which occurred at a Bruton Fair see Appendix 2) (5).

c)   Bruton Feast.

The third custom which was supported by all levels in society was the parish feast, which historians agree was one of the most important holidays for ordinary people. It was a major time for enjoyment and helped to make them feel that they were an integral part of the community. When Revd. James Woodforde and various members of his family attended the Races at Burrowfield, which were part of the Bruton Feast in September 1795, he noted, "The Races were very indifferent, but a vast Concourse of People attended, both gentle and simple."

Bruton Feast was very much under the patronage of local landed families, for example, in the 1750s the Honourable Charles Berkeley provided annually a Laced Hat for the winner of the Sword and Dagger contest. In the early nineteenth century the Hoares, as Lords of the Manor, regularly subscribed £1   11s   6d to "Bruton Annual Amusements" as they had become known.

It is no longer possible to pinpoint when the Bruton Feast began. As parochial feasts were often associated with the festive day of a particular saint it may well have been medieval and linked with the 8th of September which was the patronal day of the Blessed Virgin Mary, to whom both the Priory and the Church were dedicated. In addition in the later medieval period a number of Wills indicate the presence of a gild in the parish church dedicated to the same person: the Fraternity of the Blessed Virgin. It was their normal practice to celebrate her day with a feast, to which outsiders were often invited. There is no evidence to suggest what happened when the Abbey obtained a Fair on that day from 1532: the feast may still have occurred then or moved to a slightly later date in the month.

Once again evidence is lacking for seventeenth-century Bruton but nationally many of these festivities declined dramatically, mainly as a result of puritanical views. A pronounced revival occurred in the eighteenth century so that in September 1738 one traveller wrote, "I am now in the Country and at that season of the Year in which Parish Feasts abound." Twenty years later a visitor to Cornwall found that "every parish has its annual feast", and it was stated that 122 towns and villages in Devon had a feast. By this stage however they had lost any religious context and were very much secular affairs. Advertizements for Bruton Feast appeared annually in local newspapers and show that it was always in the week after the September Fair. When the calendar was amended in 1752 it also advanced eleven days like the Fair and so became staged late in September, usually after the 22nd of the month.

By this time of the year the harvest was generally well advanced or completed and there is some evidence that these celebrations became linked with the harvest at times. In September 1756 a local newspaper commented, "It's thought 'twill be the largest Feast known for many Years, by Reason of the forwardness of the Corn-Harvest."

While all levels of society and all ages attended Bruton Feast the most active participants may well have been the young as it was an ideal opportunity not only to have respite from their labours but also to meet members of the opposite sex, as John Clare observed:

> Where the fond swain delighteth in the chance
> To meet the sun tann'd lass he dearly loves
> And as he leads her down the giddy dance
> With many a token his fond passion proves
> Squeezing her hands or catching at her gloves
> And stealing kisses as chance prompt the while.

For all, young and old, however, it was a time to meet friends and renew acquaintances in a very informal setting. Servants would be given permission to attend, as on 26th September 1769 Revd. Woodforde noted, "My Father's Maid Eliz Clothier returned this evening from Bruton Feast where she had been two whole Days and one Night." As with Bruton Fairs, the Feast also lasted three days. In September 1767 Woodforde recorded that his brother John spent the whole day there on the 21st, went again early on the 22nd and this time did not return until the evening of the 23rd.

Once at the Feast drink was abundant in the large number of inns and alehouses in the town and food was also plentiful. An advertizement in 1791 stated that 'ordinaries' would be held at the Bell Inn and the Sun Inn each day and at the Blue Ball Inn on just one day. An 'ordinary' was a public meal at a fixed price and at a set time, for example at the Blue Ball it was two o' clock. An account published in 1868 recalled that fifty years before "The three days was one jollification, eating, drinking, and, we might also say, *ergo* drunkenness and debauchery."

Stalls appeared along both sides of the main streets "where abominations in the shape of villainous compounds of paint and sugar were retailed to the junior portion of the public." A range of sports and pastimes of the period took place, for example, for the ordinary people there were "blind-fold races with wheelbarrows........to which, in addition to the possibility of broken legs, was in this case added the attraction of seeing some of the unfortunate drivers of barrows run into the stream at the bottom of the hill – where there was no bridge as now – in the midst of which they plunged and floundered about until they were half drowned."

There were also the usual violent sports of Sword and Dagger, Backsword, Singlestick and Cudgel playing. These seem to have attracted not only the experienced players but also amateurs such as apprentices who tried to win a prize but "often before they had finished, losing their tempers and having a set-to with their fists in earnest, to the increased delight of the spectators." Such contests were well supported by the wealthier members of the community, "great Encouragement will be given by the Gentlemen", declared one advertizement in 1750. "As a finale on the three days proceedings, a regular Donnybrook fight on Maiden Hill used to take place which enabled many who took part in it to carry home momentoes of their pleasure in the shape of cut faces and blackened eyes."

For those who considered themselves more refined during the course of the three days there were plays, games of cards and a Ball. For every one there were the races, although often only the wealthy had sufficient money to gamble for long. (6)

d) Markets.

While Bruton Feast was an annual event and the Fairs staged at least twice a year, the market was held weekly and provided an opportunity for people from all levels in society to meet together on a regular basis, although in this instance the purpose was primarily commercial. It was nevertheless the occasion to spend a few hours away from the drudgery of everyday life and possibly even to wear different clothes. That a market was granted to a particular town or village was of course not the origins of regular trade there but an indication that this trade was already at a sufficient level for a market to be established. The general presumption was that the Lord of the Manor would erect and be responsible for the stalls and would charge a ground rent as a way of obtaining a financial return on his investment. In addition in the days before newspapers and other forms of mass communication it was the place to exchange news and gossip, to find out what was happening elsewhere in the county and further a-field

Markets such as the one in Bruton, were often the centre for the sale of locally produced commodities such as wool and grain. The increase in prosperity of a town then encouraged craftsmen to move into the area as there was a developing demand for their products. They were often followed by other traders who acted as middlemen and brought in products which were not produced locally, such as salt, ironware, earthenware and fish. While most of those who attended a market were from the immediate area some people buying could come from up to twenty miles away. From the thirteenth century the recommendation had existed that to avoid direct competition markets should be at least six and two-third miles from each other, although this was often ignored as long as the markets were on different days, for example while Bruton market was on a Saturday that at Castle Cary was on a Tuesday. It has been estimated that nearly seven thousand labourers and artisans obtained weekly corn and meal from the markets of Bruton and Wincanton in the sixteenth and early seventeenth centuries.

This in itself is an indication of the number of people dependent on a market, the movement on the roads that there must have been on market days and the social mix.

The origins of Bruton market are no longer possible to determine but as there was a Mint there before the Norman Conquest, from at least 997 to 1003 and from 1017 to 1035, this probably suggests a trading centre as well and so one may have been established at that time. It was certainly in existence by the early twelfth century as at some stage between 1135 and 1154 Alexander de Cauntelou, one of the main tenants of the Tancarville family, granted the market to the prior and convent of Bruton. It was clearly successful in the medieval period as in 1330 men from Glastonbury were travelling to it to buy goods and a market road ran between the two places, passing through West Pennard and Norwood Park towards Glastonbury Tor. In 1611 the road from Babcary that passed to the west of North Barrow to Bruton was called 'the Market Way'.

After the Reformation the market was let to Sir Maurice Berkeley in 1545 and sold to him the following year. Twenty years later in May 1565 he received an additional licence or a re-grant to hold a market every Wednesday "for fish, woollen and linen cloth and thread and wool." As with the Fairs, the tolls of the market were leased by the subsequent Lords of the Manor to the same family. If Wednesday was the original market day, by the early seventeenth century it had moved to Saturday. (7)

The market itself became established at the point where the High Street and Quaperlake Street are met by Patwell Street and Coombe Street. There may originally have been a market place or square at this location but if so this has been filled in with later buildings. On the other hand, from that starting point various standings or shambles and pent-houses spread west along the High Street so from some stage the market may have been more linear in form. The success of the market led to the construction of two buildings associated with it: the first was the Market Cross. This Cross, was built, according to John Leland by Abbot John Ely, apparently within a year of being elected to office and following on from the success of his predecessor in that office in obtaining a licence for two Fairs. "There is in the Market Place of the Town a new Crosse of six arches, and a piller yn the middle for market folks to stand yn, begon and brought up to fornix by Ely laste Abbote of Bruton. A.D. 1533."

The Fairs and the Market Cross together indicate an on-going concern for the prosperity of the town by the Abbey, a prosperity from which they, of course, would directly benefit.

Subsequent descriptions of the Cross referred to ribs of the arches which diverged from the centre column to each one of the outside pillars "whence springs a flat arch which forms the Roof in Stone and is branched every way in Gothic ornaments." The Cross stood in the road just to the west of the Ward Library building where the land slopes away down Patwell Street, which suggests that there was probably a significant space under the Cross. In fact a Survey in 1669 stated that since October 1633 Robert Maydman held in the name of Agnes his wife "One Standing adioyning to the high Crosse of Brewton and a parcell of Ground in the high Crosse of Brewton called a Roome under the staires of the said Crosse."

The Market Cross was eventually taken down in 1787-8, probably to ease the flow of traffic at that point. In 1788 the Surveyors of the Highway had to pay 10s "towards repairing the road where the Cross stood." In 1803 some of the stone from the Cross was still lying near a barn in Old Barton, "The open space before it covered with the stones of the Old Cross." Unfortunately no picture or sketch of the Cross seems to have survived. (8)

The second building was the Market Hall which was constructed in 1684 by public subscription. The Berkeley family were deeply involved in this enterprise as indicated by a letter sent out to various wealthy local landowners soliciting donations. It was simply signed 'Fitzharding'. "Ye concerne of this place to see yr Servants & severall others who frequent this Market endure the much severity as often they doe by rigeur of weather have set them on a very good Worke ye building a Convenient Market house but it will be too hard for them without great assistance." The Market House was built on the north side of the High Street, along the eastern side of the present Warren Barton. That this Market House was established so far along the High Street, at some distance from the Market Cross, does again suggest the linear nature of the market by that time.

The site originally contained a tenement owned by the Visitors of Sexey's Hospital and was leased to Thomas Penny, yeoman, in 1632 for 99 years. A Survey in 1716 noted that it was "now Converted into a Markett house for the benefitt of the Towne & People comeing to Brewton Markett & now in the possession of Mr John Cheeke." In later years it was sometimes referred to as the Town Hall, for example in May 1766 Robert Pavy leased "a stable situate lying and being at the upper end of the backside belonging to the Market house or Town Hall of Bruton together with the Garden and backside thereunto adjoining & also free ingress egress and regress in and thro' the said Market house or Town Hall to & from the Stable backside and Garden." Originally therefore it would seem that Warren Barton was not a passage through to Higher Backway but the entrance on the High Street merely gave access to the garden and stable behind the buildings which fronted the street.

It is not surprising that the Market Hall should be called by different names as it was used for various other purposes. The most important was that for a hundred years the first floor served as the Courtroom for the meeting of the Quarter Sessions which were held in Bruton each April or May. In addition it also seems to have been a place of worship for Quakers as "The market-house in Bruton" received a Meetinghouse licence on 13 July 1736. It still appeared on a Return of Certified Places of Worship in 1752.

In the decades following the construction of the Market House the market continued to be extremely successful and in the mid-eighteenth century was reported to be selling each Saturday, "Corn, Butchers meat, Garden fruits, Butter, Cheese and sometimes Fish." In fact in January 1749 a lengthy Notice in a local newspaper had announced that there was to be "a Market for all sorts of Cattle, Pigs, Cheese and Barley: where great encouragement will be given to all Farmers and others that shall bring any of the above mentioned.............The Market for all other Commodities as usual." It was subsequently claimed that drovers regularly came from near Taunton. One Pilton farmer in 1684 estimated that once he had fattened his stock on the Somerset Levels he could make a £1 profit by going to Bruton market.

For a day or two either side of market day the roads and lanes around the town must have been a scene of constant movement as animals and birds were driven to market at a slow pace and then onward after sale and men and women carrying other goods for sale or home after purchase. A somewhat idealized general description was written in 1838:

Top of Market Hall showing date 1684

"The footpaths are filled with a hardy and homely succession of pedestrians, men and women, with baskets on their arms, containing their butter, eggs, apples, mushrooms, walnuts, nuts elderberries, blackberries, bundles of herbs, young pigeons, fowls, or whatever happens to be in season. There are boys and girls too, similarly loaded, and also with baskets of birds' nests in spring, cages of young birds and old birds, baskets of tame rabbits, and bunches of cowslips, primroses, and all kinds of flowers and country productions imaginable."

By the 1780s the market had declined as in November 1788 sixty-one local men signed a declaration that while the Market "has not for many years past been so much frequented as formerly" they believed it should be re-established and committed themselves to attend it on 15th November and regularly thereafter. The list of signatories included thirty-seven yeomen, seven mealmen, six maltsters and five butchers. Their attempt may not have been entirely successful as early in 1808 another attempt was made to re-start it and "the first market for the sale of cattle and grain, which, notwithstanding the severity of the weather, was numerously attended." Cattle prices were reported to be good and "wheat, barley, pease and oats met a ready sale."

The decline, however, seems to have continued as in January 1818 another group of "Gentlemen, Farmers, Graziers and Tradesmen of the neighbourhood" met and resolved to establish a monthly market "for cattle, cheese, corn, butter etc." In the next twenty years or so the market was variously reported to be small, discontinued or still in existence. These differences may be explained by the failure of the large market for cattle and grain but the possible survival of a small market for more general goods on Saturdays. In 1821 Pigot noted that there was a "Market every Saturday, and a large market, called the monthly market, the last Saturday in every month." In 1850 the 'Yeovil Times' reported that the market-place had been converted into a potato ground which may substantiate the view that the cattle market had failed and as that was more likely to have been held on the old Fair ground rather than in the High Street in the mid nineteenth century, it was that which was dug up for potatoes and not one of the main streets.

One final attempt was made in the nineteenth century to re-establish a market and that was at a meeting in August 1855. Local inhabitants considered that the imminent opening of the Wiltshire, Somerset and Weymouth Railway, with a station at Bruton, would be a beneficial time. In September 1855 notices were placed in local newspapers giving information about a Corn and General Market weekly and a Cheese and Cattle Market monthly. By December they were operational but once again with limited success as by 1861 they were felt to be "of little importance."

It is far from easy to explain the decline of a market in Bruton from the late eighteenth century, at the very time when more non-food producers lived in the town than ever before. Certainly the development and expansion of markets in other towns such as Frome for cattle and corn must have had a large impact. The very prosperity of Bruton attracted more and more traders to settle there and open their own businesses which increasingly catered for the everyday needs of the majority of the inhabitants. By the end of the eighteenth century and into the nineteenth century there were thirty-three butchers shambles alone on their site immediately to the east of Chapel Barton. In addition, the development of transport, including improvements to roads and the coming of the railways, meant that it was no longer essential to sell goods in the location in which they were produced, for example, by the end of the nineteenth century local farmers such as Josiah Jackson of Durslade Farm regularly sent milk to London.

While there can be little doubt that the markets in Bruton changed significantly through time, to specialize more and more in cattle and corn, they did, especially in the earlier part of the period, provide an opportunity for all levels of society to be involved and to interact with each other. There was of course the odd occasion when this interaction was judged to be too much as in October 1615 Roger Wilton and Rosa Walter of Wyke Champflower were presented before the Church Court for adultery, "And that hee frequenteth her howse both earlie and late verie often in the absence of her husband And that they meete together att Brewton market, where they doe place them selves together." For these activities he was fined the large sum of 20s.

Just as on fair days the sight of so many goods on the stalls was too much of a temptation for some of those who attended the markets. The desperation of poverty may have been an explanation or simply greed. In March 1621 John Carey "had a peece of Lynnen Cloth Stolen from him out of his standinge" but the theft was witnessed and so he "went and apprehended the ptie wich was one Wynfrett Davis and found his goods uppon her." In September 1653 Melior Virgin of Wincanton reported that she "saw one Christian Parfitt take and unpin one lace neckcloathe from the Standing of Agnes Gill" valued at 8d. After a search the item was subsequently found in her basket and "the Constable tooke and secured the said Woman that she might aunswer for what she had done." Nearly one hundred years later in November 1751 Joan Dally approached the standing of John Penny of Evercreech in Bruton Market "and without asking the price of any of his meatt Took up one peice of

Beef" and walked away. When challenged she denied the action but the beef was found under her apron. (9)

As this chapter has demonstrated there were opportunities for all members of the community to come together and be involved in common activities. In reality, of course, there were differences between the activities, customs and leisure pursuits of the wealthy and the poor and these became more and more pronounced as the centuries advanced.

4. FOR THE WEALTHY.

In 1751 Henry Fielding wrote, "To be born for no other Purpose than to consume the Fruits of the Earth is the Privilege of very few. The greater Part of Mankind must sweat hard to produce them, or Society will no longer answer the Purpose for which it was ordained." For the nobility and landowners leisure time was available because they had a veritable army of servants, both indoor and outdoor, to cater for their every wish and to do the necessary work. Their houses were the most comfortable in the land and through the centuries their possessions increased dramatically with more furniture, paintings, sculptures, china as well as more clothes and personal items. In the levels of society below them including traders, merchants, lawyers and craftsmen the same process was happening but to a lesser degree and with few of the refinements of the nobility.

Already in the late medieval and early Tudor periods the surviving Wills for Bruton inhabitants show that as well as cash and tools of their trade some people, both men and women were identifying specific household goods to leave to members of their family and others. In her Will of 1517 widow Alice Brymmore left "ij Spones of Silver" to each of the children of her deceased son Richard. Three years later in 1520 Richard Holmede, a tucker, left to his daughter Christian "vi platters, six podingers and six sawcers, too crockes, a basyn, a laver of brasse, a chafing disshe, iiij candlestyckes, a new flock bed." In 1543 William Gane left his servant Isabell Mog "a pair of sheets, a pair of blankets, a coverlet, a bolster and two pillows, half a dozen pewter vessels, a cow and a heifer." His son John, along with money received "a great crock and iiij silver spoons" and his son William, money and "a great crock, a cow and a bed."

When local landowner Sir John Fitzjames of Redlynch made his Will in October 1539 there was a very long list of items which included "to my wife plate value £100.......two of the best beddes of downe at Redlinch.....three featherbeds and thre mattras with coverledds and blankets". There were references to tablecloths, napkins, flat bowls with covers, silver basins and ewers, silver cups, dishes and plates. It revealed a very comfortable lifestyle at that time for the man who had been the Chief Justice in England.

The Will of widow Agnes Morris in January 1633 identified a wide range of household and personal items for distribution: feather beds, feather bolsters, blankets, canvas sheets, rugs, table boards, stools, brass pans, kettles, spits, crocks, chests, table napkins and a cup with a silver handle. In addition she bequeathed, several petticoats, aprons, a whittle, 'wastcoat', hats and gowns, making a clear distinction that her daughter in law should receive the gown which "I doe weare sondaies" and Katheren Perry the one which "I doe weare satterdaies." She was clearly a woman of some substance.

Over one hundred years later a list of paintings hanging in the Hall and adjacent rooms of Bruton Abbey contained at least eighteen portraits of various members of the Berkeley family and the Royal family, several of which were by Van Dyke and Sir Peter Lely, and also included two self portraits, one by Van Dyke and one by Rembrandt. It was not just the very wealthy who had pictures as an Inventory of "Wadden" House on the death of H.S. Michell in 1831 listed thirty-four paintings, drawings, engravings and prints. When the contents of Tolbury House were auctioned after the death of Mrs Goldesbrough in 1855, as well as many prints, there were over six hundred volumes of books.

The Georgian period was a time when a man or his family could display not only wealth but also taste or even character by the nature of the style of the house or rooms, the decorations and furnishings. Shortly before Bruton Abbey was demolished an observer noted that, "The rooms were fitted up with cornices of stucco" and there were numerous inscriptions throughout the building, including over the study door of the last Lord Berkeley, "Quid verum atque decens curo et rogo, et totus in hoc sum." ("That I care about and seek truth and propriety, and I am devoted to this.") One of his sundials advised "Vestigia nulla retrorsum." ("Search for nobody in the past.").

One visitor to Redlynch House in 1754 commented, "The house is well furnished within, and there are many good pictures in it." Eight years later Horace Walpole gave a more detailed description of this "comely dwelling, a new stone house with good rooms." He noted that over the fireplace in the entrance hall was "a bas relief, a sacrifice to Diana" and the salon was "hung with green damask and pictures. The chimney piece from one Inigo Jones….. The next is a drawing room, hung with tapestry of the months, manufacture of Mortelack. Ebony table, glass and stands, ornamented with silver." He found that even a dressing room was "hung with green damask and pictures", while the Great Bedchamber was "very handsome room…… dressing table in gilt plate, and a rich bason and ewer, in good taste." There were busts in the passages and above the library a billiard room hung with portraits.

While leisure and recreational pursuits could dominate the lives of landowners they had to ensure that their estates were run efficiently, which usually involved the employment of a bailiff, steward or other agent. After Sir Stephen Fox purchased the Manor of Redlynch in 1672 he was for more than thirty years almost entirely non-resident. For some of this time the estate was managed successively by two of his brothers, John and then Thomas who supervised the activities of a tenant bailiff, Penny. Penny seems to have been very ineffective as in February 1689 a neighbour wrote to Fox, "As to old Penny he hath been a long time bed-rid, nor can I imagine what use he ever was to yor Honour… It is a certaine rule of wisdome among country people to devour absent landlords." After Sir Stephen's death in 1716, his son Stephen settled at Redlynch, devoted much time, effort and money to the estate, was created Lord Ilchester in 1741 and Earl in 1756. (10)

a)   Violent activities.

For nearly three hundred years after 1500 the wealthier inhabitants remained very close to the rural population in general. It meant that they supported explicitly or implicitly their leisure activities, many of which were violent in nature. The wealthy could be found patronizing cockfighting, cock-throwing, badger- bull- and bear-baiting, all of which occurred in the Bruton area and all involved some degree of cruelty to animals and birds. In the mid-eighteenth century the Berkeley family was still providing prizes for annual Sword and Dagger contests at Bruton Feast.

Such a situation was unsurprising in the earlier part of the period as some landowners were themselves involved in activities which led to brushes with the law: James Fitzjames was implicated in two murders in the 1550s; the sons of Sir Maurice Berkeley were alleged to have taken part in illegal deer killing and assaulting other men in Selwood Forest in 1572; and Sir Henry Berkeley was involved in countless quarrels, disputes and hostile encounters in the 1590s and into the 1600s. By the 1700s many of the gentry strongly believed that it was in their own interests not to create hostility or tensions in the countryside and so there was a general tolerance and acquiescence in what was happening within the lower orders. In September 1759 Revd. Woodforde recorded that he "went to the Bear-baiting in Ansford" and in August 1770 attended a boxing match at Ansford Inn "between one Mellish of Bruton and one Bond of Evercreech. Mellish the Crack was beat." This was clearly still a very popular sport as he added, "Great number of People came to see it."

Attitudes, however, were changing for a number of reasons. The spread of education in the sixteenth century led to considerable development in the concept of what constituted a gentleman: it was no longer good enough just to be able to fight to serve the monarch as a knowledge of literature, art, music and architecture was required as well. The presence of a Free School for boys in Bruton from at least the early sixteenth century, which was attended by the sons of many local men, must have had a cumulative effect through time. It was after all designed to create scholars, "for the founders of the said scole intend wt our lordes mercy oonly to have the grammer of latyn tongue so sufficiently taught that the scolers of the same profiting and proving shall in tymes to come forever be after their capacities perfight latyn men." Increasingly London became the cultural centre for the wealthy, followed by many provincial towns of which Bath was a prime example. These centres began to be places for the leisure activities of the wealthy, the arbiters of fashion, manners, refinement and lifestyle.

More and more the gentry withdrew from continuous active involvement in the countryside. Servants in country houses such as Redlynch and Bruton Abbey had a separate servants' hall in which they congregated and ate away from the family. Wealthy farmers no longer had their labourers and female servants living in the farmhouse and eating at the farmer's table. Increasingly they had to rent whatever cottages they could find, no matter what the distance from their place of labour. The educated wealthy began to reject the age-old rural superstitions, such as those involving witches and illness or death caused by some supernatural force. Even the eighteenth century economic theory of mercantilism caused the groups to move further apart as it led many to regard the poor as in some way inferior as national wealth, the theory postulated, depended upon large numbers of poorly paid labourers. Very few mill-owners as a result were ever generous with their wages. Finally changes in farming techniques and developments in transport significantly increased the mobility of labourers which led to the gradual break-up of traditional communities.

It comes as no surprise, therefore, that many of the activities in which the poorer inhabitants in the countryside had traditionally indulged faced severe and developing criticism and some faded away. On the other hand the pastimes of the wealthy seem to have escaped serious attack.

b)   Hunting, shooting and fishing.

Hunting had a long history in this country and had been pursued with a passion by William the Conqueror. There were very strict laws on who could hunt, for example, as early as 1389 the qualification to hunt game was fixed at £2 and from 1670 a man had either to be the lord of the manor or have a substantial income from land to even kill a hare on his own land. In the eighteenth and nineteenth centuries more and more laws were passed by Parliament against unqualified hunting for a wide range of animals and birds. These became known collectively as the Game Laws and carried severe punishments including fines, imprisonment and transportation.

Originally much of the hunting had been for deer but they became a recognised part of the landscape when men like Capability Brown designed whole estates with them as an integral feature. By the seventeenth century deer were included in the Park attached to Bruton Abbey and in the early eighteenth century were present at Redlynch as well. This meant that there was a significant movement towards hunting other animals such as hares and foxes. As guns improved there was yet another development with the deliberate breeding of game birds such as partridge and pheasant and the preservation of this game became much more common. It is no coincidence that as the Game Laws became more extensive in the eighteenth century so did the number of cases of poaching brought before local Justices of the Peace, themselves landowners.

Hunting was clearly popular in the medieval period by the canons of Bruton Priory and may well have been taken to excess as in April 1452 included of Bishop Bekynton's Injunctions to the Priory was a ban on hunting as "the practice of hunting has led to many evils among the canons, and especially to dissoluteness, incontinence and great ill-repute." He did however add the proviso that hunting could take place with the permission of the Prior or Sub-prior and as long as it was in their presence or that of another senior canon. The punishment imposed upon any canon who breeched this Injunction was abstinence from flesh for a week.

Various members of the Redlynch House family embraced hunting and shooting with considerable enthusiasm. In November 1748 Lord Ilchester stated that most days he went "to the Forest for 4 or 5 hours. Woodcocks scarce. Pheasants and Hares not scarce." He then added, rather immodestly, "By the by, I really shoot exceedingly well; you can't imagine how few shots I have missed lately." In December 1872 the Earl was joined for the day by HRH

Prince Arthur to take part in a shoot on his estate. The amount of game which could be shot was prodigious, for example, on one day in December 1875 the Earl with six others "made an excellent bag, 986 head of game." The Hoares on their estates had not been quite so successful, nevertheless for the season 1832-3 Sir Richard Colt Hoare noted 1,121 game killed: 500 pheasant, 223 partridge, 179 hares, 112 woodcocks, 42 snipes, 38 wild fowl, 12 widgeon, 11 Readheads and 4 handrall. Between 1822 and 1833 the average number of game killed each year on their estates amounted to 1,352.

No wonder that each local estate employed several gamekeepers and under-gamekeepers to ensure a regular supply of birds and to check the activities of the poachers. On the day of a shoot large numbers of beaters would be employed to ensure that good sport was obtained. It is clear that shooting was an expensive recreation and so remained restricted to the very wealthy. Hunting too could entail considerable expenditure, as a pack of hounds could change hands for up to £2,000. By the early nineteenth century the whole system had become highly organised and books were written regularly on the subject. "Every field sport is here become a science. Hunting, coursing, shooting, each has its own season, its well-defined bounds, its peculiar horses, dogs, and weapons..... Through the winter, then up to the very approach of spring, hunting offers whatever charms it possesses: pheasants, woodcock, and snipe shooting, in the woods and by the streams, are all in their glory."

For other wealthy men of leisure to hunt legally after 1784 a licence had to be obtained on payment of a duty and by 1790 seven of those who qualified in Bruton had obtained the necessary Game Certificate: John and Ludwell Dampier, Revd. John Goldesbrough,

John Hoddinott, Henry Albin Martin, Revd. Edward Michell and George Ward. The brother-in-law of Revd. Woodforde, John Pounsett of Cole also had a certificate so the Parson recorded on 1st September 1786 that the latter killed four brace of partridges and on 7th September 1793 one of his guests at Cole, William Webb of Wincanton, "Killed a brace of Partridges, a Hen Pheasant and a fine fat Rail." More generally hunting seems to have become associated with Bruton Feast as in 1791 it was noted, "An excellent pack of hounds will attend each morning on Creech Hill."

Two types of hunting for recreational purposes seem to have remained popular in the Bruton area. The first was hare coursing in which a hare was pursued by dogs, usually greyhounds, by sight and not by scent. The main aim of hare coursing was not necessarily to kill the hare but to provide a competition between two dogs. As early as 1560 the Duke of Norfolk had devised a complicated means of assessing the performance of the dogs based on the extent to which a dog forced a hare to move away from the straightest line of its escape. It did of course offer the possibility of gambling for the wealthier members of the community. In 1776 Lord Orford founded the first Coursing Club.

Although the Revd. Woodforde does not appear to have been an avid sportsman, he did take part occasionally in this activity as on 27th October 1763 when a hare was found near his house in Ansford, "Mr Cross and myself went out and coursed it before breakfast and killed it with Mr Cross's dogs and a good course it was." In September 1786 he was still enthusiastic if not completely successful, "A Hare was found sitting near Lisbury and Mr Pounsett and self went out and saw her coursed – soon killed. After that Mr Pounsett and self went out a coursing till dinner time, coursed a brace and killed one."

Over eighty years later in April 1869 members of the Hadspen and Shepton Montague Coursing Club celebrated their first anniversary with a dinner at the Blue Ball Inn for eighty men "including many of the principal residents of the town and neighbourhood." They were referred to as "the lovers of this good old fashioned sport." The following year before the dinner, "Over 49 horsemen put, or rather galloped in an appearance, while crowds of individuals who adopted more primitive and less imposing means of locomotion, also attended and took part in the thoroughly English sports of the day. 49 hares were found, 29 of these afforded capital sport, which eight paid for with their lives."

Subsequent reports indicate that the enthusiasm did not diminish. As late as November 1897 Josiah Jackson noted, "went over to Godminster to the fag end of a coursing (Hare) meeting." The numbers involved make it clear that this remained a popular sport not only amongst the wealthier members of the community who took an active part but also with labourers as well, although for them it was often a case of following on foot.

The second form of hunting was for foxes which were perceived as a perennial problem in the countryside, especially for anyone who bred or kept game or domestic birds. For that reason no property qualification was required for fox-hunting and, although it remained dominated by the aristocracy and country gentlemen, in the second half of the eighteenth century it attracted many farmers and wealthier professionals and tradesmen. This new breed of hunter could become very irate if they discovered that landowners were deliberately trying to get rid of foxes to protect their game. In the early nineteenth century one of Sir Richard Colt Hoare's gamekeepers was caught transporting foxes out of the county. It was not unusual for hunters to bribe gamekeepers to leave foxes alone but in this instance the aggrieved fox-hunter complained to Sir Richard that the gamekeeper defended himself by stating that as he "had never seen the colour of my money I could not expect & should not have any Fox of his catching."

At the end of the nineteenth century at Durslade Farm Josiah Jackson made many references to fox hunting and the regular meetings locally and on his land, for example in November 1895 he noted, "Fox Hunters met Redlynch Gate this morning" and March 1897, "Fox hunters here." When he knew that the hunters were expected he made the necessary arrangements such as in November 1897, "Had locks took off gates for Fox hunters tomorrow." Needless to say he was not always pleased with the results of their visits but as a tenant farmer there was little that he could do, "This day some of the Fox Hunters, about 7, rode across my Winter Beans and wheat top of Hill, about 6 acres each lot and did considerable harm."

On one occasion in February 1863 a particularly cunning fox appears to have had a very lucky escape. When it was being pursued by the Mendip Fox Hounds towards Wyke Champflower, it took refuge upstairs in a house. It managed to hide while the huntsmen searched the building but was eventually spotted as it climbed a ladder which led to a garret. It did however escape though an open skylight and reached its home safely, "and thus cheated its pursuers of the intended prize." (11)

Although rabbits had been bred in the medieval period for their fur and as food, as witness the rabbit warren of Bruton Priory and another at Cole, in later centuries they became a major pest and were extensively hunted. The problem for many tenant farmers was that by the terms of their leases they were not permitted to kill these rabbits until after the passing of the Ground Game Act in

1880, no matter how much damage they did to crops. Prior to that date the landowner hunted them himself or leased the right to do so and hence in 1873 T.O. Bennett, a Bruton Land Agent, leased "Cogley Wood & Durslade Shooting", and in a letter to Sir Henry Hoare in September of that year he claimed that Mr Herrington, the tenant of Durslade Farm at that time "Has full confidence in me as to the Rabbitts, and you may depend on my having them kept down as much as possible." At the end of the century a later tenant, Jackson, was still plagued by them but at least by then he could do something about it. On 24th January 1899 he noted, "Went Rabbiting, killed 20." They could do considerable damage, "Went to Cogley Wood & had a look at the damage done by Rabbits to underwood" and he decided as a result to put up wire netting in an attempt to protect a large area. On 16th November he shot nine rabbits and thirty-five more the following day. While for some men there was sport in this activity, for Jackson it was also an absolute necessity.

A range of other animals and birds were hunted and shot for recreational purposes by the wealthier members of the community. Revd. Woodforde recorded somewhat despondently in his Diary on 11th January 1764, "I afterwards went out a shooting for about two Hours, and Killed nothing but a Crow." In 1876 after the presentation of a silver hunting flask to J.P. Fitzgerald who for twenty-two years had been the land steward and agent of the Earl of Ilchester, a stag hunt had been arranged. A buck and a pack of hounds were brought to Creech Hill and the former released. It was chased through Lamyatt to Evercreech and back to Spargrove and Pinkwood and was finally caught near Bruton Railway Station.

Otters were regarded as a threat to the sport of fishing and as late as 1889 one local gentleman was reported to have offered 5s a head for each otter destroyed. In October 1795 Revd. Woodforde recorded "Caught a very large Bitch Otter in the Garden today with a large Gin" at his sister's house in Cole. In January 1875 J. Balch and J. Hoddinott shot a dog otter weighing nearly twenty-five pounds in Wyke Champflower and four years later Mr Glynn of the Glen, Bruton, shot a fourteen-pound otter which was three feet six inches long.

Pigeon shooting also seemed to have had its supporters in Bruton although in 1718-1719 Thomas Vigar was fined 10s for "Shooting Pidegeons" illegally. From the middle of the nineteenth century it had become a much more organised activity. In December 1856 a shooting match was arranged by the landlord of the Sun Inn but bad weather meant that the participants spent more time inside enjoying a dinner. Twenty years later a shoot took place on Atkins's Hill but the reporter had to record "of the sport itself we can say little, except that most of the pigeons fell to the 'irregular troops', who had, as usual, posted themselves out of bounds."

Although Revd. Woodforde was not a great hunter he was clearly passionate about fishing as his Diary contains many references to this pastime. In September 1768 he recorded, "I caught 4 brace of Tench very fine ones out of our Pond-Close this morning in less than an hour", aided by his father's drag net. In July 1786 when he was staying at Cole, "After breakfast I walked out a fishing, had not put my Line in Water more than five Minutes before I caught a fine Trout of one Pound and a Quarter with a Grasshoper. It measured in length 14 Inches." Three years later once again in Cole "I spent most of the Day a fishing, caught a brace of Trout and three Eels." For those men who had the necessary wealth or the leisure time it was an ideal existence.

The canons of Bruton Priory had their fishponds close to their monastery and at Brewham, but in their case they were a source of food rather than sport. Once the Berkeleys were installed in the Abbey they continued to maintain the fishponds which became part of their pleasure grounds to the east of their residence. "An arch over the road led to some ponds in the meadows on the other side, by which were some walks." It is highly unlikely that fishing by any local inhabitants was permitted and the same may be said of the ornamental lakes created in Redlynch Park, especially in the eighteenth century.

The wealthy protected their hunting, shooting and fishing avidly so other local residents fell foul of the laws relating to these, most of which centred on poaching. In November 1765 John Chaffin was fined the standard £5 for killing a hare using a dog and a gun. The Magistrates' Entry Books in the second half of the nineteenth century contain numerous cases of 'Trespass in search of Conies', the local name for rabbits, with the usual fine being 5s and 5s 6d costs, for example Stephen Cocks in September 1855, William Gover in August 1868, Thomas Rendle in March 1871 and Henry Balch in 1881. Unauthorized fishermen faced a fine if caught, for example in 1712-13 Richard Fenn was fined 10s and Thomas Vigar the same in 1719-20. Similar fines were imposed upon Albert Chant and William Longman in May 1881 when they were found "Illegally fishing in the River Brue at Pitcombe." Thomas Vigar does appear to have been particularly inept as in the same year as he was fined for fishing he was fined another 10s for "Shooting Pidegeons."

With so much hunting and shooting accidents became inevitable. When pigeon shooting was taking place in December 1856 Edward Ashford was eighty yards away when he "met with a shot in the eye, the sight of which will be entirely lost." No compensation was payable in those days. In January 1876 when the Earl of Ilchester was leading a shooting party a boy who was beating with his father "received a charge of shot in his leg." At least he was treated by the local doctor, Dr.Heginbothom, and installed in the Blue Ball Inn. Both incidents seem to indicate remarkably careless shooting by the hunters. Even the aristocracy could be injured as in December 1895 T.O. Bennett added a note to a letter to the Earl of Cork and Orrery, one of the Visitors of Sexey's Hospital, "I was very sorry to observe your Lordship's accident in the Hunting Field & sincerely hope you are recovering."

As well as for recreational purposes game was important for one other reason to the wealthy and that related to the custom of gifts. Such presents were regarded as an important method of cementing social relationships, of gaining gratitude and hence maintaining the peace and stability of the countryside. In 1532 Canon Richard Bishop of Bruton Abbey wrote to Lady Lisle, "my master hath him recommended to my lord and to your good ladyship, and do thank your good ladyship for his venison and for manifold kindness besides." On 1ˢᵗ September 1795 Revd. Woodforde, staying at Cole, noted, "old Mr Dalton called on us with two fine Pheasants in his Pocket as a present to us." A few days later he received "a fine Cock Pheasant" from Mr Webb of Wincanton. In fact Woodforde became quite annoyed if a hunter shot on his land and did not give him some of the result as on more than one occasion he recorded that sportsmen had been successful "but never sent me a single Bird." In 1807 approximately one third of all the game killed on Sir Richard Colt Hoare's local estates went to farmers in the area. In most years in the 1890s Josiah Jackson received a brace of pheasants from his landlord, Sir Henry Hoare, or from the Earl of Ilchester. (12)

c)   Other Outdoor Pursuits.

While hunting, shooting and fishing constituted the major part of the outdoor activities of the wealthy, there were several other pursuits which appear in the Bruton and the surrounding area. Bowles were clearly important in the early seventeenth century as in 1633 the curate Emmanuel Mason was accused of neglecting his duty, "he beinge att bowles in the parke." The reference to the Park suggests that the game was taking place on land belonging to the Berkeleys and therefore likely to have been patronized by them. Horse racing was popular in the eighteenth and nineteenth centuries, "Racing, every one knows, is a matter of intense interest with the greater portion of the nobility, gentry, and others." It was probably the source of the most common form of gambling amongst the wealthy. In August 1789 Revd. Woodforde and several other gentlemen bet on two horses running at Kingweston, "I lost as all the others Losers did 1   1   0." Although much of the organization was controlled by the wealthier members of the community, it was a sport which appealed to all levels in society. The same clergyman also noted that at Bruton Races in 1795 "a vast Concourse of People attended, both gentle and simple."

Horse or pony racing also occurred at the Bear Inn in Dropping Lane as in August 1749 John Cheeke placed a Notice in a local newspaper, "That on Monday the 7th day of August, will be run for at Dropping Lane, near Bruton, in the County of Somerset, a handsome Saddle, the value of Two Guineas, by Poneys not to exceed Twelve Hands and half, carrying each a Feather." There were to be three heats, each four miles in length. Cheeke added, "Any Gentleman that has a mind to send their Poney may depend on great care taken of him." Twenty years later it was still a popular location as in August 1769 Revd. Woodforde reported that his brother "John spent his

Afternoon &c at Dropping Lane, Horse-racing there." Like other wealthy men John Woodforde was prepared to travel some distance to races, such as to Bath in September 1770. By the late nineteenth century local horse racing had become centred on Wincanton.

Earlier in that century there had been a revival of interest in archery. Whereas in the medieval period and beyond archery had been crucial for warfare by the 1830s it was for competition and social purposes. In February 1832 a local newspaper reported that, "The gentry of the eastern part of this county have lately formed a Society, called the 'Selwood Foresters,' the principal object of which appears to be the amusement and practice of archery." Its patron was Sir Richard Colt Hoare of Stourhead and others involved in its management were Henry Hoare and Henry Hobhouse. It was following the example of one which already existed in the western part of the county.

Throughout the 1830s meetings occurred, usually at Stourhead on the terrace near Alfred's Tower, with spectacular views "at which were present nearly all the nobility and gentry for many miles around." It is interesting to note that while a "number of splendidly dressed ladies dispersed over the grounds", others took part in the competitions themselves. It was clearly viewed as an activity suitable for ladies. The prizes could be somewhat unusual, for example in July 1834 the first prize was "an antique cameo set in silver, supposed to be a head of Alfred, and presenting an additional local interest from having been found within the purliens of the Selwood Forest."

These archery meetings or fetes were significant social gatherings during the day and were followed by evening activities. "Dancing was kept up in the evening with great spirit, under the spacious tent which had been prepared for the company." They were not without the occasional problem as in September 1834 a local newspaper reported that while Rev Dr Colston and his family were attending a meeting "some evil-disposed person stole the front brace from the carriage.......by which the lives of his family were endangered in descending the precipitous hill from the Tower."

Football was often viewed as rather violent and barbaric and therefore only suitable for the masses, whereas cricket was more refined and genteel. It was thus perceived as more appropriate for gentlemen and so it was not surprising that a few games began to emerge in the neighbourhood in the eighteenth century. In August 1772 a cricket match occurred near Dropping Lane between the Gentlemen of Bruton and the Gentlemen of Redlynch for a purse of twenty guineas. It was obviously not an isolated occurrence as in September of the same year a newspaper noted, "We hear from Bruton that there will be a grand match played there on Tuesday next, between the gentlemen of the said town, for 30 guineas aside."

As the nineteenth century progressed and King's School moved further and further away from its free school origins and became much more a fee-paying institution, attracting the sons of wealthier families, cricket developed there. It was very well established by 1867 when one report commented that the School had "a capital eleven" with a very strong captain, H.P.Price, who in one match made seventy-five out of the 115 runs and bowled out seven of the opposition. Subsequent reports in local newspapers indicate that the School remained strong in this sport in the decades which followed. One unfortunate aspect for the Cricket team was that they had to share the Abbey Field with the football team until 1893 when the latter moved to a new location at Markesdanes. The following year the Editor of the 'Dolphin' magazine recorded, "We must congratulate the School on the generous gift it has received in the shape of a new Cricket Pavilion. The building is of wood with a tiled roof."

One master, Littleton Powys, who taught at the School between 1896 and 1901, recalled, "And to me, who loved cricket, as I did, those summer terms were delightful. I and other keen cricketers spent many happy hours on that beautiful cricket ground that lay between the church and the railway. In those days the numbers of the school were scarcely sufficient to provide an eleven strong enough to play the better local clubs without the assistance of some of the masters." By 1903, however, the position had clearly improved so much that one former pupil, Geoffrey Cator, noted that in that year, "we were good enough to earn a mention in the Public Schools section of Widen - then a five-star rating." At least two of their old boys played for Somerset in 1914 but as Cator added, "Poor boys, within a few months they were both dead in Flanders." (13)

    d)   Food and Drink.

For the wealthy eating and drinking were important leisure activities which often occupied several hours at a time. Breakfast was usually at nine or ten o'clock in the morning and Dinner in the early afternoon, although this became gradually later in the eighteenth century as it interfered with the hours of hunting. For some the day was then rounded off with Supper. Some types of food found their way almost exclusively onto the plates of the gentry, for example, in the mid 1750s in Bruton it was claimed, "Trouts and Eels not in quantities for sale, the Lord of the Manor reserve them for his own use."

Those of the aristocracy, gentry and wealthier members of the community who gave their time to act as Governors or Trustees did ensure that after their meetings they were sufficiently fed. In 1692 the Governors of the Free School agreed that in future "we will not have above 12 Bottles of Wine spent at ye next general meeting & and that we will not pay for the Ordinary of any person that Dine here, but the Governors, Tenants, the Schoolmaster, the Minister of ye Town & ye Steward." Incomplete records make it impossible to determine how much wine was being consumed at these meetings before 1692 or how many other people turned up and were fed, but that it was felt necessary to impose such a restriction may suggest a very large number.

In August 1791 the Treasurer paid £16   15s   0d for the dinner of the Visitors of Sexey's Hospital after their annual meeting and a further £1   12s   0d for that of the members of the Corporation, a substantial difference for approximately the same number of men so the Visitors must have really dined in style. Every time that a Visitation occurred in the Church the Clergy dined afterwards, for example, in 1769 Revd. Woodforde paid 3s   9d for his dinner at the Unicorn Inn which in his opinion "is not near so good as Ansford Inn. The Dinner was tolerably good – we had Venison there." The following year when he dined with nineteen other clergy at the same venue "my Dinner and Liquor" cost 3s   6d.

For the wealthier classes dining at an inn was an accepted leisure pursuit from at least the early seventeenth century. "1627 payd to Mr Chick for the Governors dyett the day that they made this Accompt iijli vs." In April 1770 news reached Bruton that John Wilkes, the radical orator, was to be released from prison and was so well received by a group of "gentlemen at their club feast at the Bell Inn…[*that they*] bespoke an elegant dinner for the day of Mr Wilkes enlargement." When Lord Ilchester came of age in 1808 "a party of gentlemen dined at the Blue Ball Inn, and spent the day in great hilarity." The development of road transport in the eighteenth century meant that several Inns in the town, such as the Old Bull Inn and later the Wellington Inn, became coaching inns and here travellers could expect a meal. In the nineteenth century a celebratory meal in an Inn became a regular occurrence: royal events, Friendly Society anniversaries and any Society's annual meeting.

The Revd. Woodforde really enjoyed his food as countless pages in his Diary record the range of items and the quantities consumed. On 1st July 1779 he noted that at a friend's house in Castle Cary six people at the dining table consumed "3 fowls boiled and a Piggs Face, a Haunch of Venison rosted and sweet Sauce, Tarts and Cheese cakes." At his sister's house at Cole on 5th July 1782 five of them ate "for Dinner some Trout, Ham and 3 Fowls, a Leg of Mutton rosted, Custards and Gooseberry Pye." One edited printed volume of his Diary which covered the years 1782 to 1787 made reference to twenty types of fish, seventeen types of poultry and game and over twenty different fruits, all of which found their way to his table.

The presence of large landed estates in or near Bruton was of significant economic value to the tradesmen of the town. Accounts for Redlynch House for the ten-year period between 1736 and 1745 indicate that the average annual payment to local tradesmen was just over £340. Not only did the Ilchester family maintain a high standard of living when they were in residence but also weekly entries, such as "To ye Butcher for ye Poors Meat   8s   11d", demonstrate that they took their social obligations seriously.

Needless to say both food and drink were taken to excess. Revd. Woodforde seems to have experienced many episodes of what he considered to be severe indigestion but which appear at times more like food poisoning, for example, when he was staying at Cole in July 1786 he awoke ill one morning and "could eat no solids all day long – in the Afternoon was very bad indeed. Going to bed I took some Rhubarb – Purging and vomiting the whole day." He experienced violent stomach pains for two days. He did admit, "I believe I made too free Yesterday with Currant Tarts and Creams &c."

In the early seventeenth century curates at Lamyatt seem to have had a particular problem with drink. In July 1629 Thomas Loyde was alleged to be "distempered with drink, read evening prayers in such manner that all took notice of it, reading forwards and backwards." Even worse was to follow for Nicholas Gawen in 1636 as after preaching in Wells Cathendral by the afternoon "hee was soe drunk himselfe that hee became an evill specticle to the whole towne", and when it came to getting on his horse to ride back to Lamyatt, "hee was hardlie able to lift over his legg to rise into the saddle." What made this such a scandal was that his sermon in the morning had been directed against drunkenness.

Revd. Woodforde's younger brother, John, certainly drank considerable amounts of various types of alcohol and was then unable to control himself in the way expected of a clergyman's son. In April 1767 he was described as "very Much disguised in Beer", and in November 1769 he was similarly "very much disguised in Liquor." In March 1771 he and three other men became drunk when they consumed "3 bottles of Wine and near 20 quarts of Cyder." Unfortunately for the rest of the family John tended to become very noisy and abusive, would swear a great deal and threaten to fight anyone. On more than one occasion James paid his brother's debts at local inns. (14)

e) Genteel pastimes.

Throughout the eighteenth century the move towards a more cultured life style continued amongst the wealthier classes. This trend was reflected in the leisure activities of both men and women as increasingly their support for the more violent of rural pastimes diminished and other genteel activities took their place.

Traditionally public assembly rooms, theatres and halls for concerts were centred in London but gradually they spread to provincial towns such as Bristol and particularly Bath. Regular visits to watch plays were just as much a part of residence in that town as was taking the waters. On the other hand, amateur dramatics flourished in country houses and in small towns. On 28th September 1762 Revd. Woodforde was given a ticket to go to Miss Chick's Play, 'The Beggar's Opera' that evening in her house in Bruton, "and it was done pretty well – Lady Ilchester, and her Daughter Fanny, a little Girl, were there – The House was quite full." Plays seem to have been staged to coincide with Bruton Feast as in September 1771 Woodforde noted that his cousin Tom and brother John did not return to Ansford until eleven o'clock at night, "They staid so late to see a Play at Bruton, being Bruton Feast."

Groups of wandering players visited the countryside as in June 1766 Woodeforde went to the Court House in Castle Cary to see a play, 'The Orphan or Unhappy Marriage' which was "performed by some Strollers, and they did it pretty well." The following month he went to see another play, 'The Provoked Husband or a Journey to London' but this was less successful as "The Company was greatly disturbed at the Play by the noise of an insolent, saucy mob outside the Playhouse." Between 14th May and 6th June 1770 a series of plays were available for him in Castle Cary, including

'The Beggar's Opera', 'Hamlet', and 'Richard the Third'. When Beresford first edited Woodforde's Diary in 1924 he did take the opportunity to make a sharp contrast with his own day as he wondered how many small towns with a population of about 1,200 would experience such a range of culture in the 1920s. For him the fault lay with industrialization, "This is an apt illustration of the deplorable decay of country gaities following on the abnormal and dismal development of industrial life in towns."

Amateur dramatics had, however, continued in the nineteenth century in Bruton as in April 1866 "an amateur dramatic entertainment was given in the National Schoolroom" by "gentlemen of the town." It was noted that, "all the principal families of the town attended, and the rooms were crowded with a delighted audience." Other dramatic performances took place at King's School, for example, in January 1888 two packed houses appreciated performances of amongst other items, 'The Adventures of a Love Letter' by Charles Matthews.

Bruton possessed its own Assembly Rooms which were opened in the latter part of the eighteenth century and belonged to the Blue Ball Inn. The building was alongside the Inn and faced onto Coombe Street. Any gathering could take place here in one of a number of rooms, including a large open space on the first floor. It was there, for example, that Subscription Balls were held.

A second genteel pastime centred on music. The expectation was that ladies in the household of the leisured classes would become proficient in one or more aspects of music and then be able to entertain others. When Revd. Woodforde was out walking at Cole in August 1793 he met "Mrs Christie as well as Miss Sampson, very great on the Piano forte – If anything Mrs Christie is greatest." In 1813 Agnes Porter, who had been the Governess of the Ilchester's

Assembly Rooms in Coombe Street showing blocked up entrance

children and who continued to live in Bruton, described in glowing terms "Miss Mary Goldesbrough, who is very good-natured, and so charming a Musician that she has melody in her throat and harmony at her finger-ends. She is indeed compleat mistress of her instrument, and gives high gratification to her hearers."

Music could be part of a general celebration, for example, on 1st January 1767 Revd. Woodforde recorded that he "spent the whole night and part of the morning till 4 o'clock a dancing, on account of Mr James Clarke's apprenticeship being expired............We had a very good band of musick, 2 violins and a Base Viol." He added, possibly rather remorsefully, "We were excessive merry and gay there indeed." In March 1863 the marriage of the Prince of Wales was extensively celebrated in Bruton with bells, parades, games, an abundance of food and drink and "The day finished (and another day begun) by a select ball at the Blue Ball Hotel. Dancing was kept up with great spirit." A Ball was even held to round off examination day at King's School: Thomas Stockwell "finally concluded the festivities of the day by giving a ball and Supper at his residence, at Coombe Villa........till long after day light had appeared."

When he was young the Revd. Woodforde seemed to have been enthusiastic about attendance at Balls. On 3rd February 1767 he recorded that he attended a Masquerade Ball at Ansford Inn, "I did not dance the whole evening. We had good musick viz., four Violins, a Bass Biol, a Taber and Pipe, a Hautboy and French Horn." Less than two weeks later on February 16th he took Miss Jordan to a concert and "a very genteel ball" at the Bear Inn in Wincanton. He regarded Miss Jordan as "the best dancer in the room" and danced each dance with her from ten o'clock in the evening until four o'clock in the morning.

By the late eighteenth century Balls had become important social gatherings. A Ball had become associated with Bruton Feast, for example, on the third day in September 1791 there was to be "in the evening a Ball at the King's Arms." There were even Balls arranged "by the batchlors of Bruton", which in May 1836 was reported to be "a brilliant ball....the whole passed off with great spirit and animation." In a carefully chaperoned situation there was clearly still the opportunity for romance to flourish.

For a number of years after 1842 Bruton staged annual Subscription Balls, usually in January. Reports in local newspapers indicate that the majority of the principal inhabitants and neighbouring gentry attended, often amounting to over one hundred people. Quadrilles, the waltz and polka were clearly the order of the day and dancing continued through the night until four or five o'clock in the morning. It was one of the major social gatherings of the year, held in the Assembly Rooms of the Blue Ball Inn.

In the 1860s references to Subscription Balls seem to cease but Balls themselves continued. In February 1867 the Bruton detachment of the 22nd Somerset Volunteers staged a public ball to raise funds; the following year J.R. White gave a Ball on New Year's Eve, "attended by most of the neighbouring gentry." The next year the location changed to Tolbury House occupied at that time by Lieutenant Colonel Hall. By 1881 an item in a local newspaper suggested that dancing had become more extensive as it reported that a Ball at the Wellington Inn on 5th May "brought to a close a most successful dancing season." What may well have started as an entertainment for a limited number of families in the Bruton area had been extended, like so many other cultural and leisure activities, to a greater section of the Victorian middle class. (15)

A third genteel pastime was socializing which became of major importance in the eighteenth century for the leisured classes. One of the key aspects of this was visiting other peoples' houses and failure to do so could lead to social exclusion and isolation. Probably for the first time in history what a house looked like on the inside developed in significance as it indicated so much about the taste of the host. Visiting of course could be a very simple affair as it required just a single room with a small amount of furniture, including a table which was suitable for taking tea. It also meant that ladies in particular had to remain familiar with the dictates of fashion or at the very least that they were appropriately dressed.

Sometimes to gain inspiration for their own homes some visitors would arrange to view the houses of the very wealthy while they were absent. On 2nd June 1772 Revd. Woodforde with several others visited Lord Ilchester's mansion at Redlynch and where he gave the housekeeper 2s. "Mr Charles Brown (Butler to My Lord Ilchester) behaved exceedingly civil to us, he brought us to drink a Bottle of red & a Bottle of white & some strong Beer." It would seem that the custom of aristocratic hospitality still existed, even in the absence of the house owners. Some twenty years later with various family members and friends he visited Stourhead where he gave the gardener 2s 6d and "Patty Collins, who shewed the House 5s 0d." Woodforde confided in his Diary, "I don't think that the Gardens or House are kept so neat as in old Mr Hoare's time." The great danger of the pastime of visiting was that it could lead to adverse comments and gossip about another person's lifestyle or taste.

While silver and fine porcelain could be an expensive proposition and so remained very much the preserve of the wealthy, manufacturers such as Matthew Boulton produced a large range of silver plated items at a much cheaper price. Josiah Wedgwood started the trend for mass-produced good quality china and George Chippendale added a range of smaller furniture which was designed to appeal to ladies. Each of these men, and a number of other designers, innovators and businessmen, appreciated the changes which were occurring in manners and culture and responded accordingly.

Once again Revd. Woodforde made many references to socializing and he recorded meticulously both those whom he visited and those who visited him or members of his family with whom he was staying. On 21st July 1793 he recorded "Mr Dalton Senr smoked a Pipe with us at Cole in the Evening", and on 13th August in the same year, "I went with my Sister Pounsett and her Daughter to Gallhampton to Willm Woodfordes in a Chaise from Bruton where we dined and spent the Afternoon with him, his Wife, my Brother and his Wife, Mrs R Clarke, Nancy, and a strange Clergyman by name Askew & lives at Honywicke." Inevitably food played a significant part as the visits by and to Woodforde often entailed dining.

Some of the visits were to take tea or coffee, the fashionable activity of the time: "I drank tea this afternoon with Dr Arnold and Dr Clarke at Justice Creed's with him and his father." More people were involved on 7th June 1770, "Mr Hindley, Mr Hayes, the Justice and myself drank coffee this afternoon with Mrs Melliar at Mr Willm Melliar's with the Countess of Ilchester, Counsellor Melliar, etc. etc." Sometimes it involved just an individual as on 22nd August 1793, "Miss Sampson of Bruton drank Tea this Aft. at Cole." The governess of the Ilchester's children, Agnes Porter, also undertook visits, for example on 5th June 1791 she recorded in her Journal, "In the afternoon, took a walk to see the good Miss Lloyds and their mother at Bruton; a charming walk, the tea was ambrosial after it – a dish of good humour, beside."

Walking out for pleasure often meant that socializing would occur when other people were encountered, for example, on 23rd August 1789 when Revd. Woodforde and his sister were taking an evening stroll towards Bruton from Cole, they met eight Brutonians including members of the Goldesbrough, Dampier and Sampson families and lengthy conversations followed.

In the evening socializing continued, often with games of cards. Woodforde's Diary contains many entries relating to this activity and his favourite and most frequently mentioned card games seem to have been Cribbage, Loo, Quadrille and Whist. An interesting sidelight on these card games is that they were often played for money, albeit small sums, a genteel form of gambling. Woodforde invariably recorded his winnings or loses which were usually between 6d and 2s 6d.

Gambling clearly remained a leisure pursuit for the wealthier part of the population. As always there were those who took it to extremes, such as Sir Henry Ainslie Hoare, fifth Baronet, who was very much devoted to hunting and gambling. By the 1880s he had lost so much money that when rents from his agricultural estates began to decrease he was forced to sell many paintings, books and some furniture from Stourhead House. In 1885 the mansion was closed and not re-opened until after his death in 1894.

Card playing was well established by the late eighteenth century as during Bruton Feast on at least one evening out of the three there was "a Card Assembly at the Blue Ball Inn." In 1812 Agnes Porter noted that Lady Susan O'Brien had come to live in Bruton, "which she finds full of good company and quite agreeable….. she is sociable and cheerfully inclined and will have her little card parties every night." The following year she gave a description of

Miss Letitia Goldesbrough as "a very sensible, good young lady. She frequently declines going to a gay juvenile party to stay at home alone with the old admiral, her father to play cribbage with him for his amusement." For ordinary people a pack of cards could be quite expensive, for example in August 1816 one pack cost John Goldesbrough of Discove 3s 6d.

In these genteel activities many of the participants were female. Their involvement marks a very large change in the role of wealthy females in society. In her Will in 1626 Dame Elizabeth Berkeley gave a glimpse of the traditional leisure activity of a woman of her class. "Item I give unto my daughter Margarett Berkeley a Needleworke Carpett of my owne making and all the Neddeleworke stooles in my Clossett not yet finished. Item I give unto my daughter Jane a Needleworke Carpett wch my Mother gave me haveinge the Killigrewes Armes there uppon." Over a hundred years later in 1733 Lucy Temple, who was the sister-in-law of William, 4th Lord Berkeley of Stratton and who spent much time at Bruton Abbey, left to one of her sisters "my Chain Stitcht Quilt of my own Work." In addition in the medieval and early modern period much of the life of a house was centred in the Great Hall which was very much male dominated, even down to the deer's heads which festooned the walls as a result of male hunting exploits.

In the eighteenth century the concept of a large dining room still remained and here the men remained after the meal to smoke and drink their port while they discussed politics, finance and other issues relevant to them. The significant development, however, was that in the design of houses of that period there was frequently another room, a Drawing Room or Salon, into which the females would withdraw (hence its name) or retire to discuss their issues. The knowledge or information which they gained from this activity meant that they were often as well-informed and up-to-date as their husbands.

Many wealthy men needed a wife who could be the manager or administrator of the house and could keep the accounts. It has been suggested that in this respect she acted essentially as his deputy, especially as many of them were very literate and well educated, even though they had not had the same formal classical education as their husbands. In many instances it was the female who was dominant in deciding exactly what went into the house in terms of furniture and floor-coverings, down to the colour of the paint and the pattern on the wallpaper. The results may be seen in spectacular furnishings and decoration in surviving country houses of that period such as Stourhead. Female involvement in interior decoration was to remain a feature throughout the Victorian era and found expression in the writing of authors such as Mrs Gaskell, particularly in 'Wives and Daughters'.

For those fortunate enough to possess wealth their lives could be very leisured and pleasurable. When great celebrations took place in Castle Cary in August 1768 to mark Lord Stavordale's coming of age, Revd. Woodforde added that the young man was not present in person, "His Lordship is on his travels abroad." A typical day in the country was described by Lord Ilchester in November 1748, at a time when his wife's health was not good and she was away in Bath taking the waters:

> "I am call'd at half an hour past eight, seldom rise till half an hour past 9, am in the Library before ten, stay there with Julian and Harry [*two of his children*] till half an hour past eleven.....

Then to the Forest for 4 or 5 hours.......To dinner at 5, always alone, read in the dining room till 7, then adjourn to the Library, drink tea at eight, and then to some book or other till 12. I think myself very happy that I can read any print by candle light as well as ever I could, without the least pain or complaint in my eyes." (16)

5. FOR THE VICTORIAN MIDDLE CLASS.

Historians have long debated the origins of the middle class: when it came into existence and what its boundaries were. During the medieval period there were broadly speaking the landowners and the masses and in very small rural villages that remained generally the case until well into the nineteenth century. In a market town such as Bruton the position was somewhat different as the economic situation meant that it attracted wealthy merchants, traders, administrators such as bailiffs, stewards and land agents, solicitors, doctors, schoolmasters, skilled craftsmen and shopkeepers, all of whom might be regarded as the middling sort of people. They formed the basis of what became the Victorian middle class.

There were many men within these groups who believed fundamentally that it was essential to build some sort of class identity within their community. They felt that leisure time and recreational activities, if appropriately organised, could play an important part in this process. It was the case, however, that as many of these men had themselves been raised in the tradition of hard work they found adaption to leisure time difficult. Nevertheless they considered that such recreation could occur between themselves as individuals and between their families. As the nineteenth century advanced they were to place great emphasis upon activities which fostered these beliefs: including voluntary associations, literary and scientific education, debating, sports, amateur soldiering as well as socializing through externally arranged dinners or gatherings in their own homes.

By the mid-nineteenth century many of the Victorian middle class were financially secure as although there were periodic crises after 1850 they were not as severe as earlier ones and the economy as a whole expanded rapidly. In addition in their businesses and other activities this class was a significant employer, for as well as assistants and apprentices many employed a gardener, washerwoman, clerks, groom and general labourers. This of course had important implications for their leisure activities as they had both time and money. As their prosperity increased they employed domestic servants, for example, the 1831 Census for Bruton lists some ninety female servants and twenty men classed as servants. By the time of the 1861 Census sixty families had at least one domestic servant who lived in. This situation meant that in these families the female members at least were freed from the routine of many domestic chores.

The middle classes tended to emulate the behaviour and cultural inclinations of their social superiors. In terms of leisure pursuits and recreational activities this was a significant matter as by 1800 so many of the gentry were abandoning traditional rural cultural activities and hence the middle classes were to follow suit. In addition many of the middle class were deeply influenced by the values which they perceived to be inherent in their evangelical or non-conformist religious beliefs, an important consideration as non-conformity had been strong in the Bruton area for centuries. They were also imbued with a work ethic which led them to believe that time should not be wasted and that there should be no frivolous leisure. Throughout the nineteenth century, therefore, they sought recreations which were compatible with these values. It was perhaps rather unfortunate that they believed that everyone else should conform to them as well.

a) Self-improvement.

A key element in the recreational time of the middle class was the emphasis upon self-improvement. This was to be achieved in a number of ways:

i) Mutual Improvement Societies.

Exactly when a Mutual Improvement Society was founded in Bruton is unclear but one was operational in the 1850s as in August 1859 one such society was reported "to be in a prosperous condition", with a balance in hand of £11   4s   0d. It was certainly staging lectures in that year, such as one in February by M. Macpherson on 'Sheridan, as Orator, Statesman, and Wit.' On the other hand, a report in another local newspaper in October 1871 stated that such a society had been formed on the 11th day of that month. Three explanations seem possible: the first is that as the Society met only during the winter months, each year it had be to reconstituted but as reports of meetings do not appear in the local press in the 1860s this may be unlikely. The second explanation is that the original society like others in Bruton, for some reason, ceased to meet but was re-founded at a later date by another group of inhabitants. A third possibility was that there was either a name change or some confusion in terminology. In February 1856 a report appeared in the local press of a series of lectures including 'Atmospheric Air', 'Antiquity of the Earth', 'On projectiles illustrative of firearms used in the present war', [*The Crimean War*]. On these occasions it was referred to as the Reading Society.

Certainly the Society founded in 1871 proved resilient and successful as reports of meetings appeared regularly in the local press in the 1870s, 1880s and into the 1890s. Josiah Jackson was an enthusiastic supporter and attended meetings frequently in the late 1880s and first half of the 1890s. The Society had for "its object the mutual improvement of the members by means of debates, essays, lectures, etc." In January 1891 the opinion was expressed that "it is hoped that the young men of the town will interest themselves in the Society by attending the meetings and entering into discussions." That observation in itself may give some indication of the age range which attended meetings and took part in its activities

At weekly meetings through the winter months members listened to lectures on a wide range of topics: 'Nature's Clockwork, or The World Inside', 'Ambulance, or The First Aid to the Injured', 'The Writings of Charles Dickens', 'Rambles through England and Wales', 'Astronomy', 'Ants', 'Women's Rights', 'Socialism', 'True Born Englishmen', and 'The Solar System'. Some talks were delivered by outside speakers but many were from members themselves, such as Dr. Stockwell and E. Clarke. When George Amor, in his lecture on 'The Influence of the Press' in 1891, suggested that some seventy-five percent of the newspapers published had a demoralizing tendency, it led to a lively debate with virtually the whole of the audience disagreeing with him. A debate on Capital Punishment in February 1888 led to a vote for its continuance, perhaps an indication of the generally conservative nature of the area.

Those delivering the lectures and taking part in debates were predominantly middle class or professional men, including the local doctor, head teacher, farmers, solicitors and tradesmen. Its Secretary for many years was E.R. Hayter, the Headmaster of the National School. As the latter was also a keen musician, it was not unusual for musical items to occur during the meetings, for example, after a lecture on 10th February 1888 Hayter conducted amongst other items, 'The Marvellous Work', 'The Heavens Are Telling', and 'Gloria In Excelsia'. When their meetings' season closed the whole evening would be devoted to musical items: solos, duets and orchestral pieces. In February 1893 they formed their own choral society and later in the year gave public performances. The extension of knowledge and cultural appreciation went hand in hand.

ii)   Reading.

Part of the process of self-improvement was deemed to be reading, particularly newspapers and periodicals to ensure familiarity with current events. Much of this reading, which often included the novels of men like Dickens which were published in weekly or monthly parts, was undertaken within the family home but some was in a more public venue. A Reading Room existed in Bruton at various times in the nineteenth century but once again it does not seem to have been the same one through the decades. In August 1859 the Mutual Improvement Society which existed at that time passed a resolution "that an additional daily paper be purchased and placed on the table of the reading-room, which was much required, as one daily paper was previously procured." This decision provides an indication that a reading room must have existed before that date. Kelly's Directory of 1861 referred to a Reading Room but did not indicate where it was located. A later Directory was more specific as in 1875 it noted, "There is a subscription Reading room in the High Street, in connection with the Bruton Mutual Improvement Society."

In March 1891 Henry Hobhouse presented the Society with the fourteen volume centenary edition of the novels of Sir Walter Scott and it was reported that by that time there was a library of nearly two hundred and fifty books. At some stage however this Reading Room either ceased to exist or more likely was judged to be inadequate for the needs of the population as in October and November 1893 Josiah Jackson was attending committee meetings for the purpose of "Starting a Reading Room for the Town." It was agreed to rent a house belonging to T.H. Jones after "some alterations necessary & putting in gas in the Rooms upstairs." By 14th December a name was agreed 'The Bruton Mutual Improvement and Reading Room Society' and "prices for members were fixed." From time to time the sale of newspapers occurred in the Reading Room for example, on 30th March 1894 Jackson noted, "I went to sale of Papers at Reading Room & bought Western Chronicle at 6d for the next three months."

Improvement was also to be achieved by listening to readings. The system of Penny Readings seems to have begun in Bruton in 1865 under the chairmanship of the Vicar, Revd. James White. The Penny Readings were designed not only for the middle class but also for the young and the working population. "We sincerely hope that the young men and labouring classes of Bruton, will show their appreciation of these efforts for combining amusement with instruction, by attending in still larger numbers."

A wide range of readings was delivered: from 'Notes of an army chaplain in the Crimea' to 'A sketch of the life of William Wallace' to Irish legends such as 'How St. Patrick got rid of the serpents from Ireland'. Each reading was interspersed with musical items. The meetings, which did seem to attract large audiences, "the room was completely crammed", continued until the late 1880s. The readings were given by middle class readers, such as local clergymen, factory owner J.R.White, Land Agent T.O. Bennett, solicitor William Muller and shopkeeper William Finch. They represented not only an easy way to be entertained and to gain knowledge but also to ensure that the required values were transmitted.

iii)   The Churches.

The local churches also played their part in encouraging self-improvement, much of it targeted at the labouring poor through the Sunday and National Schools. To encourage the concept of discipline and some degree of physical fitness, a Company of the Church Lads' Brigade was formed in March 1898 with their drill instructor being E.R. Hayter, who as well as his connection with the National School had for many years been a Sergeant in a volunteer company of the Somerset Light Infantry. In addition regular sermons were used to exhort congregations to lead a more virtuous and constructive life.

Each of the churches gave their support to the temperance cause and as the Congregational Chapel had several large rooms as well as the main worship area it hosted a range of lectures, such as in July 1859 by Mr Mackintosh of London on Astronomy "to a numerous, intelligent, most attentive, and delighted audience." Another lecture in November 1882 examined the social, moral and religious position of the Jews and their future relation to the church and the world. Members of the Methodist Chapel conducted their own Wesleyan Mutual Improvement Class which in February 1888 presented a piece of silver plate to their class leader, Mrs Amor, "as a token of love and esteem." (17)

b)   Entertainment.

Throughout the nineteenth century the middle class rejected the traditional violent entertainments that had for so long been the staple diet of the rural population. They sought to find ways to occupy their leisure time with entertainments that were genteel and family orientated, which were educative, self-improving and morally uplifting. Entertainments, which were staged predominantly, but not exclusively, indoors, fall into three broad categories: those arranged by local inhabitants, those performed by travelling groups or individuals and those which were ad hoc to celebrate a particular event.

i)   Locally arranged entertainment.

As well as the amateur dramatics already described, music featured significantly in the lives of the middle class just as it did in that of their social superiors. Various town bands appeared from time to time, played at a local function, led parades and were part of the celebrations. In August 1855 "The Bruton quadrille band was in attendance" at the National School children's treat on the Parsonage lawn. In the 1870s a Fife and Drum Band existed under the direction of E.R. Hayter who was presented with "a very handsome walnut wood inkstand, fitted with crystal tray" by them in April 1879. In March 1891 the Bruton Philharmonic Society played some instrumental music during intervals at a Mutual Improvement Society Meeting and in 1893 the Bruton Excelsior Band was formed. The latter was still in existence in the twentieth century, winning a prize at the Bristol Eisteddford in March 1907.

The real strength of Brutonians, however, was in arranging and staging concerts. For those who wished to develop good habits the discipline of the adult choirs and the programmes which placed an emphasis upon sacred music and songs were key elements in moral training. The sheer number that took place, particularly in the second half of the nineteenth century, is indicative of a remarkable level of musical talent and enthusiasm in the town, with once again E.R. Hayter, who as well as being the headmaster of the National School and the church organist, was one of the principal driving forces. He started giving an annual benefit concert as soon as he was appointed to the local school in 1870 and continued to do so for the next thirty-eight years until he retired. The concerts were staged in the National Schoolroom which was usually full. The nature of the audience may be judged from an observation made during a report of the 1886 concert, "the reserved seats being filled by the elite of the town and neighbourhood." Hayter was in fact following in the tradition of benefit concerts which had been established by previous organists, such as Perry Williams in the late 1850s. Under the latter's direction instrumental music seems to have reached a high standard but "of the vocal music we have little to say – it probably was as good as amateur performances are in general."

Many other concerts were staged by different groups, for example, in November 1875 and in May 1889 concerts of sacred music were performed in the Congregational Chapel, both with lengthy programmes and appreciative audiences. Earlier in 1889 the Bruton Conservative Association had staged "a very successful smoking concert" in the Blue Ball Assembly Rooms which were reported to be crowded. The attendance list once again was almost exclusively made up of members of the middle class or local gentry.

In the 1890s the Bruton 'Blackbirds' provided musical entertainments which were lighter in character with more popular songs of the period such as 'She's Coming Home Tomorrow' and 'Must We Leave The Old Home'. They seem to have been following more in the tradition of the Bruton Glee and Madrigal Union which was giving performances, mainly of glees and choruses, in the late 1850s and early 1860s. The Bruton Harmonic Society made its first appearance in May 1863 "for the practice of a superior kind of vocal music, such as oratorios", but accounts under that name do not seem to appear in subsequent months. It was initially under the presidency of local solicitor Henry Dyne and the Church organist,

Churchill, was the conductor. Bruton Choral Society was reported as newly formed in December 1879 and was still giving annual concerts in the early twentieth century when in December 1904 their performance of 'King Olaf' was believed to have been "the stiffest piece of work the Society has undertaken." By that stage they were under the direction of R.T.A. Hughes, the choirmaster in the parish church and another local solicitor.

Some indication of one individual's involvement in attendance at concerts in Bruton may be judged by the entries in Jackson's Diary as between February 1890 and January 1897 he attended at least ten different concerts. Many of the concerts were designed to raise money for a particular cause or institution, with the National School being particularly prominent but also the Working Men's Club and to provide the funds for teas for the elderly.

As sometimes happened in small communities there were disagreements and disputes, along with damaged egos. A classic example occurred in January 1859 when a local newspaper had to explain why the 'Red Cross Knight' was sung rather than played as a Saxhorn quartet. It appeared that a certain person who usually performed a solo on the Saxhorn "and having taken offence at not being treated as his exalted(?) position demanded, not only refused to play himself, but withdrew the Saxhorns he had lent to other gentlemen." This revelation apparently elicited an interesting response, "It was somewhat amusing to hear a little boy exclaim, he hoped as Mr - had drawn in his horns, he would keep them there. We are informed that the little urchin has been severely whipped for his impertinence."

As well as adults children made a musical contribution to the entertainment scene, especially as it was considered that choral music was important for instilling good habits. In December 1855 about eighty children from the National School gave a concert for their parents based on Christmas Carols, songs with choruses and four-part rounds. Such entertainments were continued by E.R. Hayter when he was the headmaster and these occasions increasingly included items which he himself had written based upon local events and topics.

As the nineteenth century progressed another form of locally organised leisure activity emerged under the direction of the middle class and that was the fete or bazaar, invariably to raise money for a good cause or worthy institution. One of the earliest recorded was a 'Grand Rural Fete' organised by the members of the Mutual Improvement Society in Redlynch Park, lent for the occasion by the Earl of Ilchester. As well as two bands the event included another of the Victorian middle class passions, outdoor sports. There were also several balloon ascents and the day was rounded off with fireworks. The Ancient Order of Foresters found that a fete was a good method of enhancing their funds in the 1860s and in the 1880s the Congregationalists and Methodists were staging bazaars, both to raise money for their respective Sunday Schools.

One of the most elaborate grand fetes was staged in August 1889 on the Abbey Field to raise money for the funds of the National Schools. As well as stalls, the afternoon witnessed an open-air concert, a public tea during which the Bruton 'Blackbirds' performed. A "Cinderella", that was a dance which ended at midnight, was held in the evening during which a full orchestra played and a choir of seventy voices sang. Needless to say the fete secretary was E.R. Hayter.

Two interesting points emerge from the reports of the fetes and bazaars in the local press. The first was that when lists of stallholders were published they were invariably almost exclusively the names of females. It does indicate very clearly one of the roles which was expected of middle class women at that period. The second was the degree of religious cooperation which existed in the town in the late nineteenth century. This was exemplified in November 1880 when the Congregational Chapel's bazaar was opened by staunch Anglican, Captain Dyne. In his opening address he pointed out that the town owed much to the Congregationalists as they had organised a Sunday School long before the Church of England and he felt that although they might have differences "in the formularies and creeds they had one thing in common.....it was their duty to teach Christ crucified."

Occasionally mention of other locally arranged events reached the local press, for example, in March 1876 details were given about the results of a Spelling Bee which took place in the Assembly Rooms under the chairmanship of Captain Dyne and with the headmaster of King's School, Revd. D.E. Norton, and a local doctor, Dr Heginbothom, as the referees. The first prize for oral spelling was won by the Minister of the Congregational Chapel, Revd. D.I. Gass, but two of the other five winners were female which indicates that this was felt to be a suitable competition for their participation. As was so often the case, during the evening there were instrumental and vocal items "by several amateurs of the neighbourhood." (18)

ii)   Externally arranged entertainment.

Developments in transport, especially the coming of the railways, meant that it was much easier for travelling entertainers to visit rural areas. Bruton certainly benefited from a wide range of such visitors. As most of them charged an entrance fee their clientele came more from the middle class than from any other section of the local population.

Once again various aspects of music were apparent: in January 1886 Madam R. Rose RAM., gave a concert in the National Schoolroom, assisted by some local amateurs. In April 1859 one report in a local newspaper enthused that, "Hoffman's Organophic Band favoured this town with a visit, and gave an entertainment in the Assembly Rooms, whose imitations of the various instruments, such as the musical box, drum, cymbals, and several others by the unaided voice, are truly marvellous." On a lighter note Christy's Minstrels used the same venue on their visits in March 1867 and October 1876 when on both occasions it was reported that they were very well received. In March 1891 it was Tute's Minstrels who performed there but on this visit, although the performances were stated to be very good, the attendance "was unfortunately not large, owing to the very severe weather."

Hand-bell ringers came to the town from time to time, for example, Josiah Jackson attended three of their sessions between 1889 and 1894. An earlier visit in December 1876 did not elicit a favourable comment in one local newspaper, "the entertainment was a very poor affair", and the vocalists who accompanied them were "far inferior to that which we have heard at amateur performances in the neighbourhood." There were clearly some Brutonians who were not afraid to make their opinions known.

Travelling exhibitions were staged occasionally, such as in March 1869 with "a curious creature known by naturalists as a 'Sea Leopard'", and in October of the same year a Fox Shark "said to be an inhabitant of the South Seas." Both creatures were reported to have been caught by fishermen off the Cornish Coast and both were displayed at the Old Bull Inn. Purchase's Waxworks Show visited Bruton on at least two occasions in November 1875 and October 1880.

For those who preferred rather more movement various forms of that type of entertainment were to be found. In February 1863 Middleton's Marionette Exhibition was in the Assembly Rooms and in November 1875 two performing seals were very popular, the "feats of the apparently clumsy animals being quite astonishing." The circus was in town from time to time, such as in June 1867, July 1869 and June 1889 and Bortock and Wombwell's Wild West Show in April 1890.

The Victorian period witnessed significant and rapid developments in science and technology and these were embraced with a passion by many of the middle class. Bruton was no different so that when some sort of scientific or technological lecture or display took place it was always well patronized. The following examples, which cover one ten-year period, are just a selection of those which appeared in the town after the mid 1860s: Mr Hall's Panorama of the 'Travels of Captains Speke and Grant in Central, South and Eastern Africa' was held in May 1867; in March 1869 there was an entertainment of 'Panoramic, Dioramic, and dissolving views' in the Old Bull Inn; another talk with dissolving views in October 1870 and a 'Scientific Seance' with "dissolving views, Polarized light, sensitive flames, improved Mctraillense &c &c"; and Davison's Panorama in February 1877.

It was, however, sometimes difficult to appreciate where science ended and magic tricks began. In January 1867 J.A. Rudge of Bath gave "an entertainment of electrical and optical illusions", whereas in July 1881 Dr Seaton was staging 'Magic and Mesmerism'. It was reported that "The tricks were performed very cleverly, while the subjects mesmerised kept the audience in roars of laughter." When the show was completed "A dark séance afterwards was well patronized." This particular report is one of the earliest references to a séance at that period in Bruton, an activity which was also gaining popularity nationally. It has been argued that it represented a denial of the finality of death as they had a belief that there could be contact with the 'other world'. The same denial was to be found on many Victorian gravestones where words such as 'sleeping' and 'resting' appeared regularly.

Further attempts were made at achieving some contact as after his performance of conjuring and magic in April 1889, Professor Dupres staged a private séance for members of the Mutual Improvement Society and it appears from one report that "The 'Dark Half Hour' was much enjoyed." The Society clearly had an interest in this area as in March 1891, for the second time within four years, Alfred Gapper gave "thought-reading séances in the National School-room," in aid of their funds and which were described as "most refined and diverting." Unfortunately no records have survived to indicate what transpired at any of these sessions.

Finally in the late 1850s and 1860s Ventriloquism was a popular entertainment and a number of showmen visited Bruton. In April 1859 Mr Thornton was "pronounced to be the best Ventriloquist who has visited this neighbourhood." In February Mr Thurton gave a similar entertainment, Mr Newman in December 1863 and Mr Trevori in September 1865, although the latter was less well received, "his entertainment would be greatly improved by introducing something new in the ventriloquial department."

The examples cited of travelling performers indicate a wide range of activities and demonstrate that the middle class in Bruton were far from isolated in terms of entertainment in their town. The descriptions of the performers in the local newspapers suggest that many of them were well known in the area if not nationally. While some of the events were pure entertainment many also had an educative value and may therefore be seen at times as part of the desire for self- improvement.

iii)   Celebrations.

The Victorian middle class embraced Christmas with considerable enthusiasm mainly because they had the money to spend on goods and the celebrations in general and they wished to emulate the customs of their social superiors. In 1834 Christmas Day was just one of the four days in the year which were regarded as a holiday. The Victorians added extensively to existing traditions and brought in their own innovations: a Christmas dinner was retained but they added crackers, cards and trees and carol singing was revived. Before the 1860s the tendency was to give presents on New Year's Day but in that decade it was switched to Christmas Day.

It was a time of year when the Victorian middle class could publicly display their philanthropic tendencies, which were fully reported in the local newspapers, for example, by 1834 Joseph Pepler of Coombe Farm provided annually a meal for ten of the oldest men and ten of the oldest women in the town; by 1864 T.E.S. Jelley of the Priory, variously described as a 'Private Resident' or Accountant, was providing annually "an excellent repast of roast beef and plum pudding for upwards of 200 of the sick and aged poor"; and in 1868 Thomas Hammond was entertaining twenty-three old women in his house in Quaperlake Street.

One of the undoubted strengths of some members of the middle class in Bruton was the way in which they could organize an ad hoc celebration for a specific event. Such celebrations were clearly important to them not only as a form of entertainment but also as a way of demonstrating their philanthropic tendencies. The fall of Sebastopol in 1855 led to bell ringing, flags being hoisted, a bonfire and fireworks. The Coronation of Queen Victoria witnessed extensive celebrations and each year thereafter Coronation Day was marked as a general holiday and usually involved some other activity as well, such as in July 1864 Stourhead Gardens were thrown open to the public and large numbers from Bruton travelled there to appreciate them. Queen Victoria's Diamond Jubilee in 1897 led to feasting, sports and a bonfire on Creech Hill.

The opening of the railway in 1856 was another day for celebrations, including a huge procession to the Abbey Field marshalled by William Finch, a meal for 1,250 people according to one newspaper report and fireworks in the evening. Finch, a local shopkeeper, was deeply involved in organizing events in this period and his particular strength seems to have been in working with gunpowder as he was the man who made and set off the fireworks used in displays. Other middle class men were also involved in committee after committee which organized these entertainments: solicitors such as Henry Dyne and William Muller and Land Agent, T.O. Bennett. The wives of the middle class men were expected to cook the meat required for large feasts and to provide the plum pudding. (19)

    c)   Outdoor Activities.

Although the traditional violent activities of the labouring population were frowned upon by the Victorian middle class, there were those who argued that some sort of sporting activity should be continued. They believed that this would encourage physical fitness, stamina, determination, discipline, teamwork and loyalty. These were judged to be among the important attributes for those who might enter the armed services or the various volunteer militia that operated in the Bruton area. In fact the Volunteer Force itself had a major part to play as it undertook regular drill, parades and exercises, accounts of which appeared in local newspapers, and required physical fitness in its recruits.

As the century advanced much greater emphasis was placed upon fresh air, organised games and some sports for entertainment. Writers such as Charles Kingsley criticized "the neglect of personal health, strength and beauty" and went on to advocate a sort of muscular Christianity and in 'Tom Brown's Schooldays', Thomas Hughes created a manly hero and role model. One of the driving forces behind the development of organised games were the public schools as men like Dr Arnold at Rugby School had long promoted such games to instil discipline and self-government in schoolboys. They would encourage personal courage which was tempered by the team spirit with respect for authority and fair play as the key values. They were felt to have broader applications as a physician at the school commented, "Games produce a just ambition to excel in every phase of the battle of life."

These were ideals and values which were soon transmitted to the generations of school children who were educated in the Board Schools which were established after 1870 to cater for the masses. "It is as true for the children of mechanics and labourers, as for the children of merchants and professional men, that manly sports, played as they should be played, tend to develop unselfish pluck, determination, self-control and public spirit." By 1887 at the time of Queen Victoria's Golden Jubilee former Prime Minister, William

Gladstone, was able to claim, "For the schoolboy and the man alike athletics are becoming an ordinary incident of life."

Cricket continued to be a popular sport, an emulation of that of their social superiors. The Gentlemen of Somerset played their first match, against the Gentlemen of Dorset, in 1845 but it was to be another thirty years until the County Cricket Club was established. Bruton Cricket Club may have originally been formed in 1856 but may not have been entirely successful as in July 1858 a local newspaper reported "that an effort is about to be made to revive the manly game of cricket in this town." A meeting early in August established a cricket club and a month later the town beat Yeovil Cricket Club by an innings and fifteen runs. In July 1877 another meeting had to be called "to consider what steps should be taken to resuscitate the Bruton Cricket Club."

The Club was clearly under middle class control as for the rest of the century its president was the Vicar, Revd. H.T. Ridley, and it numbered amongst its other officials solicitors, a land agent and the local doctor. The membership of the teams varied but once again the middle class remained well represented with local clergy, solicitors and shopkeepers. During each season their exploits were meticulously recorded in local newspapers and, as with all teams, their fortunes varied significantly.

As the Club had no permanent base of its own, the players were dependent upon renting a field for each season. In March 1891, for example, the Club turned its attention to Hyde, then leased by Josiah Jackson of Durslade Farm from the Hoare Estate. He agreed to let them have forty-five square yards at a rent of £8, "The club to fence it out & not to molest or do me any injury……. But they do not play cricket until after mowing is done." As in so many other activities, the agricultural year had to take precedence. In practical terms the Club do not appear to have used this site until June of the following year, "A Cricket match was played in Hyde, the first that has been played there." The Hyde location, bordered by the railway line and the road was to be their home ground for the rest of the century.

Another successful cricket team seems to have flourished in the nineteenth century at Hadspen under the patronage of the Hobhouse family. According to the recollections of W.E. Cooper, it was started in 1852 by his father, E.Y. Cooper of Wincanton who became the Honorary Secretary, and Henry Wyndham of Roundhill Grange near that town. It was clearly very select as "Our members were all balloted for, after being duly proposed and seconded, which kept the club extremely harmonious." It was taken very seriously as the gentry were reported to come from miles around and Cooper himself claimed as a young man he used to walk eight miles to be there. Its members included Captain McNair of Bruton, Revd. A. Byron of Corten Denham, old Etonian Charles Plucknett from Holton and the Revd. Henry Newbolt of Somerton, who was obviously very committed to the game as he was a member of seven or eight local clubs. Hadspen Cricket Club also enlisted the services of two boys from King's School in Bruton, Ernest Cassan and John Baulch, "both of whom were fast bowlers, and the former had a very peculiar delivery, with much screw from an old gun-shot wound, and was then reckoned one of the fastest amateur bowlers in England." The Club played teams throughout Somerset and Dorset, had their own marquee with tables for refreshments but it was only in April 1854 that they took steps to level the ground on which they played.

As football had such a violent reputation, it was not embraced so quickly or so enthusiastically as cricket by the Victorian middle class. For much of the century it lacked standardization or a coherent set of rules. In some areas a small hard ball was used and in others a large bladder. Sometimes the ball could only be kicked but at other times it could be picked up and thrown. In reality it was a game which required so little equipment that it remained well within the financial scope of many within the labouring population. It is likely to have been played informally in many places, especially as half-day working on Saturday became more prevalent.

A football club had been formed in Bruton by the 1870s as at that time they seem to have been playing matches on part of the Abbey Field, possibly sharing the space with King's School. Their problem was that there was no permanent pitch and the players seem to have negotiated some suitable land on which to play on a yearly basis. In September 1893 a group of young men approached Josiah Jackson to discuss the possibility of the town club playing on part of Hyde, but nothing seems to have resulted from the request as in February 1894 he noted that he "went to a Football match at marks dean", which once again the town club seems to have been sharing with the School. Late in August the following year he was approached by the Bruton Juvenile Football Team for permission to play on "little Bay Close", a request to which he acceded for a rent of 35s. Two years later he agreed to permit the town team to erect two goal posts on Horse Mary Down and play there until Lady Day 1898, the rent being 15s.

Reports of matches appeared regularly in the local press towards the end of the century and Bruton Town certainly seems to have had some good seasons, for example, their first eleven statistics for 1902-1903 were played seventeen, won eight, lost five and drawn four, while the second eleven played ten, won five, lost two and drew three. There was sufficient interest and talent by that stage for the town to field at least two teams throughout the season. Once again many of those playing or negotiating on behalf of the Club were from the middle ranks of society in Bruton, especially the shopkeepers or their sons, such as in the 1870s, a blacksmith, game and poultry dealer, baker, confectioner and J. and R. Newmarch, two of the sons of the owner of the Glen.

Although the Football Association had been founded in 1863 it spent the first twenty years of its life trying to sort out the differences in the rules of play, many of which came from the various public schools which had revived the game. The type of football played in the 1870s in Bruton would scarcely be recognised as the modern game. In one match played between Wincanton and Bruton Football Clubs on the Abbey Field in April 1874, Wincanton had thirteen players and Bruton fourteen, which was alleged to include eight members of Frome Football Club. The match was well supported, "the presence in the field of a number of ladies and gentlemen, and the boys of the King's School tended much to enliven the game and encourage the players."

It had been agreed beforehand "that for the first half the game should be played under Rugby Union Rules." Play moved rapidly from end to end as "one player after another attempted carrying the ball through" but "scrimmage after scrimmage ensued." When the time was called there was no score. "Ends were now changed and the Association Rules came into force" and after another hour in which "every player engaged, entered so heartily into the struggle" there was still a draw. The comment at the end of the account of this match is very revealing as it indicates what must have happened in some matches. "We must congratulate all engaged on their pluck, endurance, and good temper, and that no accident or mishap of any kind occurred to mar the pleasure of the afternoon."

As well as the town, King's School also played football, although initially not in a competitive way. One former pupil, Christopher Welch who left the School in 1851, recalled that there was no football team. "I can recollect only one game of football, to play which we went to the top of Creech Hill and set up poles on the sheep-sleight, having previously told off a small boy to blow up a pig's bladder with a quill, the ordinary way of inflating the ball at the time." About 1862 "football of some sort was played in the meadow by the river", and it was noted that "A man from a pastrycooks' sold light refreshments."

In the decades which followed football became more organised and matches were played on the Abbey Field until a new pitch was obtained first at Markesdanes in 1893 and then Jackson agreed to rent for £5 "a part of Hyde about 100 yards long by 60 yards wide (The ground not to be fenced out)." They remained on this site for the rest of the century, despite some criticisms that they shared the land with cows.

All sorts of helpful suggestions were made in the School Magazine, 'The Dolphin', to improve football, including that the captain should be more punctual after the end of school to ensure a longer game and that he should arrange to have the ball blown up and delivered to the field, "did the captain think the ball had legs so that it could walk up to the field?" A rather more practical suggestion was that there should be goal nets to avoid any doubt about a goal.

After the opening of Sexey's School in April 1891 the boys also played football, but as the numbers on roll were so small before 1900, much of it was informal on the field alongside the School. Nevertheless they did manage to form a team as Harold Scott who joined the School in 1900 recalled, "In horse-drawn brakes we travelled to our matches to the schools in the neighbourhood at Shaftesbury, Gillingham, Wells, Frome and Shepton Mallet. In the winter we sat crowded together for warmth, with a horse-cloth over our knees and our collars pulled up around our ears, and at every steep hill we had to get out and walk." For the School the major development in football came after the First World War when a field on the top of Lusty Hill was purchased as a Memorial Field for the Old Boys who were killed in the war.

The third of the outdoor areas favoured by the Victorian middle class centred on what were usually referred to as 'rural sports', which could be generally classed as athletics, and which particularly developed from the middle of the century. They were not of course limited to children. After the meal at the opening of the railway in September 1856, as part of the celebrations "rural sports and dancing were introduced." The Grand Rural Fete at Redlynch in July 1859 staged sports which included hurdle races, 'jumping lengths', 'jumping heights', run and jump, flat races, throwing the hammer and archery. When the owners of the silk mill gave their workmen a treat later in the month they also arranged various sports "which highly gratified the younger branches." At the time of the Royal Wedding in March 1863 Sergeant-Major Melhuish supervised a variety of rural sports. Lists of prizewinners show the usual middle class involvement with solicitors, farmers and shopkeepers.

Newspaper reports in the following decades indicate that at many of the National School and Sunday School treats, sports of some kind were arranged. Celebrations for jubilees and fetes, particularly those organised by the Foresters also witnessed the same activities. Similar reports appear later in the century for King's School but as one pupil recalled, "Athletics proper were not highly regarded."

He did however add "that in my early days each boy selected his own colours as trimmings for running vests and shorts, and very peculiar some of the combinations were! It must have been a bonanza for the local draper, especially as shorts came almost over the knees and vests had to have sleeves."

In the 1890s a Golf Club was established and once again its membership consisted of the local middle class such as solicitor R.A. Hughes. As well as allowing local men the opportunity to play the game it also staged matches against other clubs such as Ivy Thorn in June 1898, a number of which were played on their own course on Creech Hill, occasionally referred to as Creech Links.

Indulging in sport, not matter how seemingly harmless, was not, of course, without its dangers and so from time to time accounts of accidents appeared in the local press. In July 1891 it was reported that James Golledge, a local actuary, broke one of the bones in his right ankle while playing tennis. He was immediately attended by Dr Stockwell as the injuries "were of a rather serious character." (20)

d) Socializing.

The Victorian middle class were very active in being members of groups, clubs and organisations which met regularly for various purposes. Invariably considerable socializing took place, especially for men but also for women. Those males who attended the Mutual Improvement Society, for example, had ample opportunity to socialize and develop useful contracts with other inhabitants.

Freemasonry provided one occasion for male socializing. Bruton Freemasons first met in 1841 in a room in the Wellington Inn and in May 1843 moved to meet in their own Lodge room in the Sun Inn as Royal Clarence Lodge No.695. After eight years the Lodge ceased to exist as "all the Members of the Town had either left the neighbourhood or resigned." It was, however, re-founded in August 1864 and met at the Blue Ball Inn. Membership tended to be small, peaking at forty-nine in 1879 and not all those were resident in Bruton itself. The surviving membership lists for the period 1865 to 1891 indicate that the majority classed themselves as gentlemen, yeomen, farmers, professional men, such as surgeons, solicitors and schoolmasters, shopkeepers, traders along with a few skilled artisans such as builders, plumbers, tailors and saddlers who were very much in a minority.

A regular feature of the Freemasons' Meeting was their dinner afterwards and this was an excellent opportunity for socializing. In fact staging a dinner and attendance at it was a significant aspect of many organizations in Victorian Bruton. As early as 1815 the Bruton Society of Tradesmen were meeting at the Wellington Inn for a dinner, although this particular group may not have survived for long. Much later in the century the first annual Tradesman's Dinner was reported in January 1886 as being held in the Blue Ball Hotel. In the middle of the century local detachments of the militia and cavalry were staging regular dinners at the same establishment. As well as all their other activities in the 1880s the Ancient Order of Foresters were holding anniversary dinners. These dinners were the occasion for loyal and lengthy toasts and optimistic speeches. These were obviously the place to be and to be seen for those who wished to maintain or advance their place within the community.

The wives of the middle class Victorians and other single and widowed females of the appropriate class played a less conspicuous role when it came to many of the public meetings and events. They were of course always there in important categories: they were prominent in the wide range of philanthropic activities which flourished in the town in this period; they organised and oversaw the stalls at the fetes and bazaars; and for public celebrations they prepared the huge quantities of food which were required. While they accompanied husbands, fathers, brothers and other respectable gentlemen to concerts and various entertainments, it is impossible to determine how many groups they formed in their own right as most, if they existed at all, went largely unrecorded. The existence of a sewing club has emerged as the result of entries Jackson made in his Diary as his wife Annie attended their meetings on a regular basis in the 1890s, and some of them were held in his farmhouse. Whether the products were for personal use or for sale at fetes and bazaars or for charitable purposes was not mentioned. Middle class ladies also emulated their social superiors by visiting each other and taking tea, but once again these have escaped a record except for a few references in Jackson's Diary. (21)

e) Bruton Agricultural Society.

The Agricultural Society, probably more than any other single society, organisation or group, epitomised many of the Victorian middle class values and aspirations. It encouraged improvement, staged competitions and shows to promote excellence, provided entertainment along with opportunities not only for socializing but also for moralizing. Such societies were also seen as a way of promoting social harmony in rural areas. When he spoke at the annual dinner in December 1834 the Rt. Hon Henry Hobhouse declared that "he thought meetings of such a kind contributed much to unite different ranks of society."

The Bruton Agricultural Society was founded in 1818 and was claimed in the 1870s to be the second oldest in the country. It amalgamated with similar societies in Castle Cary in 1888 and Wincanton in 1891 to form the East Somerset Agricultural Society. Such a union had first been proposed in the 1850s on the grounds of greater efficiency, less movement of stock and higher prizes. In the end the motivating factor was probably cost, especially as the apparent depression in agriculture intensified in the 1880s and 1890s and each year the local committee had to meet together to decide if the annual cattle show was feasible.

The principal event in 1818, and in each year for the rest of the nineteenth century, was their Cattle Show which seems eventually to have replaced the September Fair. As it had no permanent home of its own it was held, initially each December and later in the century in October, in various locations, such as The Grove, Jubilee Park and a field near the railway lent by Jackson. The primary purpose was to show off animals, based upon the simple rule that all stock exhibited had to have been bred by or have been in the possession of the owner for six months, or in the case of pigs for three months. Gradually the range of exhibits was extended to include horses, dead poultry, cheese and butter.

In many years the Show was popular, for example, in 1892 it attracted 448 entries. The Prize Lists were published year after year in local newspapers, and indicate that great emphasis was placed upon the 'best of breeds' and 'second best' categories. The Show was clearly highly regarded not only in Bruton and its neighbourhood but also further afield as competitors came from most of the rest of Somerset and parts of Wiltshire and Dorset.

The Agricultural Society wished to encourage farmers and landowners but in addition labourers and servants. Cash rewards were given annually "for long and faithful servitude", and so, for example, in 1841 James Williams received two sovereigns for thirty-one years service with John Card and in 1842 Henry Hill received one sovereign for fifteen years service with Alfred Priddle. One of the longest periods of service was forty-six years by John King with D. Symes, for which he received £2 in 1859. Rewards were also given for exceptional feats, such as to a shepherd, Thomas Knighton, who received £2 for rearing 246 lambs from 240 ewes for John Saxon in 1847 and to James Clarke who reared 339 lambs from 322 ewes for William Cary in 1863.

The reward system was extended gradually and by the 1850s included female servants on farms as well, for example, Mary Baker received £1 10s in 1863 for twelve years and nine months service with Mr Gifford, senior. Another category rewarded was that of the labourer under twenty-one with the longest period of service with the same employer and in 1863 this was awarded to Silas Laver with thirteen and a half years with Thomas Gifford, senior. Such payments continued for decades so that in 1888 Thomas Butt, an employee of Messrs Jones & Sons, received £1 10s. That those under twenty-one were being employed for such long periods of time is very indicative of the presence and continuation of child labour in the Bruton area even towards the end of the nineteenth century. In addition by implication these rewards may be seen as an element of social control as not only did they reward those who had performed as was expected but also encouraged those who had not achieved similar results.

The same exhortation to encourage improvement was evident in the various agricultural competitions which were established at various times in the nineteenth century. In 1854 the 'Association for Awarding Prizes to Good Labourers in Husbandry' was formed by the Agricultural Society. In that year it organised competitions in mowing, reaping and ploughing at the appropriate times of the year. The usual first prize was £1 10s which Benjamin Williams won in July for mowing half an acre in two hours and twenty-five minutes, and William Bishop won the ploughing contest in October. It is unlikely that these competitions continued through the decades as in November 1880 a local newspaper referred to the third annual ploughing match organised by the Agricultural Society which does suggest a break had occurred.

These competitions were regarded as important events and in some parts of Somerset were said to rival the enthusiasm for, and the festivities on, Club Days. Large numbers of people turned out to watch the skills of the various competitors and judging was thorough and the winner became a local hero. As always refreshments, particularly liquid ones, were available, often in a marquee and the competition was followed by a dinner, prizes awarded, toasts and speeches, after which the remainder of the evening would be spent "in harmony", a phrase beloved by local newspapers of that period. "The competitions induce thoroughness. They create a desire to do the best. They make a perfect workman."

Another important aspect of the Agricultural Society, already suggested by the competition days, was the opportunity for socializing. In 1860 one local newspaper reflected on this: "What an agreeable phase of our social life is the agricultural-meeting system, which is now in its zenith, all over the country. It brings farmers and squires, landlords and tenants, together….. Long may these agricultural gatherings be the honest, hearty, friendly meetings they now are." The newspaper could have added that the gatherings were welcomed by tradesmen and shopkeepers as well as a result of the influx of trade which they brought into the town.

The highlight of the social calendar on Show Day for many was the dinner which ended the day, presided over by a member of the local gentry, often from the Hobhouse or Hoare families. It was a time not only for a substantial meal in a local inn such as the Blue Ball or the Wellington Inn, but also for the presentation of prizes and for speeches. Some of these speeches, judging by the reports in the local press, were very long and must have seemed interminable.

The scope of the speeches was broad but always started with the loyal toast and that was usually followed by one to the Church, next to the Army, Navy and Volunteers, and then to the Lord Lieutenant and the Magistracy. Each of these speeches required a response which could be very wide-ranging. There was then a toast to the Agricultural Society which would lead to lengthy responses relating to agricultural issues. Interestingly however some speeches commented upon contemporary issues, for example in 1866 the factory owner, J.R. White, made reference to the unrest in Ireland, the threat of a French invasion and to the 'Alabama Case' which had arisen as a result of events during the American Civil War.

The speeches were of course an ideal opportunity to moralize and to remind the labouring classes of their duty. In December 1853 William Miles, M.P., used the occasion to remind his listeners in Bruton that "the first duty we have to teach the poor is their duty to God, and then follows the inculcation of their duty towards man......and they may come out useful members of Society." The following year one speaker encouraged labourers to develop their skills, especially with new machinery but added the implied threat that, "If they did not take care to improve, masters must employ others instead of them." Much later in the century as the East Somerset Agricultural Society, a much more practical approach was taken towards education when it financed three scholarships of £10 each for three years for boys at Sexey's Trade School.

The entertainment aspects of the Agricultural Society must not be overlooked. Watching the various competitions which it sponsored and the activities of the Show Day provided a wealth of entertainment not only for the middle class but also for many labourers as well. In fact the whole of Bruton seems to have taken the annual Show Day very seriously. A report in 1892 stated, "The town, too, was, also gaily decorated, the main streets being lined with shrubs and overhung with tastefully decorated arches bearing appropriate mottoes." In the cold and dark of winter this event must have been a welcome diversion. The reporter went on to comment, "In fact the quaint old streets of Bruton seem particularly adapted for decoration, and the Brutonians always take full advantage of this whenever opportunity offers."

For a number of years towards the end of the nineteenth century the committee of the Society made arrangements to provide specific entertainment. It may well be that a decrease in either interest or attendance in what were very difficult decades for agriculture prompted this action. In October 1892, for example, they paid up to £150 for the tight-rope walker, Pierre Blondin. He performed his high-wire act, "for an hour in the afternoon, and also in the evening, midst fireworks" in front of "a large crowd of spectators." In his Diary Jackson recorded the preparations which were necessary on Hyde for the performance including digging holes for the poles and laying planks. It is possible that Blondin gave repeat performances in subsequent years such as 1896 and 1902, or another performer was by that time using his name.

As the Agricultural Society operated for more that eight decades in the nineteenth century it was inevitable that its popularity should vary. It does seem to have faced a difficult period in the 1850s as in December 1859 one reporter commented on the success of the Show that year but added, "This is the more gratifying from the fact that for some years past the Bruton show appeared to be rather declining than improving." The upturn was attributed to "The energetic exertions of the gentlemen of the committee, and the hon. secretary (Mr. Dyne)."

Some problems were self-inflicted as internal division arose in the early 1870s. The committee seems to have become split along political lines with the Conservative group championed by T.O. Bennett who claimed, "My supporters are the Cream of the Agriculturalists in this neighbourhood", and the Liberal group led by Henry Dyne. Bennett noted that, "Mr Dyne's great supporter is Mr Sutcliffe, the radical whip here." He went on to allege that Sutcliffe, who was a Glass and China Dealer in the High Street, "was of so rude a nature to all but his own Party that it was quite impossible for us to remain in the Room, or to have anything further to do with him in his capacity as Treasurer to the Society." Not for the first time nor for the last did disputes of a political, religious or personal nature divide a local community. Nevertheless despite suggestions that the Show should not take place, it continued to be staged, perhaps Bruton as a whole had too much to lose.

Finally two items, which appeared the local press, throw a different light upon the Agricultural Society. The first emerged in a law case following the December 1870 dinner. As the dinner cost 2s   6d, many men did not attend but waited outside and when it was over rushed into the room as a "disorderly mob" to hear the speeches and the list of prize winners. In this year the committee tried to stop that happening but in the general confusion a miller, Thomas Pike of Shepton Mallet, who had attended the dinner but had just left the room for a moment "received, somehow or another, a blow from the fist of defendant (*farmer Thomas Gifford of Hadspen*), which furnished him with a plentiful supply of Claret gratis." Gifford apologised profusely but the local Magistrates still fined him 6d with costs.

The second item appeared in December 1863 under the heading "Colloquy at the Cattle Show."

"Fair-haired gentleman(?) to stout young lady, 'Good morning, Miss, have you been to see the fat pigs?' 'No, Sir.' 'Oh, *you* should go and exhibit yourself.' 'Thank you, Sir, when *you* take your *carrots* to Shepton Horticultural Show, *I* will take myself to Bruton Cattle Fair.' (Exit carrots, feeling smaller.)" Political correctness was still a long way in the future. (22)

The overall impression created by the activities of the Victorian middle class in terms of their leisure pursuits and entertainments, was that they aimed for propriety, for the sedate and the genteel. Much of it was family orientated, sometimes arranged by themselves and sometimes by travelling entertainers. Throughout there were the themes: self-improvement, educative and morally uplifting. At times it appeared sentimental and moralizing as illustrated by the songs sung at entertainments in Bruton. 'Sell No More Drink To My Father' and 'See That My Graves Kept Green.' There was even their own ballad, 'Bruton Town'. (See Appendix 3)

6. POPULAR CULTURE.

For the great majority of ordinary villagers whose lives were dominated by unremitting toil, there were essentially two principal types of leisure activities: those associated with the main holidays and special festive occasions and those which were everyday, common activities such as a drink in the alehouse, gossiping with neighbours in the street or at the common well, or exchanging news and information on market days and fair days. So much of this second type, which was of course predominantly oral and thus has left little trace, was based upon their sense of belonging to a particular locality for it covered their everyday experiences in their cottage, street and village and was about what was important to them at any particular moment. It reflected the uncertainties, problems and hardships of their lives, the details of which could be shared with family and friends.

For the historian the leisure activities of the ordinary people, especially those of an everyday nature, create a particular problem. They were of no interest whatsoever to the wealthier, literate members of the community and hence were virtually never recorded. In addition the leisure pursuits of the masses on holidays and festive occasions were so common place that for centuries they too were hardly ever written down. It is clear, however, that there were already cultural differences between the mass of the population and the wealthier members by 1500 and these were to intensify in the sixteenth and seventeenth centuries.

Many of the popular recreations were based upon traditions and customs and had no permanent base. They were very much public and gregarious: they occurred in the streets, the market place, the churchyard and in the fields adjoining the village or town and so occasionally a surviving field name may give a clue to some activity. Until the eighteenth century little written evidence has survived for popular recreational and leisure pursuits for ordinary people in Bruton and the surrounding areas. For many of those which do emerge in that century it is possible to speculate that they had existed for a considerable period before then as references may be found to them at an earlier date elsewhere in the county, region and at national level.

So much of the popular culture was male dominated as women were excluded from many of the points of contact with it. Very few females, for example, in the Bruton area served an apprenticeship or were skilled enough to belong to a gild. As the alehouse attracted large numbers of men, females often felt uncomfortable going there, at least on a regular basis. Women do seem, however, to have been the spectators at many events.

Although much popular culture was oral, it also had a visual dimension as small inns and alehouses were compelled by law from at least the early seventeenth century to have a sign outside. It was also common for shops to have some sort of pictorial sign to advertise their presence and nature, such as the outline of a fish or a loaf of bread. At hiring fairs men would either wear different colour ribbon in their caps to indicate a particular skill or carry an appropriate tool such as a shovel or wool comb. As with the oral aspects the signs have also disappeared.

For centuries children had devised their own entertainment and activities in the precious moments when they were not required to undertake other more laborious tasks. In the rural area of Bruton boys from as young as six years old were expected to perform useful functions at various times of the agricultural year such as leading the horse when ploughing occurred and frightening away the birds as the young crops grew. The evidence of John Sharrer Ward suggests that huge numbers of young children were part of the domestic system in the production of cloth as they helped their parents in their own cottages. Childhood as such was not a concept which was prevalent for the masses until at least the middle of the Victorian era.

Simple games did exist however, but once again were hardly ever recorded as it was taken for granted that this was what children did, were of little consequence to literate adults and were rarely organised. In one of his poems John Clare described the unbounded pleasures experienced by boys released from the classroom after a day in school:

Harken that happy shout – the schoolhouse door
Is open thrown & out the younkers teem
Some run to leap frog on the marshy more
& others dabble in the shallow stream.

Many of their activities used the most basic of props: racing sticks on the river or skimming stones. Larger sticks could be used as wooden swords for play-fighting – possibly an early training for some of the more violent leisure activities later in their lives.

A fortunate few might have been able to obtain some sort of homemade ball which could be used in their version of Fives or kicked around the streets as a football. Some may even have managed to obtain a wooden hoop and then got a stick from the hedgerow with which to hit it. By the nineteenth century marbles were popular and glass ones could be found in the tops of many glass bottles which were often just discarded.

There are occasions when an odd isolated reference leads to more questions than it answers, for example, in July 1816 the Churchwardens paid Miss Mussell 7s 6d "for wherlegig at Grope Alley". This was presumably a merry-go-round for children but why the Churchwardens should finance it and why in that location remains unclear.

Other pastimes had an oral basis and various traditional rhymes opened up the development of collective activities with "Ring a'ring a'roses" long being a favourite with children in many areas from the seventeenth century. In the Victorian era and probably long before, skipping, especially for girls, was very extensive in the Bruton area as all that was required was a piece of rope and a whole range of rhymes were chanted. One relating to drinking gin may well have had its origin in the eighteenth century when gin was particularly prevalent and indicates its potential consequences:

> A house to let, enquire within;
> People turned out for drinking gin;
> Drinking gin is a very bad thing,
> So Polly come out and Kate go in.

As their names were called the girl who had been skipping ran out and the other took her place.

Another rhyme which was very popular was,

> Red currant, black currant, raspberry jam,
> Tell me the name of your young man
> ABCDEFG, (etc.)

The letter at which the skipper was caught was supposed to give the initial of her sweetheart's name. The girls usually had two goes – the first letter was the Christian name and the second the surname.

Finally it is important to stress that at a time when the mass of the population found their lives dominated by strenuous and often monotonous labour and the daily struggle to survive, involvement in the various activities and entertainments which made up popular culture was a significant safety valve, a method of dissipating popular frustrations. In that way paradoxically it helped to reinforce the authority of the wealthier members of the community, to maintain the status quo.

a) Violence.

i) Towards each other.

Some of the earlier leisure pursuits and entertainments contained a level of violence which later generations were to find unacceptable. They did nevertheless occur, finding widespread support and patronage and perhaps reflected very much the society in which ordinary people lived. The most common time for this organised violence was during Bruton Feast, after Bruton Fair, in September of each year.

One of the most popular of the contests in the eighteenth century was Sword and Dagger. This sport would appear to have been prevalent in various countries in Europe throughout the medieval period, for example, competitions between groups of Italian youths were recorded in the twelfth century. A contemporary woodcut of the Cotswold Games of 1612 shows two adult figures with wooden swords and daggers. Wooden swords and daggers had in fact been used for practice purposes for centuries as it avoided serious injury to participants and prevented damage to valuable metal weapons.

Sword and Dagger was certainly patronized by the local gentry as each year in the middle of the eighteenth century and beyond the

Berkeley family provide the main prize for the first day's winner. This was "a Lac'd HAT: valued at 27 Shillings" in 1750; "a Silver Lac'd Hat and Knot" valued at one and half guineas in 1768 and two guineas in 1774. At Castle Cary the prize was slightly more ornate as it was "A Gold Laced Hat." After the death of the last Lord Berkeley the prize became cash, so for example in 1791 there was "a Purse of Five Guineas." If Sword and Dagger occurred on a second day there was usually a guinea for the winner and half a guinea for the runner-up. It may well be the case that the first day attracted those with some expertise in the sport and the second day if it occurred was for young hopefuls such as local apprentices. The Silver Laced Hat fought for and awarded for decades was clearly an important status symbol within a community and took precedence over cash. The man who won it could expect to be regarded as a local celebrity and its presence was evident much, much longer than cash.

The other patrons of such contests were local alehouse keepers, for example, in May 1749 John Cheek of the Bear Inn in Dropping Lane advertised that in Whitsun Week there would be a Sword and Dagger contest at his Inn for "A Handsome Silver Bowl, of the value of three pounds." It was specified that, "He that breaks most heads, and saves his own to be intitled to the Bowl, clear of All Deductions, except Five Shillings to be spent in the House." Clearly bringing trade to the inn was an important consideration as alcohol would be consumed in abundance. The timing of this contest was of course significant as it indicates the continuance of the festivities at the Whitsuntide period.

While the aim of the contest was to draw blood from the head, various rules were imposed, such as "The Gamesters to mount the Stage exactly at One O' Clock in the afternoon each Day, ready dress'd." It was carefully laid down what was required to receive the prizes, "the person that breaks most heads and fairest to have the Hat, and the second best the Knot." The inclusion of the word 'fairest' may well be an indication that there were very few rules once the match had started and that all sorts of dubious practices were used. It has been claimed that some of the contests became so personal that they resulted in a general fight with fists as well. To prevent one man dominating the stage for a long period it was stated that "when 2 heads are broke by one man, he is to go off and after 5 o'clock each day, there are to play out the tiers." As the contest was to last for four hours before the knockout stages, it obviously attracted many participants, not only from Bruton but also from other areas, for example, an advertizement in 1751 stated, "It is said that the famous NUTH, of Wells, and Mr Hunt, of Glastonbury, will play for Eight Guineas upon the said Stage at Bruton."

Many spectators attended the competitions as most advertisements in local newspapers ended with words such as, "NB. Very good encouragement will be given to good players." To ensure that there would be a regular source of new talent, young men were encouraged to start, "and prizes each morning for young gamester to play for." Sword and Dagger matches, therefore, lasted the whole day with varying degrees of skill on display. They took place on simple wooden stages which were erected in convenient open spaces, such as the market place or in large yards behind inns such as the Old Bull in Patwell Street.

The other most popular violent entertainment was Backsword or Singlestick, with the first name being the one which was generally used in Bruton itself except on odd occasions. For this contest only one arm, usually the right one was used and the other often tied down so that it could play no part. The contestant held a thin stick which was about three feet long and which had a small wickerwork basket at one end to act as the hilt to protect the hand. The object once again was to draw blood from the opponent's forehead.

In most of the middle years of the eighteenth century the winner could expect to receive one guinea and the runner up half a guinea. By 1791 the overall purse, as for Sword and Dagger, had been raised to five guineas. The contestants fought on the same stage, starting at the same time but usually on the second day of the three-day Bruton Feast. Other towns may have been more generous as an advertisement in September 1790 for backsword at Wincanton offered the same prizes but in addition, "Every man who mounts the stage and plays will be entitled to a dinner, &c, gratis, at the Swan Inn." This represented a powerful inducement to young men who may have not always had a varied or substantial diet.

How many injuries were sustained and how serious they were is impossible to determine but as the object of both of these contests was to draw blood from the head, the danger to eyes, nose, mouth and ears is obvious. After mounting the stage it was customary for each man to say "God save our eyes," before the competition started. Attempting to damage an opponent's hand would also place him at a serious disadvantage. It is interesting to note that of twenty-five men from Bruton imprisoned in Ilchester Gaol between September 1824 and July 1839, no less than fourteen were recorded as having cuts or scars on their forehead or face. While these could have been received from their occupations or other violent activities, their position does suggest that these sports may have been involved in at least some cases.

Specific references to Backsword in Bruton cease at the end of the eighteenth century but contests continued in the neighbourhood.

In October 1806 a Singlestick contest was held at the George Inn in Castle Cary for "a Subscription Prize of Ten Guineas", and in June 1811 for a purse of twenty guineas another competition was staged at Queen Camel: "Somersetshire against all England." One late reference appeared in September 1863 when George Mapstone of Wedmore took up the challenge "for 200 Guineas and the Champion's belt" of Simon Stone of London, "the champion of England." The meeting of these two was intended to take place at Bruton later in the month but no evidence survives to suggest that it did in fact take place there.

Cudgel playing, which was the third violent activity, also occurred in Bruton, although sometimes the various names were used interchangeably. In its purest form a cudgel, which was a short stout stick or club, was used in an attempt once again to draw blood from the head of the opponent. In addition the contestant had as a guard on his left arm a second cudgel with a large hemisphere of wickerwork attached to it to act as a shield and with which to defend himself. In a Reply to the Society of Antiquaries in the mid-1750s it was noted that the sports "of the County people at the Feasts are cudgelling at which they are bold, hardy and dextrous." In 1754 notice was given that at Bruton Feast, "there will be Cudgel Playing as usual." Revd. James Woodforde attended some cudgel-playing contests in the area, for example, on the anniversary of Coronation Day in 1769 in Castle Cary he recorded, "Cudgell playing at Crokers.... At the Cudgell Playing I gave 0 4 5." While part of this sum was probably for gambling, which was common at such events, it was also customary to reward with small amounts particular players as a result of their efforts. On 17the September 1772 "gave to the Players there   2s   6d", and the following day "To the Cudgell-Players this afternoon gave 3s   0d". In addition a seat usually cost him 1s   0d.

125

The main evidence for the interchange of names comes from Woodforde's entry for 21st September 1771 when with others, "went to the Cudgell-Playing (alias Back-Sword) at Crockers, where was good sport and a vaste concourse of people." He had in fact been in attendance the previous day as well but on that occasion he recorded "we had but bad sport, the Gamesters playing booby." Over the two days he spent 4s 6d. Whatever the correct name, violence remained as a form of entertainment that continued to attract not just the ordinary people but some from the wealthier classes as well.

Woodforde rarely attended such events alone, "I was there with the Gentlemen." What remains fascinating is that despite his background, education and profession, Woodforde, at least for the first thirty years or so of his life, remained interested in violent activities and sports. He developed pronounced opinions about the quality of much of what he witnessed and gave significant amounts of detail in his Diary. On one day in September 1772 "There was but indifferent playing there" but on the following day, "We the Gentlemen all went in the Afternoon to Crockers to see some more Cudgell-Playing, and we had very good Sport today, and one Ford, a Dorsetshire Man, got the Silver Cup – he played very well and behaved very civil withal." Perhaps Woodforde was typical of his generation which did become less keen on such leisure pursuits by the later decades of the century.

The most unusual entry in his Diary occurred on 21st September 1759, "Went and saw women playing Cudgels." This is the only reference which has so far come to light in this area to indicate that females participated in this activity. Although he was at Ansford at the time he did not record where the event took place.

Boxing was a particularly brutal and violent activity as there were virtually no rules for these bare-knuckle fights and by the late eighteenth century it was being increasingly attacked as it caused deaths and serious injuries. No evidence has emerged of boxing contests in Bruton itself but it was prevalent in the area as on 2nd May 1769 Revd. Woodforde reported that, "Brother John went to Cannards Grave this morning to see a famous Boxing match between Parfitt Maggs and one Darck a Londoner and the Londiner beat Maggs." Just over a year later in August 1770 Woodforde himself attended one as he noted, "There was a boxing Match at Ansford Inn today at half an Hour after one, between one Mellish of Bruton and one Bond of Evercreech. Mellish the Crack was beat, Great number of People came to see it."

Men were prepared to travel some distance to attend boxing events as in May 1770 Woodforde's brother John journeyed to near Bristol to be present at a fight, "to see two famous Boxers fight – George Maggs and Melsom the Collier – two Cracks." When John returned home two days later it was to report that Maggs had been beaten in a few minutes and "A great deal of money was lost there, the Betts being for George Maggs." Once again for many men the gambling element was an important part of the event.

Wrestling was common in some counties such as neighbouring Devon but no evidence has emerged that it took place in Bruton. Such sports gave a rare opportunity for ordinary men to acquire prestige, self-respect and personal recognition. It must not be overlooked that such contests provided local people with a topic of conversation for months after. John Clare appreciated the status which could be achieved in wrestling:

> For ploughman would not wish for higher fame
> Than be the champion all the rest to throw

And thus to add such honours to his name
He kicks and tugs and bleeds to win the glorious game. (23)

    ii)   Towards Animals.

As well as violence against humans various animals and birds were used in cruel activities to provide entertainment, not only for the ordinary labourers but also for the wealthy who used the events for extensive gambling. Only from the mid-eighteenth century, and then very slowly, did attitudes begin to change amongst some in society and opposition to various blood sports developed and eventually to have some effect. It was not, however, until the Cruelty to Animals Act 1835 that all blood sports involving animal baiting were made illegal.

Bull-baiting.

This activity seems to have been common in Somerset as in the seventeenth century Fuller claimed, "The Gentry and Commonality of this County are much affected with Bull-baiting for which purpose there are very good Mastiffs." In some parts of the country butchers were even required to have a bull baited before it was killed. The usual method of baiting was to tie one end of a rope around the base of the horns of a bull and the other end to an iron ring driven into the ground. The rope would be about fifteen feet in length so the bull had a circle some thirty feet in diameter in which to move. Once this was done a dog was released. The injuries caused were extensive as dogs were gored, had their stomachs ripped open or were thrown considerable distances and heights, resulting in broken bones. The bulls suffered deep scratches from claws and had large chunks of flesh torn away.

Some of these contests were sponsored by the owners of alehouses and staged on land adjacent to them, for example, an advertisement appeared in a local newspaper in April 1748:

"To be sold at the Bear in Dropping-lane, near Bruton, Somerset, a Beautiful Baiting Bull, three years old, at a reasonable rate. He is to be baited on Easter Monday next." Once again the time of year is significant as it indicates the continuance of the traditional holiday with festivities at that period. It is possible that the Bull Inn, or the Old Bull Inn as it became known, in Patwell Street also staged contests at some time but there is no direct evidence for this beyond its name. There was however a large open space behind the street frontage with a barton which gave access to Lower Backway.

Other bull-baiting contests took place in suitable pits such as old quarries and one probably existed outside of Bruton, just above Coombe Farm. In a Survey of the property owned by the Visitors of Sexey's Hospital in 1717, Henry Albin was listed as leasing, amongst other lands, "One orchard in ye South east of Comb brook, supposed to be ye Plott by ye Bull Bayting place." By 1798 this land was leased by Richard Goldesbrough and referred to as "Bull Plott", and consisted of one rod and thirty poles, or nearly half an acre. The name then changed completely so that by the time of the survey for the Tithe Map in 1838 the property was listed as "Bear Garden." It was located on the western side of the road leading from Bruton towards Creech Hill, just before the turning to Coombe Farm. It was at this point as well that the old track which started in Higher Backway as Chick's Lane joined the road to Creech Hill, having passed over the hill. An ideal location for bull-baiting as it was outside of the town but easily accessible from several directions.

Although bull-baiting itself was very unpleasant on a lighter note a "mock bull" from the town was provided as a form of entertainment at Redlynch House at Christmas 1746. What exact form this took was not specified.

Former Old Bull Inn (on left) in Patwell Street.

Bear-baiting.

Bear-baiting was staged less frequently than bull-baiting as bears were not as common and were expensive to obtain. In this activity the bear was tied to a post and a dog released. As the bear was able to stand upright it could use its front paws for defence and strike the dogs some terrible blows, many of which were fatal. If a dog managed to get its teeth into the flesh of the bear, the unfortunate animal would often roll on the ground to crush its attacker.

No accounts of bear-baiting in Bruton itself have survived, although it is possible that the Bear Inn in Dropping Lane derived its name from this blood sport. Bear-baiting certainly occurred in the area as may be seen in the matter-of-fact way in which Revd. Woodforde noted on 5th September 1759, "I went to the Bear-baiting in Ansford", and four days later, "At the bear baiting at Ansford Inn."

Cock-fighting.

Much more prevalent was cock-fighting and this seems to have occurred for several centuries, being once again actively supported by all strands in society. Large scale betting took place on individual battles and on overall totals in more extensive contests. Considerable injuries could be suffered by the birds, for example, when John Swallow the younger of Castle Cary complained to a Justice of the Peace in August 1657 that John Francis had stolen his fighting cock he was able to identify it by the fact that it had already lost an eye and sustained several other injuries.

Game cocks were obviously bred in the area, for example, in June 1703 Jonathan Williams, Edward Gapper and Benjamin Roberts were alleged to have stolen six Game Cocks and two hens from John ffarthing of Zeals. In the end each man offered to pay the

131

owner one guinea by way of compounding, that is compensation and so avoid prison.

Once birds were old enough to take part in contests they were handed over to men known as "feeders" whose task was to look after the birds, feed them, train them and keep them in practice, and were expected to bring them to the cock-pit at the designated time in a fit state to fight. All birds had to be at the pit at least one and usually two or three days before the fight to be weighed, allowances made for a difference of an ounce or two in weight and the silver spurs, with which the birds were armed, were examined. At this stage lists of the birds fighting were printed and circulated.

In the eighteenth century it was the Ansford Inn which became the centre of highly organised large cock-fighting contests and where the landlord gave away grey pea-soup and bacon to the spectators. Year after year local newspapers announced these contests, usually between the Gentlemen of Somerset and the Gentlemen of Dorset, and occasionally of Wiltshire. The one for 1740 is typical:

> "This is to give Notice, That there is a great Cock-match to be fought at Ansford-Inn, by Francis Newman, Esq., and the Gentlemen of Dorset against the Gentlemen of Somerset and the Gentlemen of Wiltshire; they are to show Forty-one Cocks on each side, for Four Guineas each Cock, and Forty Guineas the odd Battle; to weigh on Monday the 25th Day of February, and fight the following three Days. Upshall and Russ are the Feeders."

Each year between forty and sixty cocks fought over two, or more usually, three days in any month from February to June. Once again each contest seems to coincide with one of the principal holidays in the festive calendar. There were prizes of generally two but up to four guineas for each individual fight and from twenty to one hundred guineas, as in 1774, for the whole battle. In 1747 the innkeeper even built a new pit for the contest because as an activity it must have brought him a considerable amount of trade. It was also very easy to stage in a relatively small space and could be inside or outside, usually with seats in tiered rows.

Revd. Woodforde's brother John was very interested in cock-fighting and seems to have attended contests regularly. Woodforde records that his brother was present on 29th May 1769 when there had been "great cock fighting." Two years later on 9th May 1771 he noted triumphantly that after a two-day cock fight at the Ansford Inn, Somerset were the overall winners and "Wilts was beat shamefully", and added, "I believe my Brother John won a good deal of money on it." That situation in fact was not uncommon as the following year he reported that John had been at a Cock Match at Bath between June 1st and 6th and won £50. In general, however, the Diarist was not a great supporter of the sport as on one occasion he noted that it was "idle work."

Cock-fighting had taken place in or near Bruton for a considerable period of time as in March 1686 Lord Fitzharding noted in a letter, "Next Wensday and Thursday are like to be bloody dayes at Bruton unless all the Cock matches be dispatched ye first day." Local tradition relates that such cock fighting occurred on the outskirts of Bruton, at the place called Cocks Plot, adjacent to the road to Godminster opposite the Park and on the hill overlooking Lusty. When council houses were built upon this site in the mid-twentieth century its name was changed to Coxes Close. There does not, however, seem to be any written evidence that such an activity took place there and old leases and surveys indicate that the site of Cocks Plot and Cocks Paddock covered over three acres, a vast area for such a sport. On the other hand the Parish Registers do not in any period which they cover after 1554 indicate a local family with that or a similar surname after whom the site may have been called. As cock-fighting was so much part of popular culture it probably did not need to be so far away from the town and was more often than not attached to a local inn. It would seem much more likely that at some stage in the eighteenth century and before there was a cock-fighting pit at the river end of Patwell Street in the Cock Inn, which was later renamed the Crown Inn. Similarly a Cock Inn existed at Redlynch, renamed the Fox Inn by 1789.

Other blood sports.

In some parts of the country where badgers were particularly common, badger-baiting was often undertaken. The usual method was to place a badger in a box and see on how many occasions within a given space of time a dog could encourage the badger to leave the box. In some places dogs were specifically bred for dog-fighting, once again suffering horrendous injuries in contests. In this sport only a pit was required and it may be that the same one could be used as for cock-fighting so the Cock Inn may have witnessed both types of contest.

Throwing at cocks, sometimes called cock squailing, was a popular recreation at Shrovetide. The usual procedure was to tie a cock to a stake in the ground with a rope which was about four or five feet long which allowed it a good degree of movement. Competitors would stand about twenty yards away and hurl a missile, usually a club, at the bird. The owner of the cock would charge one or two pence for three throws and if the thrower could knock the cock down, run and grab it before it regained its feet, it was his as a prize. More often than not the cock was either badly injured or killed.

While no direct evidence has yet emerged to indicate that any of these last three entertainments took place in Bruton or the surrounding area, such occurrences would not be surprising in a rural area. In addition apart from the animal or bird required for each of the activities considered, very little else was needed and so many of these sports would have been so easy to stage in a relatively short time in an appropriate location. As was so often the case something which was commonplace went unrecorded. It was just part of the accepted practices of the countryside prior to the late eighteenth century.

As attitudes began to change in the late eighteenth and early nineteenth centuries, however, a series of campaigns were fought which aimed to ban some of these traditional rural activities. In February 1784 one local newspaper was delighted to report, "It is with pleasure we learn that the inhuman practice of cock-squailing is now generally discountenanced and decreases every year. Indeed, none but persons of no education, or who are of an unfeeling disposition, will indulge themselves in so unmanly and unchristian a practice." The reformers' cause was greatly stimulated by the formation in 1824 of the Society for the Prevention of Cruelty to Animals which was soon initiating prosecutions. (24)

iii)   Humiliation and Punishments.

Watching a punishment, especially one which inflicted pain and some degree of humiliation as well, was part of the popular culture of previous centuries. While punishments were designed to deal with those who had been found guilty of committing a crime and to serve as a dire warning to others, they also provided a public entertainment spectacle. It is, for example, well-recorded that hundreds watched executions at Tyburn in London, and hundreds more the victims being transported through the streets from

Newgate Prison. It was no coincidence that when the Quarter Sessions in Bruton imposed a physical punishment on a criminal it was specified that the sentence was to take place on a Saturday, which was market day and the occasion when the maximum number of people would be in the town.

A public whipping became a common occurrence, especially for the mother of an illegitimate child, such as Alice Dagge in 1612, Anne Stephens in 1618, Agnes Brown and Mary Stevens in 1620. The Constables' Accounts indicate that in 1740-1741 one Constable spent 6d "when John Jacob's son was whipt", and 2s 3d the following year when James Spencer and James Lumber were whipped.

For more than a century after the Restoration of Charles II in 1660 the annual Quarter Sessions held at Bruton, usually in March or April, provided a steady flow of candidates for whipping. In most years those sentenced to be whipped consisted of between 9% and 12% of all men and women convicted. The whippings took place along the High Street for maximum effect, "to be forthwith publicly whipped as usual from the Market Cross in Brewton to the West End of the Town." In many cases the actual time was specified, generally between noon and two o'clock, the time when the greatest number of people would be attending the market. The procedure was for the victim to be stripped to the waist and tied to the back of a cart for the slow progress along the High Street. Sometimes the sentence imposed included more unpleasant details, "Let them be publickly whipt till the blood comes." For an age which was used to violent activities it provided a good source of entertainment.

The Quarter Sessions also imposed branding as a punishment for theft, "Let him be burnt in the Hand and marked on the brawn of the left Thumb with the letter T." While this procedure also tended to be performed in Bruton immediately after the sentence had been pronounced, no specific details have survived as to where it took place although in the Pillory beside the Market Cross would seem likely. As it was usually in public, more entertainment could be expected for those who wished to be present.

Humiliation was one of the main punishments imposed by the Church Courts as they were prevented from administering a physical one but they too could provide entertainment for others. Cases involving immorality tended to receive a punishment of penance which entailed standing at the front of the Church during Morning Prayers, dressed in a white sheet and holding a white wand. The numbers who witnessed this may not, however, have been very large. Throughout the medieval period such penance also occurred in the market place and although this procedure had declined by the sixteenth century it did still occur. In 1574 Elizabeth Combe was found guilty of adultery with Thomas Bradford so in "the market place in Brewton the next market daie shee shall stand in a whit sheet." Such a punishment would of course have been witnessed by a much larger number of people and being in the open would have allowed much more verbal abuse of the offender.

Humiliation and violence came together in three other punishments which were practiced in Bruton: the pillory, the stocks and the cucking stool. The first had been in use in England since before the Norman Conquest and was a wooden construction which resembled the letter T with the offender standing behind it with head and hands pushed through holes in the cross bar. Stocks seem to have come into use from the early thirteenth century and by 1405 each village was required to have its own. Stocks were much lower than the pillory with the offender sitting on the ground or a wooden seat and with his or her legs clamped between two horizontal wooden planks.

Considering that both were in use in Bruton for so long a period, very few references have survived, and these usually concerned repairs. The pillory was probably close to the Market Cross as shambles are mentioned as being near it. The stocks may also have been in the same vicinity or possibly near Patwell. In these locations there would have been maximum visibility to the greatest number of people. The entertainment value for local inhabitants was considerable as not only was there the mocking potential through verbal abuse but also any items could be thrown at the offender who had little scope to avoid them.

The stocks were a good place to hold those suspected of a range of petty offences, such as being a vagabond or idle. From 1606 one of its main uses after the Drunkenness Act was detaining drunks for several hours. The pillory could have a similar purpose although more serious cases may have ended up in it and it is possible that criminals were held in place here while branding was performed. For some offences noses were split and ears nailed to the cross bar. One unpleasant episode occurred in Bruton after Richard Vowles "foolishlie, lewedlie and slanderoselie" complained to Henry VIII in 1537 about the Chief Justice of England, Sir John Fitzjames of Redlynch. Vowles was sentenced to the pillory at Westminster and Bruton "and to loose at each place an eare." Humiliation and pain came together in another public spectacle.

The cucking stool seems to have been in operation much less frequently, only when a person offended the community in some way. It was a simple stool or chair which was used to carry the offender through the streets or place them tied to it outside their own door. Once again there are some isolated references to a stool being made or repairs carried out but nothing has survived for Bruton on the nature of the offences or the exact process followed. Humiliation, however, was clearly present and the opportunity for verbal or physical abuse.

The final form of popular humiliation and violent behaviour came with Skimmington Riding, which probably derived its name from the skimming ladels used in butter and cheese making and which were originally the instruments with which the unfortunate victims were beaten. In Skimmington Riding the local community took matters into their own hands to punish one or more of their number who had caused offence in some way. The offender was carried on a pole or in a cart and paraded through the streets, accompanied by a great deal of noise made by banging pots and pans together. While it was originally used to punish sexual misdeeds, a wife who dominated her husband or a husband who could not control his wife, it was gradually extended to any offence which displeased the community. In 1901, a local historian, George Sweetman of Wincanton , in his 'Glossary of Local Words' defined it somewhat ironically as, "Mob music, when pots, pans, kettles are beaten, horns are blown, in honour of some-one who has offended the moral sense of the mob."

Through the centuries significant criticisms were made of skimmington riding as it was argued that if large numbers were involved there could be a threat to public order and property; that it was an assault upon the victim; that malicious motives could be concealed within the activity; that the humiliation experienced was disproportionate to the offence; and above all, many inhabitants felt that it was an ideal opportunity for the more disreputable members of the community to cause trouble. One interesting allegation which surfaced was that some of the men who took part against others were insecure in their own masculine role, as it was pointed out that the targets were usually women and that there were no examples of sons taking action against fathers who beat or assaulted them or of male assaults on other men generally. One witness at a skimmington ride at Ditcheat in 1653 commented later that "not ten of that company would charge an enemy." In similar vein the writer Jonathan Swift remarked of those who mocked a beaten husband:

> Those men who wore the breeches least
> Called him a cuckold, fool and beast.

Fragmentary evidence from the Bruton area, however, suggests that the practice was carried on. One reason for its continuance was that it was too infrequent an occurrence in any one place to arouse a great deal of hostility. It was also in its own way just another form of the humiliation punishments which were officially sanctioned elsewhere. In addition it did deal with issues which were important to all classes in society, such as relations between husbands and wives. Above all, of course, such events were very deeply imbedded in popular culture and they were a great form of entertainment.

The major problem for later generations is the lack of evidence because it was unofficial, often impromptu, no record was ever kept and so it is by chance that some examples have survived. In fact no cases have emerged for Bruton itself but it occurred in the surrounding areas, for example in 1607 in Wells, 1611 in Beckington near Frome and 1653 in Ditcheat when both the Constable and the tythingman attended.

In 1871 one incident occurred in Shepton Montague when two boys had gone to fight and were stopped by Betsy Peach. For this action she was subjected to this ordeal. One witness, Edwin

Brown, an apprentice to a harness maker in Bruton, described a crowd of about fifteen or twenty people in the road and stated that he had been beating a kettle. The episode only came to light as a result of some stones being thrown, one of which struck an old woman who subsequently died. Henry Trim, a twenty-four year old carpenter, was charged with manslaughter but eventually the case was dismissed. Noise, rowdy behaviour and popular involvement remained a feature of Skimmington Riding.

There were other examples in the area in the nineteenth century but the details and references to them are meagre. In 1900 it was claimed that there had been two or three cases of Skimmington Riding in Castle Cary in the previous thirty or forty years. In the same period George Sweetman recalled just one case in Wincanton involving a tradesman who was said to have beaten his wife.

Slightly more detail may be found on two other cases but they also indicate how attitudes were changing. The first occurred near Castle Cary in 1872, "An adjoining parish has been made lively by skimmerton riding. In this case it is said that one of the gentle sex soundly beat her lord and master. If the statements openly made have a tithe of truth in them they should be investigated." Attitudes to such events were clearly changing as the local newspaper added, "Such conduct cannot be properly dealt with by a skimmerton band." The second example came as late as August 1900 when six men from Evercreech were charged with assault connected with skimmington riding. Their solicitor defended them unsuccessfully on the grounds that "they had been keeping up a very old custom, still common in this county."

The last five words were particularly significant as they indicate that this type of entertainment was still very prevalent. In addition in none of the small number of reports which appeared in the local press was any need felt to explain what skimmington riding actually was. Such was the strength of the custom that it was still general knowledge, its noise and its violence lived on. Through the centuries it was a form of popular entertainment that cost virtually nothing to arrange and the materials needed were easily to hand. Many more cases must have taken place in Bruton and its neighbourhood which were never recorded or have been lost through time. (25)

b) The role of alcohol and the alehouse.

Alcohol played a crucial part in the lives of the poorer members of the community through most of the centuries under consideration. Cider was traditionally produced in great quantities in the West Country and survey after survey for Bruton made reference to the orchards in the area, some of which undoubtedly contained cider apple trees. In 1830 it was claimed that, "Devon and Somerset are over-run with common sheds by the roadside in which cider is sold in great quantities to people of both sexes." Many farmers gave their labourers their poorer quality cider as part of their wages.

It was ale however, or from the sixteenth century, hopped beer, which was the common drink. Ale was brewed from malt infused with water and had some basic spices added. It tended to be a heavy, thick drink which deteriorated quite quickly and so needed to be drunk soon after production. There were two main types of ale: strong or good and small or common, with the latter being made by pouring more water over the residue in the vat after the strong ale had been drawn off.

Increasingly beer became more popular and in this case hops were added to fermented malt and water. It had various advantages such as that the preservative effects of the hops meant that it could be stored for longer, could be transported more easily and was more economical to brew and hence was cheaper to buy. It was claimed for example that a bushel of malt could produce eight gallons of ale but eighteen gallons of beer. It became possible to brew strong beer such as March and October beers which were kept for a year or more to mature.

Both ale and beer were important in the lives of labouring people especially as increasingly sources of water became polluted. In Bruton, while most of the houses of the wealthier inhabitants had their own wells, nearly all of which have now been filled in and sealed, the poor had to fetch their water from common wells, such as Patwell, Coombe Hill Well, Wynes Well and at least one other spring in Shute Lane. Some small cottages grouped around a courtyard also shared a common well, such as those in the Square and in the area known as Old Barton on the eastern side at the top of Cats Lane, the present day St Katherine's Hill. In the late sixteenth and early seventeenth centuries the six cottages which comprised the Almshouse, which Hugh Sexey maintained before the building of the present Hospital bearing his name, also shared one common well located behind them, access to which was specified in the residents' leases.

The major problem relating to water was that as the population increased, public health developments did not keep pace and by the latter part of the nineteenth century most of the sources of water were reported to be contaminated.

> "There are many house-wells in Bruton, but the water in a number of them is so unmistakeably polluted that the people do not use it for drinking or cooking, but resort to the public wells which are supplied by deep springs. Of these the one

most in repute is Patwell, which is within 15 feet of the Bru stream, and is from time to time flooded by it. As house drains conveying excremental matter open into the Bru, a few yards above the well thus exposed to be flooded, the alternative choice of people in Bruton for water would seem to be a poor one."

Milk was available but as it was so easily adulterated it was often regarded with suspicion. Far more serious was the fact that infected milk supplies caused outbreaks of scarlet fever, which with no effective medical treatment, led to local epidemics. Tea and coffee, for much of the period until the later nineteenth century, were both expensive and therefore beyond the reach of many labouring people. In these circumstances it was hardly surprising that the majority of the ordinary inhabitants turned to ale, beer and cider.

While spirits were regarded as important painkillers, it has been argued that ale was vital to the well-being of the poor as much of their food was of low nutritional value. One biased source claimed that ale was "most cherishing to poore labouring people, without which they cannot well subsist, their food for the most part of such things as afford little or bad nourishment." Many labourers felt that beer gave them strength. If this claim was valid in any way, then alcohol was not only a part of the popular culture of the masses but also essential for their very survival.

There were also those who believed that ale was beneficial in protecting the poor from the harsh conditions of their existence. One Tudor song related:
>Much bread I not desire
>No frost nor snow, no wind I trow
>Can hurt me if I would

I am so wrapped and thoroughly lapped
Of jolly good ale and old.

   i)   Prevalence of Alcohol.

Ale was the main drink throughout the medieval period and clearly much enjoyed in the monastery, for example, in August 1430 on the anniversary of the death of its patron, Sir John Luttrell of Dunster, the canons were provided with fourteen gallons of beer and the Prior with one gallon of wine. Not all the ale brewed there was of the appropriate strength as during his Visitation in 1452 Bishop Bekyngton found the ale "to be too thin" and the prior promised to put the matter right. While it may have happened on that occasion in a subsequent Visitation of the Abbey in 1526, three canons took the opportunity to complain that the ale was weak and watery, one making the allegation that other things such as oats had been added to the barley.

On many occasions administrative tasks were accompanied by alcohol, for example, when drawing up a taxation list in 1576, "& for our drinking at Haywardes xiiijd." When an Apprenticeship Indenture was signed a drink would be taken, "1667 August 23. Paid for beer when the Churchwardens and Overseers duly placed Margiry boy apprentice with Mr Swanton 1s   6d."

Alcohol flowed freely at the main rites of passage such as baptism, marriage and death. It is only for the latter that evidence from Bruton is clear. In 1584 the funeral expences of William Walter were 22s 0d, which included "the meat and drinke for the neighbours after they came home from the buryall." This figure in fact represented a substantial amount and was an indication of the status of the deceased. The implication in this instance was that the food and drink was provided in the dead man's own home.

On other occasions the drinking could take place in the churchyard itself or in a local alehouse, where simple food such as bread, cakes, biscuits and buns was also available. In November 1641 Thomas Albin's widow, Tabitha, allowed £1   10s   0d for his funeral expences, which included "making the grave, ringing the knell, for Dakes beere." Paupers too received similar treatment on death, although on a much reduced scale, for example, the Overseers paid 1s in 1661 "for beere when Peter Walters child was buried." On 1st July 1680 it cost them 3s "ffor beere at Rich Wayte death & burial." Over a century later in March 1780 they paid John Duffet 2s   6d "for a Shroud & Liquor" when he buried "a Stranger."

The last example indicates the way in which labourers could expect alcohol as part of, or a small addition to, their wages. When the Constable required support from local residents to assist him in performing his various functions, he could provide alcohol, for example, in October 1688 "To a Guard in searching after Wm Gibbs in Beers 6d", and in June 1693 "to the Watchman drinke 6d." In 1705 he paid 1s "in Brandy" to men who watched a fire in Quaperlake Street.

The Churchwardens too were lavish in their supply of beer as the following examples indicate:

1737	Pd for Beer abt washing the Chancel	7 1/4
1754	Pd Harry Corp beer for Workmen	7 9

This was a much larger figure as they were "rough Casting the Church & for Whitewashing the inside of the Church."

1815 Oct.	Pd for Beer for Masons at Bow Bridge	6
1828 Ap.	Beer to Men at raising &c of the Tenor Bell	4 0
1831 Sept.	Paid Beer at trying the Fire Engine	5 0

1840 Ap.	Paid Beer for Men White washing the Church	2	3
1845 May	Paid for Beer for Masons on laying foundation of the		
	Wall for New Burial Ground agst Abbey Green	1	0

Considering how cheap beer was during this period the quantities involved could be large.

After some events beer was a welcome reward, especially, for example, in the case of fire, which could be accompanied not only by hard physical labour when carrying water but also by possible dehydration. This was one of the items that was usually, but not always, the responsibility of the Constable. On one occasion when there was a serious fire in Coombe Street the Constable spent £2 "for such as Laboured therein in drink", and a further 5s to labourers "in Bread and Cheese and drink", presumably as they removed the resulting debris. In the Overseers' Accounts for 1766 there is the simple entry, "Liquor at the Fire 13s." The provision of drink at such events was clearly the accepted custom for Revd. James Woodforde noted that when the Parsonage chimney at Ansford caught fire in March 1776 many local inhabitants flocked to help, "My Uncle sent down some Cyder in Pails to the people and we gave them more."

The Overseers also provided alcohol on other occasions such as 1s in 1820 to James Clarke's men "for Beer at putting down the new floor" in a room in the Poorhouse. Their Accounts show that once this institution was opened in June 1734 one and a half pence was paid each week for "Ale at washing", a hard physical activity for some of the female inmates.

The major occasions, however, when alcohol flowed abundantly were during festivities and celebrations of any kind. When peace was declared in 1697 the Constables spent £5 on "two hogshead of beer" and a further 3s for a bottle of brandy. This was a not inconsiderable quantity of beer as it represented over one hundred gallons. Anything connected with royalty could instigate a celebration at which drink was a significant constituent. When William of Orange was proclaimed king in February 1689 the Constable spent £2   12s   0d on wine and beer. When Queen Anne was proclaimed in March 1702 the response was much more muted as just 3s was spent "in drink at Wm Gibbs." In June 1727 £2   12   0d was paid to "John Martin for Beer when the King (George II) was proclaimed." Over a century later on the Coronation of William IV in September 1831 "about eight hundred were regaled with roast beef, plum pudding and strong beer."

The Jubilee of George III in October 1809 produced similar celebrations, "At six o'clock commenced a plentiful and judicious distribution of beef, bread and strong beer, to every poor family in the parish." The Marriage of the Prince of Wales in 1863 led to a similar distribution to 600 poor people. Finally when the railway was opened through Bruton in 1856 some three hogshead of beer were consumed on the Abbey Field. The merriment which must have been enjoyed by the poorer inhabitants on these occasions would have been a very welcome relief from the general drudgery of their every day lives. Alcohol could certainly make a difference for some of them.

In a rural area it was the custom, and so there was also the expectation, that there would be a celebration when the harvest was completed. As these were such localized matters arranged by individual farmers no specific accounts of gatherings seem to have survived from the Bruton area in the earlier part of the period. An eighteenth century poem gives an indication of the general tone:

Our Master joyful at the welcome sight,

Invites us all to feast with him at Night,
A Table plentifully spread we find,
And Jugs of humming Beer to cheer the Mind. (26)

ii)   Drunkenness

One unfortunate consequence of the prevalence of so much alcohol was that drunkenness was rife and regular yet tolerated on festive occasions. Excessive consumption of ale and beer was, however, seriously frowned upon in the Priory for as early as 1452 in Injunctions issued after his Visitation, Bishop Bekynton had no hesitation in condemning the "drinking-bouts and gluttonous feasts (*which*) have heretofore been held in the canons' private chambers." He went on to order that "no one take any food or drink into the dormitory, under penalty of keeping complete silence for two months." Similarly any canon who left the dormitory "for a drinking-bout" was to "abstain from flesh food for a week" for a first offence and for a second, "he shall fast on bread and water every Wednesday and Friday for three whole months."

There seems to have been more drunkenness in Tudor and Stuart England as the beer was cheaper and stronger, many labourers were in poor physical condition and so more susceptible to intoxication, more went to alehouses as the atmosphere was more relaxed than in the house of an employer or even their own family and most alehouses were open all hours. The result was that as early as 1606 the Drunkenness Act condemned drunkenness as a "loathsome and odious sin" as it led to "many other enormous sins, as bloodshed, stabbing, murder, swearing, fornication, adultery and such like", as well as "the general impoverishment of many good subjects." The Act specified that drunks were to be fined 5s or spend six hours in the stocks.

One of the commonest sights throughout the seventeenth and eighteenth centuries will have been a person sitting in the stocks in Bruton as a result of drunkenness. In 1716-17, for example, the Constables paid 1s for "a warrant to set men in the Stocks for drunkenness." Once the 'Roundhouse' was in use in the eighteenth century this provided an alternative location for a drunk to be detained over night if he or she was unable to get home. The standard wording in Apprenticeship Indentures, especially the ones issued by the Visitors of Sexey's Hospital, was that "during the said term Taverns Inns or Alehouses he shall not frequent." This requirement clearly did not work in all cases as in May 1658 Henry Colman, a cloth drawer, complained that his apprentice, John Manning "was a comon alehowse haunter, swearer & drunkard."

Persistent drunkards often ended up being presented by the Churchwardens to the Church Court at the annual Visitations. In 1600 Radulph Petty was cited as a drunkard and again in 1612. Robert Corpe was condemned as a common drunkard on at least three occasions in 1612, 1626 and 1634. In October 1605 William Gregory was excommunicated as "sometimes hee hath bin overcome with drinke." The problem was certainly not unique to Bruton as in January 1616 John and Thomas Jelly of Pitcombe "weare taken in the tyme of evening prayer by the Churchwardens so drunke that they weare not able to go out of the place."

The nineteenth century Magistrates' Entry Books indicate that despite the best efforts of the Temperance Movement, drunkenness remained a problem in Bruton. By far the largest number of prosecutions were for drunkenness alone, followed by drunk and disorderly and then drunk and riotous. While most of those charged were male, some females such as Jane Andrews, Ann Lord and Elizabeth Bryant made more than one appearance before the

Wincanton Bench. Between 1858 and 1878 between 23% and 24% of all prosecutions in that court involving Bruton residents were for drunkenness related offences.

As the cases were often reported in the local newspapers interesting excuses began to be heard. When a labourer, Thomas Hunt, was charged with being drunk and abusive in July 1862 he claimed, "he was not making any noise, but some one called out 'Bob', and he answered. The Magistrates thought it rather odd that he should answer to another man's name, and fined him 5s, including costs."

The great concern amongst many inhabitants of the town was that drunken behaviour would get out of hand and lead to damage or other unwelcome consequences. Joseph Kittle, a local blacksmith, clearly had a violent temper and this may have been accentuated by drink, for example, in November 1704 he threatened James Armstrong of Discove with a knife and in July 1705 he was standing outside of the door of Richard Lumber, an alehouse keeper, throwing stones and dirt, and Lumber claimed that "he did heare the said Kittle Swear ffive evill oaths." On the same day he abused Thomas Gane, a beer-maker, threw stones at him and threatened to kill him.

When William Oxley was assaulted in April 1764 it was in "the publick House of Mr Walter called the White Lyon." Revd. Woodforde was not immune from the consequences of drunkenness as on 15th July 1770 he recorded that while he was preaching in Castle Cary Church, "One Thos Speed of Gallhampton came into the Church quite drunk and crazy and made a noise in the Church, called the Singers a Pack of whoresbirds and gave me a nod or two in the pulpit." He was detained by the Constable. (27)

iii)   Alehouses.

In the days before village halls, schoolrooms and other large interior open spaces the public house was the foremost meeting place for all members of the community, in fact in most villages and towns it was the largest open space apart from the parish church. Inns tended to be large, offering wine, ale and beer along with elaborate food and accommodation, especially for travellers in the heyday of coaching. In relative terms they tended to be expensive for while French wine was 8d a gallon in the fifteenth century by the late sixteenth century it had risen to 8d a quart which in part explains why there was a growing taste and demand for cheaper Iberian wines.

Certainly wine was passing through Bruton in great quantities, for example in 1539 William North, who was described as a 'vyntenar', owed £49   6s   8d for purchases which included five 'tons' of Gascon wine, that is some 1,260 gallons; and a decade later his account showed that he owed £108   15s   0d and this time as well as for Gascon wine it included 252 gallons of 'bastard' which was a sweet Portuguese wine and 882 gallons of 'seck' which was a dry amber wine usually imported from Cadiz or Jerez in Spain. In 1587 "at Palme Sundaie Even and against Easter Daie" the Churchwardens of Mere purchased over six gallons of wine "at Sherwoode of Bruton" at a total cost of 17s   10d.

Taverns were smaller than inns, sold wine which generally appealed to the wealthier inhabitants and had limited accommodation but this was not a term which seems to have been widely used in Bruton or Somerset as a whole. While a Survey in 1577 found 215 alehouses and 100 inns in the county there were just sixteen taverns. It was therefore to the alehouse that the labouring population turned with its ale or beer and its basic food, often buns and cakes which were cheap and easily prepared. The same Survey found that there were some 15,095 alehouses nationally. One problem which does emerge, especially in Bruton, is that there was a tendency to use the terms interchangeably so on some occasions a building is referred to as an inn and on another as an alehouse.

In one respect alehouses did face a significant amount of competition, especially in the earlier part of the period as in the West Country a substantial amount of cider was produced by farmers while most monasteries and larger houses brewed their own ale. These drinks would then be given to the monks and labourers and servants, often as part of their wages, so there was no need for them to go elsewhere to buy them. Much later in February 1767 Revd. Woodforde recorded, "I got up at 3 o'clock this morning to brew a hogshead of strong beer........and did not go to bed this night as we could not tun our liquor till near two in the morning." Three days later he was brewing again, "I got up before one this morning and brewed a 3 quarter barrel of strong beer and some small beer and had it all cool and tunned by four o'clock in the afternoon."

At a time when the cottages of the poor were small, cold, damp and often very crowded, the alehouse was a place of warmth as it had a fire, companionship and conviviality, a centre for conversation, gossip, the exchange of news, refreshment and entertainment. It provided a sanctuary from the cares of the world, whether the misery of repetitive outdoor labour or the drabness of the cottage. In addition for some men their 'leisure' time was the result of enforced idleness caused by such things as seasonal work, an accident which prevented full-time employment or significant weather occurrences such as prolonged severe frost or snow.

Within its walls the cultural character was what the drinkers wanted it to be and outside genteel influences were minimal. One observer commented that the village inn "is a club where the labourer can feel at home and can talk over those matters which affect him closely. In summer, he sits on the benches in the open, in winter, in the settle round the blazing fire, the workaday world shut out by the red curtains drawn across the windows."

The furnishings within the small rooms were basic and cheap with trestle tables, benches, stools and the odd chair. The ale or beer was drunk from earthenware or stone drinking pots, occasionally wooden ones and in a very few instances pewter. Most alehouses sold their liquor by the crock or bucket for people to take away. In general alehouses were towards the edge of towns or outside on busy routes and it may well be the case that in Bruton most conformed to this pattern, being towards West End, along Quaperlake Street or Coombe Street rather than in the High Street.

Many of those who ran the alehouses were poor, such as widows, and took up brewing to try and avoid destitution. This plan, of course, did not always work as it was said of one alehouse keeper in Charlton Horethorne, "being a very poor man, is not always well supplied with drink." Some sellers fell foul of the various regulations, for example, in 1629 John Stacey of Bruton was taken to the Quarter Sessions for tipling and selling ale without the necessary licence. In his case he was discharged after the inhabitants of the parish testified that he was a poor man with many children: they clearly recognised the economic value of his continuance in the trade to avoid him and his family becoming a burden on the poor rates.

For other people it was an invaluable secondary income, especially craftsmen and small holders, expressed in poetic form in the early seventeenth century:

> I see by my labour but little I thrive
> And that against the stream I do strive
> By selling of ale some money is got
> If every man honestly pay for his pot
> By this we may keep the wolf from the door.

The poem does indicate one problem which many alehouse keepers faced and that was allowing too many of their poor customers to run up debts which were unlikely to be paid in full. Operating an alehouse had various attractions such as in the earlier part of the period there were very few regulations, no special training was required and there was a substantial demand for drink. For some women of course it did offer the opportunity for a degree of independence.

In the late nineteenth century Richard Jefferies claimed that, "As a rule the beerhouse is the only place of amusement to which he (*the labourer*) can resort: it is his theatre, his music-hall, picture-gallery, and Crystal Palace." In fact after the local gentry it was the publican who sponsored, arranged and staged many of the popular recreations, all of which of course were good for trade. The very names of some Bruton public houses may imply that a particular activity associated with popular entertainment took place there: the Bull, the Cock and the May Pole. Inside many of the alehouses games which were linked with gambling took place, most notably cards and dice, both of which once again apprentices were supposed to avoid, "at Card Dice or any other unlawful Game he shall not play."

Singing and dancing were taken for granted in alehouses and inns and so virtually never recorded and hence the true extent will never be known. Needless to say as soon as Oliver Cromwell attempted to suppress this form of entertainment in the 1650s examples started to emerge as some of the inhabitants of Bruton took little notice. On 30th April 1655 Thomas Haine, one of the tithingmen, was sent by the Constable "unto the Howse of one Richard Maby of the said place Alehowse keeper & there to remove those who were there singinge & keepinge of disorders." He discovered three men inside including William Whitacre, a gardener, and when he ordered them to go home "the said Whitacre replyed to this depent beinge Tythingman, Will your heare a good Songe" and refused to leave. The Constable was called and subjected to much "opprobrious language."

On the evening of 5th January 1656 another tithingman, Robert Oram, "heard Singinge att the Sighne of the Unicorne wch Mr Cheeke doth keepe." He attempted to gain admission by "knockinge att the doore to see what Company were so disorderly", but it took a while for the door to be opened. Inside he found one woman and three men, including William Plumer whom he alleged "strucke him this depent ten tymes att least in the stomacke." In these two instances the effects of too much alcohol were probably well demonstrated.

The Church had traditionally taken the view that people should not enjoy themselves at certain times, most notably during Divine Service and occasionally someone was presented for that offence. In July 1593, for example, at a Visitation, Henry Hatch was reported "for dauncinge att Service tyme", although the location was not specified.

Singing and dancing obviously continued for a report in a local newspaper recorded that in June 1800 "Whit-Sunday at least eight old men accidently met in the Sun Inn, Bruton, whose age together amounted to six hundred and seventeen years. In a convivial and jovial manner they regaled themselves with some October, had a dance, sang several loyal songs, and concluded with 'Old Ally Crocker'." This example also indicates that Whitsuntide was still being celebrated with enthusiasm, at least by some old men. There were those within the area who could provide accompaniment to such entertainment, for example, on 27th September 1786 Revd. Woodforde noted that while at Cole he gave 1s, "To poor old John Tally the Fidler."

Evidence from Somerset as a whole indicates that folk songs, especially carols and wassails were particularly popular. Carols were originally associated not only with singing but also with dancing. One favourite was the 'Joys' of Mary and in this county the singers managed to find twelve:

> The first girt joy that Mary had,
> It wer' the joy of one,
> To see her own son Jesus,
> To zuck at her breas' bone.

> The next girt joy that Mary had,
> It wer' the joy of two,
> To see her own son Jesus
> To make the lame to goo.

and so on upto twelve. Needless to say the wassail songs tended to focus on alcohol:

> Wassail, wassail all round our town,
> The cup is so bright and the ale is so brown,
> Our bowl is made of the good old ash tree,
> So now my brave fellows let's drink unto thee,
> 'Tis your Wassail, 'tis our Wassail,
> And jolly come to our jolly Wassail.

Chorus

Harm, me bwoys, harm; harm, me bwoys, harm;
A liddle mwore zider wont do us no harm.
Hatfuls, capfuls, dree bushel bagfuls,
And a gurt heap under the stairs,
    Hip, hip, hurrah!

How far singing continued in the public houses in the nineteenth century is impossible to determine with any degree of accuracy. It does appear that songs and ballads were passed on from generation to generation and probably continued to find expression in these locations. Certainly there is at least one dialect story which indicates that the local police constable would threaten to clear out a pub because of the noise, which may imply singing. "If any o' the chaps were a bit noisy in the kitchen o' the 'Kings Arms,' he did go to the door an' holler out: 'Now I do know which o' ee 'tis an' I shall be back-along in vive minutes look-ee-zee'." As has been seen, however, music was an important element in the lives of the Victorian middle class and with so many opportunities for participation in choirs and various bands established in Bruton it is possible that they attracted some labouring men. If that were the case then there would have been a significant change in content as so much, but not all, of the Victorian music had a sacred or sentimental element.

In the seventeenth century bowls were popular and this game certainly occurred in the Bruton area, with at least the Bear Inn in Dropping Lane having an appropriate area for play. Bowls, with its related gambling, did cause some disquiet in religious circles as some men played the game rather than attend church on a Sunday. The result was that they could find themselves being presented before the Church Court. In 1613 John ffookes was reported "for prophaninge the Saboathe Day by playinge att bowles verrie unlawfully and for great sums of monie." In the same year William Trimway of Bruton was discovered in Shepton Montague "playeinge at bowles very unlawfully and for great sumes of monie", when he should have been attending "his owne pishe Churche upon a Saboath Daye." In fact such was the power of the preaching of the Puritan Richard Allein at Ditcheat that one parishioner was convinced that, "it was a greater sin for a man to play at bowls on the Sabbath day than to lie with another man's wife on a week day."

The Bear Inn was also the location of other entertainment, particularly in the 1740s with bull-baiting and pony racing. One of the main Bruton inns was most likely to have organised the hunting on Creech Hill during the Bruton Feasts in the 1790s and while the wealthy were the ones who took an active part in the chase, it was followed on foot by many ordinary men and women. In the nineteenth century it was the Sun Inn which was responsible for arranging pigeon-shoots.

In the late eighteenth and nineteenth centuries many workingmen took advantage of the opportunities available in Bruton for some protection against illness when they joined one of the Friendly Societies. Traditionally these societies were based in local inns and once again conviviality was an important aspect. After 1760 local Friendly Societies became based in the Blue Ball, the Bell, the Old Bull and the Sun Inns. In the nineteenth century the Ancient Order of Foresters had their headquarters first at the Sun and then the Blue Ball, while for a brief period in the 1840s the Manchester Unity of Oddfellows met at the Old Bull.

The local public houses also had other functions but while they could hardly be described as entertainment, they do indicate the central role that they played in the life of the community in general. As the nearest prison or House of Correction was at Shepton Mallet and then Ilchester, it was the usual custom for the Constable to arrange for a prisoner to be detained and guarded at a local alehouse.

24 Dec 1691	ffor a guard all night on Jane Budd and expenses at Wm Gibbs in beere ffire and Candle		
		5	0
20 July 1705	Expenses two days and one night at Wm Gibbs wth a guard on Wm Lumber and carrying him to prison about a base child		
		9	0
30 Jan 1701	Charges in apprehending two Souldiers and a guard 2 days & nights		
	the expenses at the Castle on them and their guard	16	0
		18	0
1728-9	pd the expenses at the White Hart whilst the Prisoners were kept there		
	3	16	4

For some of the poor one essential business which was conducted in a public house by the landlord was that of the pawnbroker. Many of the poor could just about manage to survive in ordinary circumstances but in times of crisis such as harvest failure, prolonged bad weather, unemployment, injury or illness, it was often necessary for them to pawn something from amongst their few possessions. Some innkeepers fulfilled the role of pawnbroker, not always legally, for example, in March 1859 Edward Ashford of the Bell Inn was summonsed for "exercising the trade of pawn broker, without having procured the necessary licence." He was found guilty and fined the large sum of £12   10s   0d. Faced with severe hardship in the 1660s a number of the poor were forced to pawn goods, for example, widow Anstice Leversuch had "pauned all that once I have", and John Collins, a carpenter, asked for help with "the redeeming of his goods." Unfortunately in these instances no alehouse is mentioned but remain the most likely location.

As there was no local hospital, a person who was ill and had no one to look after him or her or who had met with an accident could be treated in an inn by the local doctor. In August 1861, for example, a labourer named Sims was loading a cart at the railway station when the horse bolted and the wheel ran over him and "injuring him so severely, that he expired a short time after he had been removed to the Crown public house." In January 1876 after the son of a beater had been accidentally shot in the leg in Redlynch Park he was treated by Dr Heginbothom when "he is lying at the Blue Ball Hotel." A few months later in July George Williamson drowned while he was swimming in the River Brue at Pitcombe and after his body was retrieved from the water it was taken to Sunny Hill Inn. It was even the case that in the winter of 1821 to 1822 the Overseers paid 7s to "Mr Hannam for taking care of a man that was Insane at the Blue Ball."

As a suitable space could be obtained in an Inn it was also on a fairly regular basis the location for the Coroner to conduct an Inquest. In the nineteenth century virtually every inn in Bruton was used at some time or another for that purpose; in April 1869 the Coroner was at the Blue Ball after Mr Beale died from a fall from his horse; in May 1870 Dr Wybrants held an Inquest at the Wellington Inn on the body of a child found dead in the mill pond; in December 1872 he was at the Sun Inn after a new born child had been buried without the necessary certificate. In January 1884 the new Coroner, Mr Muller also held an Inquest at the Wellington Inn following a death on the level crossing at Sheephouse. Over twenty years earlier in October 1862 Dr Wybrants had been at the Wellington Inn for one Inquest when he was required to stage a second. The first Inquest was on the body of John Inderman who had been the station master at Bruton railway station but left as a result of depression and some six months later he was found dead in the River Brue at Batt's Hole. While this Inquest was in progress Charles Huish, a labourer at White and Bord's factory, was crushed to death when a length of wall collapsed on top of him. As the same jury was still available Dr Wybrants held a second Inquest.

Other formal business was also conducted in appropriate rooms in local inns. In January 1732 for example evidence was taken from witnesses to the Will made in 1726 by John Walter, who lived in Templecombe and bequeathed land there to Sexey's Hospital. As he left a life interest in his estate to two nieces it was to be more than a decade later before the issue was resolved in Chancery. Any organisation which required a large space for a meeting could hire a room, so, for example, the Bruton Turnpike Trust regularly used the Wellington Inn for public meetings in the nineteenth century, such as on 28th July 1842 to discuss the erection of a new Tollgate within their system and in most years, often in September, for holding the meeting at which the Tolls were let for the following year to the highest bidder.

While there had always been itinerant entertainers who frequented local markets and fairs, it was only in the nineteenth century that under the watchful eye of the Victorian middle class these entertainers staged their exhibitions, displays, lectures and musical events in local inns (see above).

That there were so many inns, alehouses and beerhouses in Bruton does suggest not only a wealth of custom from local inhabitants but also that there was a considerable number of people travelling for one reason or another and who stayed in or were fed in these establishments as the need arose. In the days of coach travel before the arrival of the railways several inns in Bruton such as the Old Bull Inn and the Wellington Inn served as coaching inns. As late as the day of the Census in 1861 there were a total of thirty-three lodgers in seven inns in Bruton, including twelve in the Old Bull Inn and nine in the Royal Oak.

Perhaps the most overlooked, and most unusual, importance of alehouses and inns was not related just to Bruton but was of national significance and that was in the production of saltpetre. Saltpetre, or potassium nitrate, was one of the components of gunpowder and traditionally was obtained by crystallizing the drainings from dung heaps, which were therefore seen as a valuable military resource. So important was this ingredient that from 1560 saltpetre men were appointed who had the authority, amongst other things, to enter dovecotes, barns, stables, pigpens and cellars to remove manure heaps, usually in barrels.

Owners of such buildings were forbidden from paving their floors with stone or brick which would prevent the build-up of the dark rich black soil. In fact this did happen so that, for example, in April 1635 the Lords of the Admiralty sent an order to the Justices of the Peace for Somerset, including Sir Henry Berkeley, drawing their attention to the fact that in their county "divers innkeepers have paved their stables" which constituted a "great disservice to his Majesty and loss to the kingdom." In July 1666 John, Lord Berkeley of Stratton, who was the youngest son of Sir Maurice Berkeley of Bruton, received a Commission "to work saltpetre and gunpowder, of which there is a more than ordinary occasion for a defence of this realm and to dig for saltpetre in all convenient places between sunrise and sunset." With so many inns and alehouses in Bruton it was to be hoped that the town was playing its part in the defence of the realm.

It is not possible to state with any degree of certainty the exact number of public houses which existed in Bruton for two main reasons: the first is that some of these establishments were very short-lived and have left virtually no evidence of their existence. Secondly many unlicensed premises existed as it was so easy to brew ale as little equipment was required. Information about these tended to emerge only if they were prosecuted by the authorities and the names of the offenders appeared in Quarter Session Records or their fines were listed by the Overseers of the Poor.

Some sort of tavern or alehouse selling alcohol had long been in Bruton. A Tax Roll for 1327 in the reign of Edward III included the name of Roberto le Taverner who was assessed at 6d. In the reign of Queen Mary in 1555 Henry Hussey of Bruton received a licence "to keep a tavern or taverns and sell wines by retail or in gross to be drunk in his mansion house or houses."

By the late sixteenth century there were at least three inns in the town: one was the George Inn which pre-dated 1577 as in his Will made that year Edward Ansley left to his two sons "a common inne or hostelry in Brewton called the signe of the George." The second was the White Hart which was first mentioned on 9th December 1588 when the Parish Registers record that George Bathrin, gent., "died at the Hart." The third was the Unicorn which in 1596 was owned by Edward Chicke. Significantly each of these was towards the eastern end of the High Street, near or in the Market area.

Throughout the seventeenth century the number of inns and alehouses remained constant but as Table 1 indicates there was a sharp increase in numbers in the eighteenth century, even allowing for the rise in the population.

Table 1 Inns and Alehouses in Bruton in the seventeenth and eighteenth centuries.

Year	Number
c1621	6
1669	6
1713	11
1734	13
1768	16
1777	17
1784	15
1798	7

As the population in 1791 was estimated by Collinson to be 1,600 the number of inns and alehouses in the period 1760 to 1780 must have represented one alehouse for approximately every one hundred inhabitants of the town. The sharp decline in the 1790s may be explained by the severe economic depression which was experienced from the middle of the decade, especially as a result of harvest failure and the resulting high prices which were accentuated by other shortages caused by the war against the French.

Table 2 Inns and Beerhouses in Bruton in the nineteenth century.

Year	No. of Inns	No. of Beerhouses
1850	6	7
1859	6	4
1861	6	4
1866	8	2
1872	9	1
1878	7	2
1895	6	2

There was much greater consistency in the number of inns in the Victorian era as may be seen from Table 2, with most being listed in a wealth of Trade Directories. There are, however, probably some discrepancies in this Table as beerhouses may occasionally have been classed as inns, especially in the 1860s and 1870s. The 1861 Census revealed that nationally there was one drinking establishment for every 189 inhabitants, whereas the Bruton figure was rather higher at one for every 223 residents and this was to remain similar for the rest of the century, although at the time of the 1851 Census it had been one for every 162 inhabitants.

The rise in beerhouses may be explained by the Beer Act 1830 which permitted any ratepayer to obtain a licence for £2 and then brew and sell beer on their own premises without reference to a Justice of the Peace – an indication perhaps of the power of maltsters at that period. In 1833 it was estimated that there were some 35,000 beerhouses in England and Wales and they were severely criticised by many people, such as Captain Chapman who reported from the West Country for the Poor Law Commission in 1832. He referred to them as a "baneful influence." Six years later Howitt was just as critical, "A new class of alehouse has sprung up under the New Beer Act, which being generally kept by people without capital, often without character; their liquor supplied by the public brewers, and adulterated by themselves; have done more to demoralize the population of both town and country, than any other legislative measure within the last century."

Operating a beerhouse or even an inn did not mean that the landlord could expect to become wealthy. As late as the 1861 Census several of them were shown to have more than one occupation, for example, James Pearce of the Castle Beerhouse was referred to as a Beer Seller and Tailor, Benjamin Hobbs of the Swan Beerhouse as a Grocer, Beer Seller and Carpenter and Frederick Davidge of the Bell Inn as an Innkeeper and Carpenter. In the same year when John Curtis of Pitcombe was fined £4 and costs for selling beer without a license he was referred to as a labourer.

On the other hand as early as the sixteenth century some innkeepers were members of the local economic elite and very influential such as the Cheeke family who at various times were Bailiffs of the Town and Hundred, Steward of the Hundred, as well as being Churchwardens and Overseers of the Poor. While John Sims operated the Sun Inn in the latter part of the eighteenth century he was also the Bailiff of Bruton. In cases such as these it was not unusual for an inn to remain in the hands of a family for generations.

With hard work and enterprise some innkeepers became wealthy men, for example when Daniel Morgan made his Will on 10th April 1853 he was the tenant of both the Blue Ball and Wellington Inns. He left all the contents, brewing equipment and horses and carriages to his wife for her life or until such time as she remarried. He also had a Life Assurance policy for £1,000 which he used to establish a Trust for his two children, a boy and a girl who were both still minors. He was unable to sign his own name, possibly either as a result of illness or as a lack of education, so just made his mark. He was buried on 22nd April 1853, aged 48 years.

(For some indication of the range of inns and alehouses, their tenants and length of operation, see Appendix 4)

Needless to say as alehouses, and later beerhouses, were the haunt of the poorer members of the community they drew considerable criticism from the wealthier classes, often because of the usually unjustified fear that they were centres of idle gossip, criticism, intrigue, unrest and crime. At times such fears also extended to inns as in 1610 there was an allegation that there was "an inn at Brewton called the Unicorne, where many lewd and suspicious persons gathered in April."

To retain a good reputation in a small community was an important matter, especially for a woman so when Jane Jelley made allegations against ffrauncis Traunter in "the howse of John Illing in Brewton called the signe of the Harte", the slighted had no hesitation in resorting to the courts. In public in the alehouse Jane Jelley "said unto the fforsaide frauncis Traunter amongst divers other persons, that she the said ffrauncis and her husband Thomas Jelley and William West were together in one Kingestones entrie a Tumbelinge togeather meaning therebie as this deponent verlie beleaveth that her husband Thomas Jelley was naught [*misbehaving or wicked*] with the said ffrauncis Traunter in the said Kingestones entrie." Such issues could so easily become the source of contention and conflict within a small community.

All that the wealthy could see was the disorder, drunkenness and immorality and that they were an institution which encouraged the impoverishment of the lower orders as they parted with their hard-earned money. They failed to appreciate them as a place of help and comfort. In 1727 an anonymous writer claimed, "The vile obscene talk, noise, nonsense and ribaldry discourses together with the fumes of tobacco, belchings and other foul breakings of wind, that are generally found in the ale-room..........are enough to make any rational creature amongst them almost ashamed of his being. But all this the rude rabble esteem the highest degree of happiness and run themselves into the greatest straits imaginable to attain it."

On a more practical level, however, there was considerable concern that at times of food shortages such as in the 1590s and 1620s they diverted grain from food into brewing. In fact in the famine year of 1630-1 the Somerset Justices of the Peace suppressed many alehouses in the county "in regard to the dearth of grain.....and the extraordinary quantity of corn that is spent in those places." Maltsters of course had to obtain a licence such as for example Roger Coles of Bruton on 15th February 1624 when he was ordered by Henry Berkeley to pay £10 "To observe his licence for maultinge granted at Mich Sesss last."

Not unsurprisingly therefore through time many measures were passed against alehouses and their activities. As early as 1552 an Act of Parliament required J.P.s to licence alehouses and further Acts in 1603 and 1606 forbade drunkenness and 'tippling', that is, sitting drinking for more than one hour in a man's own parish, mainly on the grounds that drunkenness could lead to other unfortunate activities. In the Commonwealth period in the 1650s a series of laws banned frequenting alehouses and various activities in them, such as singing and dancing upon a range of fast days and during the time of Divine Service on Sundays. If all else failed there was always the stocks. A sustained attack was to develop in the late eighteenth century and especially in the Victorian era. (see below)

No matter what the wealthier members of the community thought about them, inns and particularly alehouses remained a vital part of popular culture, entertainment and leisure time for centuries. The fact that a town the size of Bruton could support so many of them, especially in the eighteenth century, is indicative of their importance in the lives of so many men and women. (28)

c) Church Ales.

Church ales, sometimes called 'revels' or 'wakes' in different parts of the country, had been a major occasion of entertainment throughout the medieval period. It was a significant convivial gathering of the community where there would be food, drink, plays, dances and strenuous games such as wrestling. In some areas it was accompanied by bear-baiting and bull-baiting. In most parts of Somerset it was not unusual for the Churchwardens themselves to brew the ale and then sell it to parishioners and so it had an important economic benefit as it was a rapid method of raising money, possibly for the church or the parish clerk but above all for poorer neighbours. In that sense it played a crucial role in helping to maintain social stability in the community.

One historian has concluded that "they were charity in the sense that the word was understood at the time, for they entailed goodwill, hospitality, reciprocity, neighbourliness, and the raising of money for a variety of social needs, including assistance for neighbours who had fallen into poverty." It was a way in which the community could look after and take care of its less fortunate members before the existence of the Overseers of the Poor with the Poor Rates and certainly long before the State assumed such a role. Bishop Piers called them "Feasts of Charity."

Church ales in Bruton have proved very elusive, especially as the surviving Churchwardens' Accounts only start in 1653. As such festivities were so extensive in the West Country as a whole and prevalent near Bruton, it is inconceivable that they did not occur in the town itself. In addition they were normally staged on a Sunday after Evening Prayers near to the patronal day of the parish church, in this case of the Blessed Virgin Mary on 8th September. This time of the year was also the occasion when the medieval Fraternity of the Blessed Virgin staged their annual celebrations and so some sort of connection is very likely. Nationally church ales were extensively attacked by the Puritans in the seventeenth century but revived after the Restoration of Charles II in 1660 and in revised forms they flourished in some areas in the eighteenth century. The similarities between church ales and the Bruton Feasts of that century are unlikely to be a coincidence and suggest the revival of an age-old custom.

Neighbouring towns and villages staged their church ales, even though they were not always popular with some of the wealthier and more puritanical members of the community, for example in 1596 Francis Hastings left bequests to North and South Cadbury, Holton and Maperton on condition that they abandoned their church ales. On the other hand the church ale at Milborne Port in 1603 was reported to have been supported by many "substantial householders of honesty and good credit." In 1607 in Charlton Horethorne Robert Smyth was said to have been drunk "three days together" at their church ale, possibly as the result of a "certain powder used there to provoke drunkenness."

In nearby Mere in Wiltshire church ales proved to be a significant source of revenue as the churchwardens reported a clear profit in 1605 of £15 6s 0d and in 1606 of £20. Nearly one hundred years before in 1517 Stogursy Parish Church had received £6 13s 4d, not insubstantial sums in that period.

The nearest example to Bruton seems to have been in Pitcombe in 1615, at a time when church ales were increasingly coming under attack. In that year the churchwardens paid the minstrels to play for dancing in the churchyard. Their successors did not approve of this use of church rates and so presented them at the next Visitation later in the year

Criticism of church ales was prevalent in the Tudor period. As early as 1547 the government of Edward VI tried to ban them when all parishes were ordered "from henceforth to surcease from kepinge any churche ales, because it hath byn declared unto us that many inconviences hath come by them." It had little effect. Increasingly religious authorities were concerned about drunkenness and the consequent licentiousness which was alleged to follow. Assuming that church ales were held in Bruton in September, the Parish Registers do not seem to indicate an increase in births, illegitimate or otherwise, nine months later. In the period 1554 to 1599 just over 6% of all christenings occurred in each of May and June, compared with 7.2% in April, 8.6% in September and 9.1% in August.

The civil authorities in Somerset, as represented by the local magistrates, were much more concerned about possible breaches of the peace and contraventions of the restrictions on the sale of alcohol. For over half a century after 1594 they waged an unrelenting campaign against the church ales in what became almost a war of attrition with Orders issued against them in 1594,

1600, 1607, 1612, 1615, 1624 and even as late as 1649. The very fact that so many Orders were issued was an indication of their lack of effectiveness. As Puritan ideas gained a hold their opposition became more and more successful and while a few church ales, such as one at Kingweston in 1653 survived, the majority did not. It was to be more than a generation before these age-old popular entertainments were revived, albeit in an amended form. (29)

d) Exuberant Behaviour.

In the nineteenth century more than one newspaper reporter commented that when it came to celebrations, their organisation and implementation, Brutonians came to the fore. The evidence available would certainly seem to substantiate that claim, although not all the popular entertainments followed the directions which the Victorian middle class deemed appropriate. At times they regarded them as in the tradition of the time-honoured ceremonies of saturnia when the common man was king for a day and the world was turned upside down. These celebrations, which led to much exuberant behaviour, fell into two main categories: the regular and the ad-hoc.

i)   Regular

One of the times of the year that became associated with misbehaviour, usually fuelled by ale, was Shrovetide. Through the centuries it had become celebrated particularly by apprentices and young people in general. In some parts of the country it was not unusual for huge games of football, sometimes between entire villages, and other sports to be arranged at that period.

The only direct evidence for such unruly behaviour in Bruton dates from February 1653 when five young men "did throwe many great

Stones att many doores." One of the perpetrators, Ralph Hardinge, confessed that "he was on Shrove Tuesday last att night att one Richard Waytes howse in Brewton Alehowse keeper about Nine of the clocke in the night, and there spent with other younge people of the said Towne fwor pence and for it a iug of Beere." Another young man, Thomas Gill, agreed that he threw stones at "one Goodman Alexanders doore" but denied breaking his window. This does appear to have been a widespread custom as reports of such behaviour have surfaced from elsewhere in Somerset and the West Country as a whole, even down to the Isles of Scilly.

This alcohol-fuelled escapade by these young men was only part of the activities of that evening as both men witnessed other events, "That about Seaven o'clock that night he saw ffive men wth visages and beatinge a brass pan went up and down the Streate, and many people beinge gathered together in great multitudes, where they overthrew one another in the streat." The implication of this statement is that there was a general free-for-all. At some stage the "Bar on Richard Illinges doore was beaten out." The number of people was so great and their behaviour so unruly that one tithingman, John Clarke, having failed to persuade some of them to stop throwing stones at doors and to go home, was so afraid "in soe much for his owne Safety, he durst not goe through the Street, but went to his Howse the backway."

It may be possible to speculate that another Shrovetide incident did occur as at festivals such as this it was not unusual for groups of armed men to invade neighbouring parishes to seize some trophy or another, to occupy an alehouse and to beat up anyone who opposed them. Even though the attack by the Batcombeites may be seen in the context of the Civil War in the 1640s and probably had underlying religious issues as well, as it occurred in February it may have been reflecting this type of behaviour and the age-old Shrovetide customs.

During the Easter season it was customary for work to cease on various days and many servants to be given time off. In some areas fairs and sports were arranged at that time but as Bruton already had its three-day fair in April, there is no evidence which has survived to indicate any other official activities around that time. One reference does exist, although well into the Victorian period, which suggests that Easter could be another occasion for exuberant behaviour in the Bruton area. While the damage caused could have been accidental, there is always the underlying suspicion that these festive seasons provided the opportunity for old scores to be settled.

In April 1870 one local newspaper reported that, "The holiday usually given on Good Friday was spent by some youths of this town in playing some mischievous pranks with the property of some farmers and others in the neighbourhood. Gates were unhung and broken, the folds were opened, and one man had the shafts of his cart broken off." As a warning the newspaper added, "The police have a clue to the offenders, and they will in all probability receive a lesson which will teach then to be more careful in the future." Despite this optimism and a reward of £5 being offered, the Magistrates' Entry Books do not show any prosecutions. In fact these Entry Books for nearly half a century do not indicate an upsurge of cases of assault or damage in the months of March and April, which may suggest that if such behaviour did occur at that time it was generally tolerated as it was so little and so infrequent.

May, with May Day, Whitsuntide and the celebration of the birthday and Restoration of Charles II, remained within popular culture a time for festivites and some excesses. Despite all the actions of the Victorians they failed to eradicate some aspects of this popular season. As the gathering of the old men in the Sun Inn on Whit-Sunday in 1800 indicated, the tradition of singing and dancing at this time of year was far from dead. It will be no coincidence that on 30th May 1881 two men were fined for being drunk and riotous in Bruton and a further ten young men were prosecuted for wilful damage, although in this case they managed to avoid further punishment by paying a total of 27s in damages.

A few days after these events the Blue Ball Friendly Society staged their annual parade and church service followed by a dinner. After the dinner came the speeches with toasts, including one to the 'Army, Navy and Reserve Forces.' While Captain Dyne was responding to this and praising the Volunteers he commanded, "Some amusement was caused at this juncture by one of the members, an old Crimean hero, named Perry, pointing out of the window behind the Captain and saying, 'better men than *they*, captain'. The 'they' turned out to be some militiamen who were reeling along the street more than 'half seas over'."

That such events were occurring when the Temperance movement had been active for decades and that children were taken out of the town on their school treats to avoid witnessing the scenes of drunkenness, must indicate a certain expectation of behaviour during popular entertainment at this time which was deeply ingrained in many within the community. The lack of earlier evidence makes it impossible to determine how much more extensive such celebrations had been in the centuries before.

In a similar way the continuance of the wild celebrations associated with 5th November was indicative of how important that date had become in popular culture. It was a time of bell-ringing, fireworks, bonfires, drunkenness, assault, mischief, damage and death.

After the assassination attempt on James I and all the members of Parliament by Guy Fawkes and others, an Act was passed which required the English to celebrate "with unfeigned thankfulness.... this joyful day of deliverance." The original concept was one of prayers and thanksgiving but through time the emphasis changed. It was certainly the case that anti-Catholic feeling remained strong, especially amongst members of the Church of England. On 5th November 1768 Revd. Woodforde read Morning Prayers at Castle Cary and noted that it was "the day on which the Papists had contrived a hellish plot."

During the eighteenth century this day was one of the most important in the popular calendar in many small southern towns with official celebrations, often with processions, the provision of wood for the bonfire, fireworks and of course drink. As with other activities which involved the participation of the labouring classes, the wealthy gradually distanced themselves, especially as in some places more emphasis was placed upon the vilification of a local person. Although the church bells continued to be rung annually in Bruton on that day until at least 1781, it became much more an occasion for celebration by the ordinary people. In 1815 the jury of the Court Leet stated that, "a Nuisance has existed and been occasioned for several Years past on the 5th of November by lighting Bonfires and letting off Fireworks in the Street." It reminded the Constable and tythingmen that it was their duty "to repress the same." As reports later in the century make clear, in this they and others were singularly unsuccessful.

Until the late 1880s or early 1890s this was the night when the authorities came closest to losing control of the town, when the labouring classes ruled the streets and, from the perspective of the wealthier inhabitants, the world was turned upside down. From 1850 the re-establishment of the Catholic hierarchy in England for the first time in over three hundred years, with an Archbishop of Westminster and thirteen diocesan bishops, gave a tremendous boost to these popular demonstrations against Roman Catholicism.

From the middle of the nineteenth century local newspapers gave annual accounts of the evening such as in 1867, "The discharge of fireworks might be heard in various quarters." Bonfires appeared on the surrounding hills and in 1875 on Church Bridge and at West End where one seems to have been lit in most years in the 1870s and 1880s. In 1880, "The boys of the King's School had a huge bonfire in their playground with numerous crackers, squibs, &c." These customs seem to have been generally tolerated but there were others which were much more dangerous and which attracted criticism.

The tradition had developed of rolling lighted tar barrels through the town which created the possibility not only of injury but also of the danger of fire. The 1880 report noted, "Tar barrels were lighted and rolled through the streets to the danger of the inhabitants." In addition, "Several of the rougher portion of the community spent the evening in throwing about balls of tow steeped in turpentine and lighted." It was a time of considerable noise as an account in 1869 indicated, "Tar barrels, torches, squibs &c and the customary hollooing and shouting having each their own patrons."

There were allegations that some of the crowd became out of control and that beer played a part, the nightmare scenario for many of the wealthier inhabitants of the town. One report referred to "the lovers of riot and disorder", and another that, "The town was as usual given over to mob-rule on Friday evening last...... and one 'gentleman' in a light felt hat, who appeared to be several degrees madder than any body else, added fuel to the flames by ladleing beer *to the multitude assembled at West End* out of a bucket, accompanying the libations with insane speeches about the rights of Britons, especially himself." Six year later it was claimed, "The annual saturnalia took place on Saturday evening. From an early hour the streets were in the possession of 'the roughs', who amused themselves by 'squibbing' women and children as they passed."

The dangers of these uncontrolled activities were all too evident as the 1881 report also mentioned, "a well-known character, who had managed to get thoroughly intoxicated was 'squibbed' till her clothes caught fire." In 1890 it was also alleged that letting off fireworks in the streets long before 5th November was causing horses to bolt and back towards shop windows. More serious in 1873 four boys belonging to Sexey's Hospital were in a group playing with gunpowder when it exploded and burnt them. Even worse in 1876 two men named Armstrong and Turner were on Coombe Farm Hill using a length of gas pipe as a 'cannon'. On the fourth firing it burst and injured a girl called Vigar who was severely cut over the eye and a boy called Newman who was hit in the face but Thomas Sly, aged eleven, "was struck by a fragment seven inches by two inches" and it "nearly split his head in two, of course killing him on the spot." A verdict of accidental death was recorded.

In fact most of these activities could be found throughout Somerset on this evening, with bonfires, lighted tar barrels, home-made cannons and squibs being particularly popular. In the mid-nineteenth century the top hats worn by the members of the new police force invariably proved to be an irresistible target for young men with their squibs. While traces of tar remained in the streets for weeks afterwards, the wild, unusual and colourful events of the evening often provided a talking point for the inhabitants for many months.

Burning an effigy, not just of Guy Fawkes, was also a popular custom, a way of showing displeasure with the behaviour of another person in the community, and the origins of which were lost in time. On 5th November 1768 Revd. Woodforde recorded that in Castle Cary an effigy of Justice Creed was carried through the streets "upon the (fire) Engine, and then had into the Park and burnt in a bonfire immediately before the Justice's House." The Justice had angered local residents when he had sent the Churchwardens to the Wells Ecclesiastical Court when they had failed to present James Clarke for an alleged "Riot in the Gallery at Castle Cary."

An example of effigy burning occurred in Bruton in November 1859, although on the 14th and not the 5th. Matthew Feltham and George Hillard, both labourers, were charged with "wantonly carrying a Burning Effigy thro' streets of Bruton 14th inst thereby interrupted free passage." Each was fined 2s 6d with 5s 6d costs or fourteen days in Shepton Mallet House of Correction. Unfortunately no other details were given so it is impossible to say if this was a continuation of the celebrations of the 5th or whether the two men were annoyed with some local figure.

Needless to say the wealthier inhabitants in the community became increasingly alarmed at the activities associated with the 5th of November, especially in relation of public order when they found streets impassable, bonfires in confined spaces, possibly made of timber stolen from local woods and property threatened with damage and, above all, unregulated crowds. They were not of course concerned about bonfires and fireworks themselves as these were part of many other celebrations but rather their use unsanctioned by them. Gradually the middle classes reasserted their control over the evening, possibly with a greater degree of self-confidence and better organisation as a result of political developments, most notably the establishment of Parish Councils after 1894. By the end of the century the Victorians seem to have succeeded in taming yet another of the traditional times of popular entertainment. One report in 1900 noted that, "Bonfire night passed off very quietly, in Bruton there was an organised procession." The year before Josiah Jackson recorded that he went to watch the bonfire held on 'Pigeon Tower Hill', a site which he had lent to the organisers. (30)

ii)   Ad hoc.

In addition to the regular dates there were also a whole range of ad hoc celebrations, many of which, as has already been established, were associated with the monarchy. At these times alcohol flowed freely but other leisure activities were organised as well.

The Coronation of Charles II in May 1661 was met with overwhelming enthusiasm in Bruton. One newsletter reported, "The latter end of Aprill and the beginning of this month was spent in several places, dayes and nights, for joy of his Majestys coronation…. The towne of Bruton in Somersetshire, for joy of the coronation, their bells all day and night ringing; their stage pageants, songs, town musick……their musketeers and pikes with great order and repeated volleys, plenty of drink." It must have been quite a spectacle and celebration for all the inhabitants lasting days. The report does contain the only reference to stage pageants taking place in the town, an entertainment which was centuries old with, for example, the medieval mystery plays.

The Restoration of Charles II continued to be celebrated in Bruton and the surrounding area for at least two centuries, so what started as an ad hoc affair became a regular one. On 29th May 1769 Revd. Woodforde noted that, "I read Prayers this morning at C. Cary, being 29 of May the Restoration of King Charles II from Popish Tyranny." In the Victorian period the day usually finished with a firework display, not always without incident as in 1856 William Finch who was "preparing a quantity of rockets and fireworks….. and trying experiments with some combustibles" suffered severe damage to his left hand when they exploded.

The Coronation of other monarchs was also an occasion for popular celebrations. For the coronation of William IV in 1831 eight hundred inhabitants were fed; for Queen Victoria's coronation in 1838 one hundred and twenty of the oldest inhabitants were entertained, the Sunday School children received a treat as did the employees of "the manufacturers and principal tradesmen." The day ended "with a splendid display of fireworks". By the time of Edward VII's coronation in1902 sports played a large part. The anniversary of the coronation day was often celebrated as well, for example, on 22nd September 1769 Revd. Woodforde recorded bells ringing all day, cudgel playing and a large bonfire, and "very grand fireworks in the evening." In Bruton in the nineteenth century the anniversary of Victoria's coronation day was usually a public holiday when all the shops were shut.

Royal Jubilees were also times of popular entertainment, for example, that of George III in 1809 was accompanied by bell ringing and the distribution of "beef bread and strong beer, to every poor family in the parish." The Golden Jubilee of Queen Victoria was celebrated with a public dinner for all residents over fifteen and a tea for all children under fifteen, along with several hours of "athletic sports." Fireworks ended the day. A decade later the Diamond Jubilee was also celebrated with dinner, tea and sports, the meals being eaten in a large tent erected in the Jubilee Park, all of which Josiah Jackson helped to prepare. He also lent a horse to transport 120 faggots for a huge bonfire on Creech Hill, one of eighty that it was claimed could be seen from that vantage point, "amid great enthusiasm."

The wedding of the Prince of Wales in March 1863 was a time of more great popular celebrations as to begin with about 600 of the poor were served with beef, bread and beer. A parade was followed by "a variety of sports, the favourite games appeared to be football and a jingling match but this latter seems to have had serious consequences, as some of our friends say they laughed until they were ill…. and the spot on which it was played appeared to be the centre of attraction." The day once again ended with fireworks.

One unusual celebration for which virtually no details have survived occurred in the late seventeenth century. According to a book entitled, 'A full description of all the principal towns of England', published in 1699, Bruton was "a Town memorable for little else than that the Noble Family of the Mohuns is here Entombed; unless we mention the late extraordinary processions which the Women of the town made on the Conclusion of the late Peace." The Peace referred to will be the Treaty of Ryswick of 1697 which ended the war against the French. These celebrations were certainly extensive as the Constable spent £5 on two hogshead of beer, 7s 6d "To the Trumpett and Drum", and 8s to "Mr Ludwell for 6 lb of Gunpowder." Why this peace treaty led to such festivities and why women in particular played such a prominent role and were selected for special mention is not clear.

All of these occasions when popular celebrations occurred must have been extremely important for the entertainment and leisure activities of the poorer members of the community. For them such events would provide a brief respite from their general toil but in reality they were few when viewed from the perspective of the year as a whole. On the other hand, so many of these festivities gave ordinary men and women the opportunity to acquire some prestige, especially if they won or performed well in a particular sport or game. For some it was an occasion to dress in their best clothes, or to ensure that their children were well-presented at a National School or Sunday School event.

At the simplest level, many of the celebrations and entertainments were accompanied by decorations and arranging these and being noticed was another way of gaining recognition within the community. In many instances the main form of decoration centred on greenery, which was readily available and cost nothing to obtain, although increasingly public houses and inns relied more upon fancy arches with mottoes upon them. When the railway arrived in September 1856 there were considerable celebrations and it was noted that, "The houses were gaily decorated with laurels." For the Foresters' Fete in August 1867 it was reported that the town "had been nicely decorated with arches of evergreens, flags and flowers." (31)

    e) Miscellaneous Games.

Throughout the centuries many different games were played in Bruton for popular entertainment and as leisure pursuits. Unfortunately, partly because these were the activities of ordinary people and partly because they were so common-place, information about them and descriptions of what was involved was very rarely written down. In addition there was a tendency to use a vague word such as 'playing' and so the exact nature of what was happening has not survived. In July 1694, for example, when Nicholas Hobs discovered his neighbour Richard Vigger beating his son, he prosecuted him. Another neighbour, Frances Cornish, gave evidence that she heard Vigger's wife, Mary, say that if the boy "would not cease of playing before her doors she would scould him to death."

In February 1691 the Constable had paid 6d "for Crying that the boys should not play in the Town Hall." This clearly did not work for any length of time as in 1693-1694 he paid 1s "for the warrant to hinder the playing in the Markett house." It is possible to speculate that in both of these instances it might have been general rowdy behaviour or more specifically football or a game of Fives which required a wall. As always playing any game on a Sunday was frowned upon and so in 1780-1781 the Churchwardens paid 6d "for Crying a Notice to prevent boys playing on Sunday." At least the town-crier was ensured regular employment. In one instance in 1701-1702 another 6d was spent on a summons "for several boys playing in the Church." It may be that the building still contained some clear open spaces and plenty of hard surfaces for a ball.

That there were many popular games and other forms of entertainment is also indicated by the many attempts that were made to stop participation in them. As early as 1452 Bishop Bekynton in his Injunctions had ordered that "No canon is to play at dice inside or outside the priory, under penalty of fasting on bread and water the whole of the following Friday." The Indentures of Apprentices always banned not only cards and dice but also specified that "any other unlawful Game he shall not play." The Foundation Deed of the Free School in 1519 did not permit the boys to play any games of relaxation or in the open "in any weke wheryn any holyday beside the Sonday shall fall or happen." The Articles of Government for the School drawn up in 1566 repeated this ban to avoid "to muche licentious libertie of playeinge", but did permit games in other weeks "if the weather so fine for one after none in the said weke."

One game which did command popular support was Fives. A major reason for this was that at its simplest level all it required was a ball and a wall. It was certainly in existence in the Free School by 1720 as in June of that year the Governors threatened to prosecute "any Boys or other person whatsoever (except the Schollars) [*who*] shall be found playing at ffives in the ffives place belonging to the School." An open Fives Court was built by Revd. J.C.J. Hoskyns Abrahall after he became Headmaster in 1826 and two more Courts were built after 1873 when Revd. D.E. Norton, senior, filled that post. One former pupil, Christopher Welch, who left the School in 1851 recalled, "It was at Fives that the School chiefly prided itself; the Bruton players being among the best of the time. We had a fine open court and practised assiduously." Matches were played against other schools such as Sherborne. In fact early twentieth century copies of the School Magazine, 'The Dolphin', show that the School was still playing against other schools and inter-house matches throughout the 1920s and 1930s.

As Fives required a fairly high stonewall to play against, the tower of a parish church was an obvious location. It was played regularly in Babcary Churchyard as on one occasion in 1764 while he was the curate there, Revd. Woodforde held a bachelors' party and he and his guests "plaid at Fives in Babcary Churchyard this evening." The following year he gave a similar party and watched fourteen gentlemen from Castle Cary play "Fives all afternoon in the Churchyard at Babcary." It is interesting to note that in both these instances gambling took place as in 1764 Woodforde lost in total 1s 6d but the following year he won 2s 9d. The game became less popular in Castle Cary as in 1768 at the behest of the Churchwardens, his father, who was the Vicar, gave them "leave to dig up the Fives-Place in Cary Churchyard."

The evidence for Bruton Churchyard seems to be more circumstantial. In November 1773 the Churchwardens paid 2d "for Crying the breaking Church windows", and in 1780-1781 a further 6d "for playing in the Chyard." A century later in March 1881 they prosecuted seven young men for "Misbehaviour in the Churchyard." The case was settled out of court and may also have been linked with rowdy behaviour at Eastertide. In none of these instances is any detail provided about what actually took place.

In reality Fives could be played almost anywhere and could be very organised for example on 24th September 1767 Woodforde noted that his brother "went to Camel this morning to see the Fives Playing there, and did not return till after 12 at night." On the other hand it could be more ad hoc as on 29th June 1773 Woodforde recorded that "I played at fives with James Clarke, 2 Games he beat me in the first Game, and I beat him the second Game." This encounter occurred at Mr Hadley's ale house at Pitcombe.

Not long after Sexey's School was opened in 1891, a Fives Court was constructed. One former pupil, Hubert Phillips who joined the School in 1904, recalled, "Fives is a grand game. Our court was constructed for what (I believe) is officially known as Rugby Fives, played not with a bat but with the flat of one's hand." He added not too modestly, "After some years' practice I became quite good at it, on two occasions reaching the final of the school championship." Such was the popularity of the game at the end of the nineteenth and beginning of the twentieth centuries that later Headmasters reported that whenever former pupils visited the School they always wished to ask about and see the Fives Court.

A newspaper report on the popular entertainments in the town associated with the Royal Wedding in March 1863 noted that one of the favoured activities was a jingling match which "appeared to be the centre of attraction." This was an extremely old and popular entertainment as it required few items: a rope, posts, bell and blindfolds. Up to about a dozen men or women were blindfolded and placed inside a square, the boundaries of which were marked by the rope joined to four posts. One other person had a hand bell and the aim was to keep ringing the bell and avoid being caught by the blindfolded men or women usually within a set time. A prize could be awarded and once again it opened up the possibility of gambling. For how long this game had been played in Bruton is impossible to determine.

Four years later it was reported that at the Foresters' fete 'Kiss in the Ring' and 'Aunt Sally' received "the largest share of admirers." In the former young men and women chased each other in a ring of participants, in some versions after a handkerchief had been dropped by the person to be chased, and when caught could be kissed. It has been suggested that this pastime originated as a fertility ritual associated with the vernal equinox but in the Victorian period it was a safe pleasure with clear rules and boundaries, a pre-ordained end and a lack of consequences. There was also a children's version linked to a rhyme:

> I sent a letter to my love,
> And on the way I dropped it;
> And one of you have picked it up
> And put it in your pocket.

The boy or girl in the centre of the circle would choose one of the opposite sex, kiss him or her and then swap places.

Free Grammar School Playground showing Fives Wall just to right of centre

The game of 'Aunt Sally' seems to have started in the mid-Victorian period but there is some suggestion that its origins lie in the older, violent cock-throwing which had died out. A skittle called the doll was painted and dressed up in a frock, sometimes with a mask or black painted face, a throwback to some depictions of the devil in the medieval period. It was not long before the representation became that of an ugly old maid or aunt so it has been claimed that there were also racist and misogynist implications as well. The doll had a clay pipe stuck in her mouth and hung elsewhere and the object was to knock the pipes off the doll rather than to tip the doll over.

In the Victorian era quoits became an organised popular form of entertainment in the town, for example, by 1870 the Quoits Club had a practice ground at Coombe Farm. In some areas this game had been played extensively in the mid-eighteenth century but no evidence has yet emerged for that to have been the case in Bruton. At the beginning of the twentieth century the town's club was still playing matches and even the Vicar's Bible Class had it own club. This was another game which required few pieces of equipment: a post and flat rings or semi-circles of iron such as a horseshoe. The rings were pitched at the stake in the ground and points awarded, with or without gambling taking place. Being so straightforward it is again very likely that this game had existed for centuries, with horseshoes as the main item. In 1759-1760 the Churchwardens paid 1s for "a Notice against Shackle playing on Sundays", and it is possible that this was an earlier form of the game.

In May 1814 a local newspaper carried a cautionary tale about Uriah Penny of Yarlington who "after exerting himself in playing at barn-ball, drank freely at a stream of water, in consequence of which he died the Friday following." Unfortunately no details were given about the exact nature of the game, although it obviously involved a ball in a barn.

Inns often had a skittle ground attached and this was always a popular leisure pursuit, where money could change hands. In October 1860 a large skittle match was played at the Blue Ball for a prize of £10 between a local team and one from Bristol, an indication that the game was well-established in the town. Bruton won the match which "caused considerable excitement in the neighbourhood, and a large company attended to witness the game."

Some popular pastimes were more opportunistic, for example, in 1882 a correspondent to a local newspaper drew attention to "the nuisance caused by shooting with catapults." He alleged that not only were boys shooting at passers-by but also "Sparrows, red-breasts, and other feathered friends generally, as well as cats, dogs, donkeys, and little children are all reckoned fair game." Boys in Bruton had probably been involved in shooting at the same targets year after year for centuries.

Another leisure pursuit was weather-dependent and that was skating on ice. The early months of 1888 were very cold and newspapers reported skating by large crowds of local people on Redlynch Lake at various times between January and March. In December 1890 Josiah Jackson recorded that he went up to the same lake to watch the skaters but does not seem to have taken part. Such entertainment was enjoyable as long as the ice was thick enough to bear the weight of the skaters and on one occasion in December 1881 it was not. "The ice in some parts was not very firm, indeed, a boy named Cary received a 'ducking' but fortunately, it being near the land, he got out safely." As there had been various ponds in and around Bruton throughout the medieval period such skating as a popular recreation was not new.

In some instances it is impossible to determine how far ordinary working people were involved in some leisure activities, for example, in 1894 Jackson helped to purchase a Bagatelle Table for the Reading Room and two years later he makes reference to the Billiard Table in the Bruton Institute but gives no other details. Billiards had existed in the area for many decades as on 23rd July 1771 Woodforde noted, "Before Dinner I went with Jack to the George Inn & played at Billiard & won of him 2s 0d." Once again gambling was in evidence. (32)

f) The Victorians strike again!

While it would be incorrect to blame the Victorian middle class alone for the attack on, and the loss of, much popular culture, they did embrace the existing criticism with enthusiasm and did their best to institute permanent changes not only in forms of entertainment but also in attitudes. The Victorian middle class, as has been discussed, did a great deal to develop for themselves new forms of entertainment and amusement which they judged to be compatible with their religious and secular views. It could be regarded as unfortunate that driven by these beliefs they thought that every one else should embrace them as well. They came to consider that they must first wean the working class away from their vicious habits, as they perceived them, and then the way would be open for some understanding and co-operation between the classes. Social harmony and social stability would thus be ensured.

A number of factors came together throughout the nineteenth century which placed severe constraints upon the working class and their culture. The first was the development of a police force so that activities were monitored more closely than ever before and the law more rigorously enforced. Once the new police station was opened in Wincanton in 1856 offenders could expect rapid transfer to its cells after their apprehension by the Bruton police constable. Enforcement was also aided by the creation of a much more organised system within the magistracy, for example, the Wincanton Division was established in 1831 and regular Petty Sessions were held which dealt quickly with alleged offenders. Various forms of licensing, especially of public houses, meant for example, that the freedom which they had enjoyed in relation to opening hours was seriously curtailed. Finally, many newspapers, both national and local, reflected the views of the more middle class within a community and constant criticism of some of the activities of the labouring population found expression in their pages.

There can be no doubt that underlying much of the fear of popular culture was the notion that if groups of people gathered together, especially in large numbers and with alcohol readily available, there was the potential for discontent, violence and riot. From the thirteenth century many bishops had attempted to remove secular activities such as fairs, markets, games and sports from churchyards. In the medieval period such gatherings were criticized as they diverted men from more useful activities such as practising their archery and preachers denounced the way that many of these occasions degenerated into drunkenness, violence and sometimes bloodshed. In fact as early as 1311 Bishop Drokensford commissioned the Bishop of Cork to visit Bruton "to reconcile the cemetery of the parish church after bloodshed." It is possible that in this case some popular entertainment being staged in the Churchyard deteriorated into violence.

Violence in the churchyard does appear occasionally such as in October 1605 when Robert Darby was summoned before the Church Court accused of "Strickinge Mr Evans the cureat in the churchyard because hee reproved him for his drunkenness And for a common drunkard." Darby was excommunicated but was absolved the following year when he claimed, "that he did not strike the said Evans willingly but throwing a stone att another bodye, it lighted on Evans." In Pitcombe in July 1588 Robert Lane was charged that "he stroaketh Thomas Mogge in the churchyard wheareby blud was shed." Stone-throwing and fighting in the churchyard did seem to occur.

Historians have suggested that in the period from about 1580 to 1640 there was a growing divergence in many communities between the poorer inhabitants and the yeomen, prosperous artisans and craftesmen. Increasing wealth played a part in this development, as did various religious and cultural factors, not the least of which was the growth of literacy amongst the more respectable inhabitants in a town or village, so the Free School in Bruton may have played its part. Not surprisingly therefore from the Tudor period more and more measures were introduced to ban secular and communal activities in general and many other small group and individuals' entertainment as well, such as singing, dancing and drinking during the time of Divine Service. Many considered that a man's very salvation was put in jeopardy. "How perilous is it then to tolerate these profane pastimes, which open the flood-gates to so much sin and wickedness."

Throughout the eighteenth century increasing refinement amongst the wealthy within society meant that gradually but relentlessly they turned their back on the traditional sports of the ordinary people such as wrestling, cudgel-playing and single stick. Many of these activities they began to perceive as primitive, immoral and likely to cause disorder. Little by little, the gentry, clergy and prosperous farmers abandoned the older ideas of paternalism within their community, when amongst many other things they had provided the patronage which some of the games and sports required. A few men began to take an active role in ending those leisure pursuits of which they disapproved. It was said of one Devon Magistrate in 1797, for example, "he was remarkably attentive to the morals of the people within his district, and successively laboured, though with great and long opposition, in suppressing village ale-houses, cock-fighting and bull-baiting."

The traditional pattern in the countryside was breaking down as families whose ancestors had lived for generations in the same village migrated to the new urban centres with their industries. Here factory discipline meant that taking time off work for a whole range of entertainments was no longer possible as the steam engines drove the machines for twelve, eighteen and, in some cases, twenty-four hours a day and labourers had to be operating those machines. Productivity was the key to economic prosperity and no factory owner was going to allow a popular entertainment or celebration to stand in the way of that.

One early Victorian writer lamented, "What a revolution of taste has taken place in the English people as regards popular festivals and festivities..........The times, and the spirit of the times, are changed: we are become a sober people....England is no longer merry England, but busy England." The Victorian middle class embraced such beliefs with open arms as labour discipline prevented idleness which they could not tolerate in any circumstances as it neglected social and religious duties. Customary holidays, of course, were responsible for the loss of working time. No wonder the poetry of Isaac Watts was so popular with them.

> In work of Labour or of Skill
> I would be busy too:

> For Satan finds some Mischief still
> For idle Hands to do.

They had found a work discipline so what was then required was a leisure discipline to complement it in order that social control could be maintained.

The Victorian middle class was aiming for respectability and self-improvement and with this came their own morality, which, amongst other things, led them to believe that some of the activities of the labouring people were barbaric and inhumane. They had no hesitation, therefore, in opposing such sports and entertainments as boxing matches, bull-baiting and cock-fighting. In all this they were aided by their religious zeal, either through Non-Conformity which was strong in Bruton or the evangelical branch of the Church of England. There developed a great suspicion of worldly pleasures, for example, on one occasion the reformer Hannah More remarked, "The amusements of a Christian must have nothing in them to excite the passions which it is his duty to subdue."

While the Victorian middle class played an important role in change it must not be overlooked that there were those within the working classes who also advocated such a situation. Non-Conformity, especially Methodism, was widely embraced by labouring people with a genuine religious fervour and they wanted to see working men being more sober, rational and far-sighted in their use of leisure time. There were also working-class radicals who believed that in order to make progress all the working classes must aim for respectability and self-improvement, ideas which were to find expression in Chartist writers and in the early trade unions. One problem of course was that the working class concept of respectability was not necessarily the same as that of the middle class. For the former it was often as basic as decent clothes, avoidance of frequent drunkenness or family brawling in public, or even just a clean doorstep.

A struggle was taking place which was to have profound cultural implications: it was a struggle between the traditional and the new way of life, rural and urban, uneducated and educated, and perhaps even between traditional beliefs and Christianity. Popular culture was increasingly marginalized and social discipline developed with more and more laws and regulations issued by the State in all aspects of life. When regulation was not possible or likely to have little effect, the Victorians attempted to move a group or customary leisure pursuit in a different direction, to reform rather than to repress. It was for them part of the ongoing process of the re-socialization of the working classes with the middle classes taking the lead in providing the new amenities and ensuring that approved standards would be maintained.

i)   The attack upon alcohol.

As far as the wealthier classes in the nineteenth century were concerned alcohol was at the root of many of the problems which they perceived to be affecting the labouring classes. As late as 1890 General William Booth of the Salvation Army was convinced that, "Nine-tenths of our poverty, squalor, vice, and crime spring from this poisonous tap-root. Many of our social evils …….. would dwindle away and die if they were not constantly watered with strong drink." As a result of his huge survey in the 1890s Charles Booth estimated that a quarter of working class incomes went on drink and more recent research has suggested that allowing for tee-total families the figure may well have been between one third and one half.

There were those who believed that recreational activities would help to fight drunkenness. In 1834 a Parliamentary Select Committee recommended, "The establishment by the joint aid of Government and the local authorities and residents on the spot, of public walks, and gardens, or open spaces for healthy and athletic exercises in the open air……..and of district and parish libraries, museums and reading rooms, accessible at the lowest rate of charge; so as to admit of one or the other being visited in any weather, and at any time." Generally the idea was not acted upon and so it is not surprising that there was an increase in regulation and a wish for temperance.

One historian has concluded, "The modernization of attitudes towards thrift, work-discipline, sobriety, orderly behaviour and respect for the law, the eradication of alternative influences to the teaching of the Church; all required the control of the alehouse."

Regulation.
There was of course nothing new in regulation as a licence to sell alcohol had long been required. There were always those who did not comply for whatever reason and found themselves prosecuted, for example, in May 1731 William Chafyn, Joseph Melhuish and Rose Berryman were each fined £1 when convicted of "keeping a Common Alehouse in Brewton aforesaid without being Lycensed according to the direction of the Statute." Mary Martin, "who kept a little Shop in this place", was less fortunate in 1738 as she ended up in Ilchester Gaol "for selling Spiritous Liquors contrary to Act of Parliament." In January 1789 William Oliver was fined £2 with 8s costs for his first offence of selling beer without a licence.

Other alehouse keepers faced fines for permitting tippling on Sundays, for example, in August 1743 the Overseers of the Poor distributed £3   3s   4d to thirteen poor people which was the total in fines on several alehouse keepers, "For Selling & Tipling Beer on Sunday 30th June." In September of the same year Anne Hill was fined the usual 10s "for keeping A disorderly House on Sunday September 14th." In September 1759 two innkeepers, James Andrews and Robert Everett of the Sun Inn, were each fined 10s for "Suffering Tipling."

The Beer Act of 1830, therefore, came as a surprise to many people as it significantly relaxed the existing system when it permitted any ratepayer to obtain a licence for £2 and then brew and sell beer. The only restriction appeared to be that on Sundays permitted opening times were between 1pm and 3pm and 5pm and 10pm. As the number of beer houses rose dramatically the Victorians responded with more legislation as in 1839 the hours for opening on Sundays were slightly reduced and in 1854 all public houses were required to close on Saturday at midnight and not reopen until 4am on Mondays, with the exception of between 12.30 and 2.30 and 6pm and 10pm on Sundays. The Licensing Act 1872 was the first attempt to prohibit night time drinking and from 1874 all public houses had to be closed from 11pm until 6am each day. It is sometimes overlooked that before this piece of legislation public houses, subject to the Sunday restrictions, could remain open twenty-four hours a day so that no matter what hours a labourer was working the public house was always available.

What is perhaps rather surprising in terms of regulation is that, if some of the public houses were as subversive as claimed and the locations of such undesirable activities, why it took so long for any significant effective regulation to be introduced. Much of the answer rests with the composition of Parliament itself as it was still dominated by landowners, many of whom drank themselves. They displayed a remarkably consistent opposition to any measures which they judged likely to interfere in local affairs. They did of course have a pronounced vested interest as well as the brewing industry was a major purchaser of their barley crops.

It is also interesting to note what support some establishments could receive. When the landlady of the Crown Beerhouse in Patwell Street, who was a widow, applied for a spirit license it was declined by the local magistrates who suggested that she wait until the next licensing day "when probably she might be married." She clearly acted upon their suggestion and married John Dobel, referred to as "a most respectable man" and the application was renewed in 1860. This time there was opposition from some inhabitants on the grounds "that there were as many licensed houses as would suit the requirements of the town." The application, however, was endorsed by the Vicar, the Revd. James White, the Churchwardens, the Overseers "and the most respectable inhabitants of the town." The spirit license in this instance was granted.

Needless to say there were many within the labouring population who viewed any restrictions as an attack on one of their popular recreations. When a proposal was discussed in Bruton in 1882 to close public houses on Sundays the meeting degenerated into "one of the most disorderly that have been held in the town for many a long day." The object of many at the meeting seems to have been to prevent the speakers being heard and when William Clarke suggested that not only should they do without beer on a Sunday but also all the time, as he had done for the last twenty-nine years, there was complete uproar.

Many publicans also breached these new regulations and a number from Bruton appeared before Wincanton Magistrates all charged with "the Sale of Beer during prohibited hours", for example, James Pearce in 1858, William Parsons in 1859, Benjamin Hobbs in 1862 and Edward Ashford in 1864. The latter offered an interesting defence: "the defendant had laboured under a mistake as to the state of his guests, believing their red eyes to be the evidence of weeping and not of drinking, and thinking they were travellers who had a right to demand liquor." The Magistrates were not entirely convinced and he was fined 5s, although this penalty was half the usual amount.

Temperance.

The other thrust against alcohol came from the Temperance Movement, which was actively supported by the two Chapels in Bruton and also by the Church of England. Exactly when a formal temperance society started in the town is unclear but it was claimed in 1871 that, "Many years ago there was a flourishing society in Bruton." Speaking in December 1882 William Clarke recalled that he had started a Band of Hope in the town, usually directed at young people, "Many years ago" but it had received little support from the Churches at that time. As he had been an abstainer for nearly thirty years such a group could have dated from the 1850s. The organisation certainly flourished after a meeting in January 1871 which attracted a large audience, "We hope…the influence of the meeting will not be lost, but that many may be induced to join the 'Cold Water Army', and fight the tyrant Alcohol." In February 1872 Good Templarism reached Bruton and the 'Hope of Bruton' Lodge was formed, which in the 1880s was under the presidency of Josiah Jackson and in the late 1890s became the Bruton Total Abstinence League. His Diary records regular attendance at committee meetings and lectures.

Certainly many people took the pledge such as seventy-two in June 1882 and forty in January 1889. There is some indication that propaganda was specifically directed at the working class and that it was having some effect as in December 1882 one speaker bemoaned "the absence of all but the working classes" at this meeting. The evidence is too fragmentary for any definite conclusions about the impact of the movement in Bruton, but for those who did accept temperance as a way of life, it did place them in a position of having more control over their lives and to support themselves and their families. Much of the propaganda distributed by groups such as the Band of Hope was designed to educate young people, especially males, about the problems associated with alcohol and so in the long run may have made a difference.

The movement was so strong in 1899 that in July of that year they staged their own Temperance Fete in Jubilee Park. Its leadership had finally realised that it could attract more people to its recreational activities than to its formal meetings with their moralistic lectures. Its message could be spread in a different way. Increasingly when public celebrations took place, non-alcoholic drinks were available, for example, for Queen Victoria's Golden Jubilee in 1887 in the committee meetings to discuss arrangements a conscious decision was made to provide "lemonade to the abstainers", and Mr Dyne readily donated twenty-five gallons of it. (33)

ii)   Changes to Whitsuntide.

One of the great successes of the Victorian middle class from their perspective was the continuation of the transformation of the Whitsuntide period from one of anything up to a fourteen day drunken holiday to a one-day Bank Holiday in the early 1900s, or in the case of Bruton, two days. While this process had been happening for decades with, for example, the gradual withdrawal of the gentry and the wealthier classes and pressure from the Evangelicals and the Non-Conformists, the Victorians added further refinements. Their principal success was in linking the Whitsun period with the activities of the Friendly Societies and in particular the Club Day. They even managed in many cases to transform that day with their own moral values.

The principal objective of Friendly Societies was to encourage working men to provide for sickness, infirmity and old age. They fell into two broad categories: those which were based in public houses and often shared out their funds every seven or eight years as a means of attracting members and secondly those which met elsewhere. In fact all the societies based in Bruton met in the various inns. In addition there were the more national affiliated orders, such as the Ancient Order of Foresters which became one of the two most important Friendly Societies in Bruton. The other one that was to gain dominance in the town was the Blue Ball Friendly Society, probably founded in 1818. In fact at various times after 1760 Societies had also met at the Bell Inn, the Old Bull Inn and the Sun Inn.

There were a number of attractions for working men that drew them to the Friendly Societies. In the first place there was the sickness benefit. The Blue Ball Friendly Society, in common with others in the area, such as at North Brewham and Shepton Montague, paid 5s or 6s a week to a sick member. Secondly, each one also paid funeral expenses, along with a contribution to the widow, and all members were required to attend the funeral with all their regalia. For many men a respectable funeral was an important consideration. Between 1882 and 1887 the Foresters expended £253 14s 3d in sickness and death benefits when its membership consisted of between 127 and 143 men. Thirdly, as many of the local societies divided their funds regularly it provided a welcome addition to the family income, for example, in 1872 the Blue Ball Friendly Society paid out £745 13s 2d to some 143 members, representing about £5 per man and included some 30% interest on their contributions.

Finally, the Friendly Societies offered conviviality and as most of the early societies met in local inns a weekly contribution of 2d was required which had to be spent in the public house at each meeting. Some societies such as the one at Shepton Montague dispensed with this requirement as it met in the local Schoolroom, and may suggest a different attitude to alcohol there.

All the local societies seem to have adopted the same Club Day format, centred on the Whitsuntide period, for example, the Old Bull Friendly Society on Whit Monday and the Blue Ball Friendly Society on Whit Tuesday. It may be possible to argue that these two days became in the late nineteenth century the principal holidays of the year for many in the community. The usual procedure was a parade, headed by a local band, of all members in full regalia through the town to the Parish Church.

This parade often entailed garlands of flowers and oak leaves carried on poles and for the Foresters the 'Chief Rangers' rode on horseback, attired in green and carrying bows and hunting horns. Most Club members followed wearing the broad sash of their Society across their chests and the Steward carried the Club staves with the brass head. In fact one procession was so large in 1893 that it was said to have had over 300 marchers of whom more than forty were on horseback and they were accompanied by two bands. In the Parish Church a service was held in which the Vicar or other Minister preached a sermon. This was followed by a further parade through the town calling at the residences of the principal inhabitants and then a dinner at a local inn or later in the century in a marquee erected on a field at West End or on the Abbey Field. Dinner was followed by games and dancing.

This pattern of events was not restricted to Bruton but could be found on these days throughout the whole of Somerset to a greater or lesser degree. Increasingly the societies laid down detailed rules to govern conduct on Club Day, for example, the Shepton Montague Friendly Society fined its members 2s if they did not attend, 6d for walking out of their place, 6d for causing a disturbance and 2s 6d for fighting, smoking or drinking in the Schoolroom where they had their dinner.

The Victorians considered that the Friendly Societies contributed to 'civilizing the masses' in two main ways. First some of the rules and regulations of the Societies were designed to maintain and improve behaviour. The North Brewham Society banned fighting along with "wrestling, stage playing, gambling or the like" and members agreed "not to join in any riot or rebellion against the present government or the laws of the land." The Blue Ball Friendly Society refused sickness benefit if the "disaster or disorder proceeds from venereal disease, or any species thereof, fighting, wrestling, profligacy, drunkenness, or any breach of the peace." There was a fine of 6d if a member at a meeting was "detected cursing, swearing, or using opprobrious language, or being intoxicated, or laying wagers, or raising any dispute to injure the character of any member, causing any quarrel or disturbance, promoting gaming, or refusing to keep silent." It was a fairly comprehensive list which was repeated in the rules of other local societies. Appropriate behaviour was not only expected but also was demanded from all members.

It became the pattern of the Club Day to involve members in harmless, healthy outdoor leisure pursuits. Year after year reports in the local press referred to games and sports which invariably followed the dinner. In 1889, for example, the Blue Ball Friendly Society staged at least fourteen different races and sporting events with prizes which ranged from small amounts of cash to hams, cheese, a garden fork and a whip.

The second way of controlling the masses was through the involvement of the gentry and the Victorian middle class in the Societies. There is no doubt that the Friendly Societies in the Bruton area were well supported by the local landowners and principal inhabitants, usually as honorary members and sometimes as officials. These men could then provide a guiding hand and a great deal of influence towards the required moral behaviour.

Once again every year their names appeared in the reports of the Club Day celebrations and at the other events. The Hoare family of Stourhead subscribed annually to the "Bruton Benefitt Clubbs" in the early nineteenth century and a report in 1843 on the Old Bell Friendly Society stated that, "most of the principal gentry are honorary members." In the 1850s the Treasurer of the Shepton Montague Friendly Society was J.P. Fitzgerald who was the Steward and Land Agent of the Earl of Ilchester. Most of the annual dinners reported in the press were under the Chairmanship of a local doctor or the Vicar, supported by a range of other middle class patrons, such as solicitors, traders and local shopkeepers. Henry Hobhouse MP of Hadspen House was an honorary member of the Ancient Order of Foresters in Bruton. When Josiah Jackson attended the Old Bull Friendly Society dinner in December 1894 he noted that eight out of nine parish councillors were there.

The dinners were invariably followed by toasts and speeches and these provided another opportunity for the honorary members to extol the required virtues. After the Loyal Toast others would include the Church, and the Armed Forces before coming to the Society itself and its officers. The whole range of required messages would have been covered from loyalty, duty and discipline to industry, thrift and provision for the future.

Even before that the sermon in the Parish Church had a part to play. In 1845 for example, a sermon was based upon Ecclesiastes IV, vv. 9-10, "Two are better than one; because they have a good reward for their labour. For if they fall, the one will lift up the other." More than thirty years later, Revd. H.T. Ridley, preached on Matthew V, v. 19, "Whosoever shall break one of these least commandments, and shall teach men to do so, he shall be called the least in the kingdom of heaven; but whosoever shall do or teach them, the same shall be called great in the kingdom of heaven."

Yet with all this moralistic input there remained a concern that the Club Days would become wild and drunken. In the 1860s, for example, the Congregational Chapel held their Sunday School treat outside of the town so that the children would not see any drunken excesses. "Whit Tuesday is selected for this treat in order to draw away the children from the scenes of drunkenness which accompany the club feasts at this period." Certainly in the late 1870s it was more peaceful as one report in 1878 commented, "P.C. Gard, who is stationed in Bruton, succeeded without any assistance in maintaining order and quiet; which, as many of our readers know, is not always an easy task on such occasions." There was still some disruption to normal agricultural activity as Jackson noted in 1891, "Men away at Blue Ball Club."

iii)   Changes at the Harvest.

Another traditional time for communal celebrations and all that they entailed had been at the completion of the harvest. The Victorians managed to change that completely. In some instances it remained with individual farmers to reward their own labourers but the format was different: gone was the provision of large quantities of beer or more likely cider and in its place the Harvest Tea, as for example was provided by James Harding, a staunch Non-Conformist, for his labourers at Whaddon Farm.

For the community as a whole two forms of celebration became the accepted pattern in the nineteenth century. The first was a religious service, the Harvest Thanksgiving. Its origins seem to have been in Cornwall in 1843 and about 1860 it had been introduced in Shepton Montague by Revd. C.F. Tink. In October 1864 a large Harvest Thanksgiving Service was held in the Congregational Chapel in Bruton when the Chapel, Schoolroom and vestry were all decorated with fruit, flowers and evergreens and suitable mottoes were also evident.

It was at this period that a number of appropriate hymns appeared, such as, "Come, ye thankful people come", in 1844 and, "We plough the fields and scatter" first appeared in 1861 in England although it was based upon an eighteenth century German song. The Harvest Thanksgiving proved to be a very popular service in Bruton, for example, in 1881 it was reported that, "Bruton Church, for a country town, is a very large one, but it proved in the evening unequal to holding the congregation that assembled, many persons being unable to obtain admittance, while not a few stood throughout the Service. " The following year it was said that, "the sacred edifice was crowded."

The second new form of communal celebration became the Harvest Tea. In October 1864 a successful united harvest tea meeting was held in the Congregational Chapel with some 300 Congregationalists and Methodists sitting down to the tea. Such teas, although not always a joint venture, were to take place annually for the rest of the century, for example, in October 1894 Jackson and members of his family went to the Harvest Home Tea at the Wesleyan Chapel.

The Church of England also accepted the idea of a tea and on occasions theirs was linked with a concert, usually in the National Schoolroom, both of which proved to be popular, for example a report in 1886 stated, "Tea was laid for about 150, but so large was the company that the tables had to be laid a second time. The room was crowded in the evening for the concert." Victorian religion and temperance had managed to eradicate another part of popular culture. What had been a predominantly male dominated occasion became one for the whole family.

iv)   Teas.

The idea of providing a tea became a well-used one in Victorian England. Most years the children of the various Sunday Schools and later the National School, had their treat which invariably followed the pattern which included a parade, tea and games. Starting the concept young was expected to have beneficial effects in the long run. In 1859 the silk factory hands of White and Bord were treated to both dinner and tea. After that, "various sports were commenced, which highly gratified the younger branches." Dancing then followed for two more hours. In March 1866 the position was reversed when the workers of Mr Boyd invited him and his wife to a tea to celebrate the first anniversary of his takeover of the factory. After tea the evening was spent in games, singing and dancing. Amongst the celebrations at the end of the Boer War in 1902 was a tea for all the children in the town. In cases such as these no alcohol appeared anywhere and the appropriate messages were being sent out.

v)   Constructive Activities.

As well as diverting the nature of popular celebrations, entertainment and leisure pursuits, the Victorian middle class also considered that it was essential for the labouring man to undertake some constructive activity at times when he was not performing his paid employment. Not only would this increase independence and self-respect, but also use up any surplus energy and keep him out of the public house.

Allotments.

Allotments were an ideal answer as they fulfilled these criteria and in addition they had some economic advantages as they would allow the labourer to grow food to feed his family. Captain Scobell of North Brewham, who was a great advocate of allotments, commented, "It keeps him from idleness, or worse than idleness." In some parts of the country it was customary for farmers to permit their labourers to have access to small pieces of surplus or fallow land to grow potatoes. In September 1823 Mr Penny of Coombe Farm allowed six of his labourers eighteen ridges of land covering three rods and twenty-one perches to grow their potatoes. In 1832 the Overseers of the Poor for Bruton reported that land "let to labourers was generally at 1s per perch, for growing potatoes." From 1830 onwards the pioneer of allotments in the West Country was the Bishop of Bath and Wells, soon supported by Captain Scobell.

In December 1840 the Bruton Field Garden Society held its first annual meeting under the chairmanship of silk mill owner, J.S. Ward. He reported that, "Two closes of land in the neighbourhood of the town, which were kindly offered for the purpose by the Right Hon. The Earl of Ilchester, and Sir Henry Hoare, Bart., have been let out to the poor of the parish from 10 to 40 perches." He added, significantly, that the more than 130 tenants "are contented, and grateful for the benefits this conferred on them." The following year solicitor Henry Dyne enthused that, "the poor are very grateful..... The system promotes industry, economy, and, above all, that in which the poor are generally deficient, thoughtfulness as to the future." On the same occasion H.L. Dampier of Collinshayes, who had originally opposed the system accepted that he had been mistaken. He found that many local men "are contented and grateful, each being aware that his occupancy depends on his own good conduct." There was some degree of security of tenure as landowners such as Captain Scobell specified that tenants could not be removed from their piece of land, "provided they are convicted of no crime, and that they pay their rent punctually."

The Allotment Movement continued to spread throughout the Victorian period and a Return to Parliament in 1890 indicated that there were seventy-one allotments in Bruton under a quarter of an acre, twenty-four in Pitcombe, seventeen in Shepton Montague and ten in South Brewham. Allotments could be very beneficial for the living standards of the poor as one report in a local newspaper noted in October 1870, "A very prolific crop of white rock potatoes had lately been dug on an allotment at Dropping Lane portion of the Bruton Field Gardens, occupied by Thomas Corp. One potato weighed one pound and three-quarters, and measured 14 inches in circumference, and several others were over one pound in weight." This particular allotment was probably located amongst those on the land where the road down Dropping Lane branches around Parkwall, forming a large triangle between the walls beside the two roads. In the twentieth century this land became a small-holding occupied by Henry Toogood, now called Park Corner.

The Victorian middle class witnessed so many benefits from the allotments as it kept labourers from public houses, decreased idleness and increased self-respect and pride, especially if they were able to exhibit and win at the Foresters' Annual Flower Show in Bruton. There was the important economic benefit that they were providing food for their families. The statistics suggest that these allotments were providing food at various times of the year for between 20% and 30% of the total population of the town. These small pieces of land promoted the values which the Victorians so admired: hard work, industriousness, forethought and planning. The tenants had to maintain a good level of behaviour or they faced losing their allotment. Perhaps above all, the labourers seemed contented and grateful so would pose no threat to the social stability of the area. (34)

Self-improvement and knowledge.

The Victorian middle class was deeply committed to self-improvement and the acquisition of useful knowledge and they were thus avid supporters of any organizations for working men which fostered the same. Mechanics Institutes had been founded in 1823 and one does appear to have made a brief appearance in Bruton. A public meeting was held in the National Schoolroom in September 1859 under the chairmanship of the Vicar, Revd. James White, and at which other clergy and solicitors spoke. As a result "upwards of fifty working men have become members of this institute." Later in the month it was reported that it was hoped to start a reading room and "several gentlemen have kindly promised to supply some papers and periodicals gratuitously." It does not however appear to have survived.

Early in 1879 a Working Men's Club was formed with the momentum coming once again from the middle class as a musical entertainment was held in February to raise money, with local clergy and E.R. Hayter of the National School, being significant participants. The following month the Visitors of Sexey's Hospital allowed the Club to lease the old clubroom of the former Bell Inn and arrangements were made to purchase new furniture. Here was the promise of a clean, furnished, well-lit and warm room, a far cry from the conditions in many labourers' houses. One local newspaper commented, "We trust the club will receive the support it justly merits from the gentry and tradesmen of the town." It was certainly still in existence just over two years later in May 1881 when another entertainment was staged in the National Schoolroom to raise money for its funds. As references to this Club do not seem to appear in the local press later in the 1880s it does not seem to have survived for long.

Nationally such clubs were seen as a way of diverting men from public houses but most of them did permit the sale of beer which provided a valuable source of revenue. In this respect their great success was that they removed much social drinking from the commercial pressures of the public house. One historian has commented, "They were genuine recuperative refuges, free from commercial pressures, ritual drinking, police harassment, district visitors and the wife and family."

Organised Trips and Outings.

Transport developments in the Victorian era, and particularly the arrival of the railway in Bruton in 1856 and at Cole in 1862, opened up an alternative recreational pursuit for ordinary people, especially with the introduction of the cheap excursion. It has even been suggested that railway outings probably did more than anything else to change the nature of some of the traditional holiday activities. In fact railway excursions were sometimes so popular that it was impossible to board a train, for example, in July 1863 it was reported that large numbers of people were left standing on the platform at Bruton as the excursion train to Weymouth was already full. Some potential travellers opted for a refund while others waited for a later train, only to be transported in a cattle truck. At least for the return journey additional space was provided as it was stated that the train reached Bruton at 10.30pm with three engines and thirty-seven carriages.

Children frequently benefited from rail excursions and increasingly Sunday School trips went to the seaside, for example, in June 1875 all the children from the Church of England Sunday School were taken to Burnham-on-Sea. On arrival they were fed with bread and meat, played games during the afternoon and were then provided with tea. In June 1862 some 150 children from the Congregational Chapel Sunday School went to Cole Station where they joined over 500 more children from chapels in Wincanton on a day trip to Burnham. Both of these outings coincided with the Whitsun Club Days and indicate the desire to remove children from the potential drunken scenes. Throughout the 1880s and 1890s the girls who were resident in Sexey's Hospital were taken on an annual trip, usually to Bournemouth but occasionally to Weymouth.

The Choir of the Parish Church appear to have had an annual trip by train to Weymouth from the 1860s. In general in the morning, "The various seaside amusements were indulged in" and then followed dinner, with toasts and speeches. The trip in August 1861 seems to have been more memorable as the bathing machine containing their clothes was hauled up the beach leaving the swimmers stranded in the sea. By the 1890s Bournemouth had become an alternative destination and the excusion seems to have been broadened, "Besides the choir, a very large number of people availed themselves of an opportunity for a long day at that favourite watering place." Employers too arranged an annual outing for their workers, such as Jones and Sons Brewery which, for example, took all their men on their annual excursion to Bournemouth in August 1890 and provided them with refreshments during the day.

The Chapels.

It is important to stress that the Non-Conformist chapels could play a very positive role in the recreational activities of labouring people. They were not just concerned with salvation, although everything which they organised was within the general context of godliness and respectability, but that in itself was an attraction for some of the poorer classes. When the Young Men's Bible Class attached to the Congregational Sunday School went on an excursion to Bournemouth from Cole in 1891, for example, they had their own saloon carriage and "The journey was enlivened by some selections of music, several of the members having taken their instruments." Although they dispersed in the resort they re-assembled at 5pm for tea in the Temperance Hotel. Once again all the required and appropriate messages were being transmitted.

The Independents who later became the Congregationalists with their large chapel in the middle of the High Street, were joined permanently in the 1830s by the Wesleyan Methodists with their chapel at West End, although they had made a brief appearance in the late 1770s and early 1780s after a visit by John Wesley in 1776. By 1851 some 35% of all church attendance in the town was at these two chapels. Together they offered companionship and conviviality along with an exhilarating experience for many of their members. Some people regarded the sermons as a superior form of entertainment and as the preachers tended to change each week, especially in the Methodist Chapel where there was no resident Minister, and where they were drawn from the congregations of the chapels themselves, there could be great variety which was often accompanied by vigorous and rousing hymn singing.

Wesleyan Methodism was seen as a counter-attraction to the beer house and there were clearly those in Bruton who were strongly influenced by both religion and temperance and who wanted to reject the traditional entertainments in favour of more 'respectable' ones. In these instances this desire was from the labouring people themselves and not imposed from above. Both chapels tended to be freer in their worship compared with the rigid format of the parish church.

In addition these chapels staged treats with food and games and excursions for their Sunday School children, outings for the whole family as well as talks, fetes, bazaars, tea meetings, concerts and various festivals. Such occasions often involved chapel members from other villages attending and so there was an opportunity to meet friends and for general conviviality. The chapels could fulfil actively a significant role in structuring leisure time, especially for children.

Mottoes.
It would seem that on every conceivable occasion the Victorian middle class used opportunities to press home the messages which they wished to impart to those of a lower social status. Every time that there was a public celebration the decorations in the streets were used, for example, when the railway arrived in 1856 it was noted that there were "several triumphal arches....bearing appropriate mottoes." Eleven years later when the Foresters paraded through the town in 1867 one arch had the motto, "May they ever be united." For the Agricultural Society Show festivities in 1899 there were arches with mottoes such as, "Little labour, little gain", "Labour conquers all", and "Industry supports us all." Few inhabitants could be left in any doubt.

Education.
It was however through education that the Victorian middle class reiterated day after day, week after week, month after month and

year after year, the values, principles and attitudes that it wished to impart, even though deep down there was the always the fear that the growth of literacy within the labouring population could lead to greater dissatisfaction with their lot. In addition there was some concern that the newly literate would turn to what were perceived as cheap, inferior and immoral novels or to newspapers which concentrated on lurid tales of vice and crime, such as the 'News of the World', which was started in 1843 and which by 1854 had the largest circulation in the world at some 190,000 copies per week.

Nevertheless the development of schools went ahead. The Independents were the first of the religious groups to open a Sunday School in Bruton, probably in 1803 when they built their Chapel in the High Street. By 1833 it had 191 children attending. In 1838 the Church of England opened its Sunday School in the western part of the former Poorhouse in Silver Street, replacing the one which had been operating for a short while in a carpenter's workshop in Coombe Street. Finally the Wesleyan Methodists opened a Sunday School in their Chapel at the West End in 1848 and eventually constructed a separate larger schoolroom on a nearby site in 1897.

The Infant and National School officially commenced in 1841 with an average attendance of at least one hundred, rising to over 200 by the mid 1850s. In these Sunday and Day Schools the children were constantly exposed to the Victorian interpretation of Christianity with its emphasis upon duty, station in life, deference to others and moral behaviour. Through the decades it became the most effective tool which could be imagined. Two hymns typical of the period serve as examples of the sentiments which found expression. The first was written for children by John Page Hopps:

> Father, lead me day by day
> Ever in thine own sweet way;

Teach me to be pure and true,
Show me what I ought to do.

When my work seems hard and dry,
May I press on cheerily;
Help me patiently to bear
Pain and hardship, toil and care.

The second from the pen of Henry Van Dyke was directed more at adults:

They who tread the path of labour follow where my feet have trod;
They who work without complaining do the holy will of God;
Nevermore thou needest seek Me; I am with thee everywhere;
Raise the stone, and thou shalt find Me; cleave the wood and I am there.

Every task, however simple, sets the soul that does it free;
Every deed of love and mercy done to man, is done to Me.
I, the Peace that passeth knowledge, dwell amid the daily strife;
I, the Bread of heaven, am broken in the sacrament of life.

For those of the labouring classes who wished to improve themselves the Victorian middle classes arranged Continuation or Evening Classes which could be undertaken when the work of the day was over. Once the new National School had been opened in 1851 the Headmaster was conducting Evening classes of one and a half hours each on Mondays, Wednesdays and Fridays. By 1893 these sessions in the winter months had been reduced to Monday and Wednesday evenings in the Infant School in the High Street and included arithmetic, mensuration, geography, drawing and wood-carving. There were also other Evening classes which were just for females and covered Domestic Economy, Dress-cutting and Dressmaking, Geography and Needlework.

As the area was still so rural there was some emphasis upon developing skills in agriculture and agricultural pursuits. In November 1893 a Butter School was started in the Assembly Rooms and had no difficulty in filling the ten places available. The opening meeting consisted not only of a lengthy talk on milk but also a demonstration lesson on the use of the cream separator and butter- making. Such a School was clearly well received as in the following month the Visitors of Sexey's Hospital arranged to pay the fees of £1 17s 6d for three of their girls to attend. By the end of the decade talks and demonstrations were being given on a range of agricultural topics such as poultry keeping, rick thatching, spar-making, orchard management and pruning. For those who wished to improve their skills there were some opportunities available and these sessions were reported to be attracting audiences of about sixty each time.

vi)   Assessment.

The sweeping changes envisaged early in the nineteenth century were not easy to achieve because as the century progressed it became clear to many within the middle classes, the non-conformist chapels and amongst some sections of the working classes that not all labouring men wished to spend their leisure time in chapels or reading rooms, attending concerts or lectures, and so other attractive alternatives were needed which would involve instruction, recreation and entertainment. In pursuance of this objective the Friendly Societies, along with some aspects of the Agricultural Society, played an important role.

Nevertheless by the end of the Victorian era the popular culture of previous centuries was almost unrecognisable. "A mighty revolution has taken place in the sports and pastimes of the common people", wrote one observer. The uninhibited drunkenness, violence, disorder and mayhem that had accompanied so many holidays and festive occasions had been 'civilized'. Gone was most of the cruelty to man and beast with its emphasis upon boxing, cudgel-playing, singlestick, cock fighting and bull and bear baiting, and in its place a more refined entertainment with its emphasis upon parades, dinners, teas, games, sports and dances.

During the nineteenth century a series of factors came into play which greatly assisted changes in, and the development of, popular culture and help to substantiate the idea that the labouring people themselves played a part in the on-going process. The coming of the railways meant that the world of the labourer was greatly extended. Cheap excursions were possible in a way which had never existed in the past, although not all of these were to the liking in the Victorian middle class, for while a trip to the seaside was judged to be beneficial, travelling further afield to a race meeting or prize fight definitely was not. The development of the local and national press with its many notices and advertisements created an awareness of leisure events which had never existed before.

Working people also benefited from reductions in their working day and working week, which by the end of the century had markedly increased their potential leisure time. The struggle to achieve such reductions had been long and protracted, with opposition from the very men as employers who aimed to transform the attitudes of their workers. While the first hesitant steps had been taken in the factory and mines legislation of the 1830s and 1840s, there were many who still worked long hours. In October 1898 a very articulate letter from an 'Assistant' appeared in a local newspaper:

> At a meeting of the Institute last year, it was proposed that a petition be signed by members and others and sent to the tradesmen asking them to close their establishments at seven pm, as is done in the neighbouring town of Wincanton, and, I believe, in Castle Cary. Only one thing prevented this being done – the assurance by a tradesman that steps were being taken to attain this end. What the steps were, or who was taking them, no one seemed to know, and nothing further has been heard of the matter. On behalf of our class, I now ask the Bruton tradesmen to follow the humane example of their neighbours. People have only to know that the shops will shut at seven o'clock, and they will get their wants supplied before that hour. The work of the assistants would be done better. Few people can work 12 or 13 hours a day in a shop without feeling the strain. 'Britains never will be slaves', No; but there are a good many in Christian England, and not a few in Bruton.

The letter did provoke a limited response as two weeks later the principal tradesmen announced that they had arranged to close at 7.30pm, but that was only to be during the winter months.

Finally there had been a significant rise in real wages, estimated to be some 40% between 1860 and 1875 and still more between 1880 and 1895 as a result of the agricultural and industrial depressions when prices fell. For the first time many labouring people had surplus cash to spend on their recreational activities often in locations that were not in a public house. At the same time more and more consumer goods became readily available such as cigarettes, tobacco, along with cheaper tea and coffee and a range of cordials including ginger beer. All of these could offer increased competition for alcohol.

On the other hand, the spectre of poverty was still there and even at the end of the century it is clear that leisure activities and opportunites remained closely linked with the poverty cycle for some men and women. Young rural labourers could well have had some surplus cash to indulge in a leisure pursuit but these opportunities declined rapidly with marriage, especially for women and more of the leisure became centred on the home, including the allotment. The presence of young children added to the difficulties but once these had started to earn money themselves and then left home the situation improved again. The poverty of old age with no income from adult children once again restricted activites. As late as 1913 in one of his surveys, Rowntree concluded that the struggle to make ends meet had cultural implications. "It means that every natural longing for pleasure or variety should be ignored or set aside. It means, in short, a life without colour, space or atmosphere, that stifles and hems in the labourer's soul as in too many cases his cottage does his body."

Overall, however, there can be little doubt that a new popular culture was being established which was no longer perceived as threatening or subversive, but in many respects conservative and respectable. Yet while there was a decreased general fear of the labouring man and his family in a public space, the Victorians were careful to keep the classes separate if possible, as may be seen for example in the different categories provided in the carriages on railway trains: namely First, Second and Third Class. Leisure had been separated from the workplace and was no longer tied to the agricultural year.

Various recreational activities had become much more organised and controlled not only with rules but also within set locations. It is very noticeable that in Bruton for example so many events start to take place in a few carefully selected venues such as the National School, the Assembly Rooms, the Abbey Field, the Rectory Garden, on parts of Hyde loaned by a local farmer and later in the nineteenth century in the Jubilee Park. With transport developments, scientific discoveries and some technological advances, the world of so many labouring men and women had been extended in ways which would have been unimaginable to their ancestors in Bruton. In that sense the workingman and woman were freer than ever they had been. The public house was no longer the centre of their entertainment and recreational world.

On the other hand, as historians have observed, the Victorian middle class "had failed to bring about a sober and Christian working class society in which leisure time was spent in a relentless search for self-improvement." Many of the activities of which the Victorians disapproved may well have continued but simply went unrecorded. In April 1800 Charles Foot, alias Davidge, a thatcher, won a contest when he "ate sixteen mutton pies, each one ounce and half, and drank two quarts of beer, in nine minutes and half." It is inconceivable that such contests and others like them, stopped dead, they were just not reported. Gambling was possible with so many different activites, although it was not mentioned publicly, such as for example in April 1843 when a young man claimed to be able to walk twenty one miles in three hours. A course was selected from Ward's Silk Factory in Quaperlake Street to the Queen's Head Inn at West End. The epic was completed with twelve minutes to

223

spare. There was always the taste for the sensational. By the end of the century Music Halls featured prominently in working people's leisure time and although one was never built in Bruton there was ease of access to other places, for example, in 1890 two Music Halls, each with 3,000 seats, were built in Bristol, but at least they did not sell alcohol unlike many others.

Whitsuntide and other riotous occasions may have been tamed but drunkenness continued, as witness the desire to remove children from the town at that time of year, and the constant stream of offenders who appeared before the Wincanton Magistrates' Bench. All that even the staunch tee-totaller Josiah Jackson could do was to note that at occasions such as at the Diamond Jubilee celebrations of Queen Victoria, "things passed off fairly well except some of my men had drunk too much and were unable to milk the cows at the proper time." In October of the same year he noted, "J. Rex and E. Morgan came back to work after a drinking bout." On 29th July 1898 he had to report, "Some of the men away drinking." At best contained but not eradicated. (35)

7. CONCLUSION.

When considering leisure activities, entertainments, customs and popular culture over a four-hundred year period various points emerge. First, the length of time during which some of the activities survived was amazing. Hunting as an organized pursuit for the wealthy was well established in the Norman period and may still be found nearly a thousand years later, albeit in a somewhat changed form and with different targets. Gambling on virtually anything remains as popular in the present time as it was centuries ago. Football, cricket, cards and dice still have their adherents just as they did hundreds of years ago.

Some celebrations, which have their origins at a slightly later date also remained popular, again possibly in a changed form, such as for example the fireworks and bonfires of 5th November, a festivity which only started after 1605. For nearly two hundred years the church bells were rung on that day, as they were on 29th May to commemorate the Restoration of Charles II in 1660. At the end of the nineteenth century, just as at the beginning of the period most of the activities remained based in the community, although transport developments did allow for travel to other locations. The village fete or bazaar, so popular with the Victorians finds support in Bruton more that one hundred and fifty years later.

Secondly, it is clear that the vast majority of the leisure pursuits and entertainments were male dominated at all levels in society. It was men from the wealthier classes who hunted and went shooting; amongst the Victorian middle class the driving force behind self-improvement organizations and other suitable forms of entertainment were men. Male labourers frequented the alehouses and took part in the more violent activities involving other males and a range of animals.

Women must have had their recreations, but these were recorded far less frequently. For the wealthier women there was the social custom of visiting, of taking tea, providing musical entertainment within the household and attending public functions, such as concerts or the theatre, usually escorted by male members of the family. They had their card circles and for Victorian women their sewing circles, all of which created a great deal of sociability. For working women so much of their leisure activity was oral, especially when working in the Bruton silk mills, or in the fields at harvest time or everyday when milking or working in the dairy. In the midst of washing, cooking and generally caring for their family, talking with neighbours or others in the street must have been a welcome relief. Of particular importance is the credit which they have been given for passing onto their children the stories and folklore of an area.

Third, it is easy to demonstrate that for at least the first three hundred years being considered, some of the leisure pursuits and the entertainment had their basis in brutality and violence. All levels in society made other creatures suffer, whether as a result of hunting, fishing, cock throwing or fighting, bull and bear baiting or shooting. Other human beings suffered for public entertainment in cudgelling, single stick, sword and dagger, as well as bare knuckle boxing and wrestling. Market days could be enlivened with one or more public whippings, or a suitable target in the stocks or pillory.

At a time when average life expectancy was much lower, when through the centuries the town was periodically ravaged by epidemics such as plague and, in Bruton's case, particularly by smallpox, when injury at work was much more common, such attitudes are hardly surprising. It has been suggested that as so many children, especially boys, were apprenticed at an early age and so grew up not within their family but with strangers, they developed a hardness and almost detachment towards others.

Fourthly, and undoubtedly most significant, it was a period of considerable change. As a result mainly of developments in education, the gentry and wealthier in society began to realise that the concept of a 'gentleman' did not just involve the capacity to fight but also a knowledge of literature, art, music and manners. In short, they became more refined and in the process many of them, albeit very slowly, began to distance themselves more and more from the great mass of the population. The activities which they had attended, had been involved in or patronized in some way such as through providing prizes, were no longer ones with which they wished to be associated.

The spread of urbanization and industrialization in the eighteenth and early nineteenth centuries witnessed the emergence of a new class in society. The middle class, profoundly influenced by the work ethic and non-conformist and evangelical religion, condemned so many of the old customs and leisure pursuits which they perceived as the path to idleness and sin. In its place they developed their own culture committed to self-improvement, knowledge and some discreet entertainment. In many respects it may be argued that they wished to emulate their social superiors but at the same time to tame the excesses of the masses.

The most radical change was experienced in popular culture. So much of this culture seems to have stemmed from the medieval period when various customs and communal festivities were ways of raising money within a parish, some of this was used for the benefit of the parish church and some for the relief of needy neighbours. In addition, of course, such activities provided a radically different experience to the harshness, drudgery and boredom of their everyday existence. At the same time social cohesion was fostered, allowing individuals or groups to be involved, succeed and so release pent-up tensions.

As so many of the celebrations and festivities within this popular culture led to drunkenness, violence and disorder, it was inevitable that they would come under attack. Even in the medieval period preachers condemned the drunkenness, brawling and bloodshed. By the time of the Reformation they were often seen as profane, licentious and rooted in popish practices with rituals and ceremonies so as a result most Saints' Days were abandoned. Many early Protestants, and particularly the Puritans in the seventeenth century, saw them as a desecration of the Sabbath and a way into sin, especially idleness. The evidence from Bruton, however, does indicate in the 1650s at least there were some within the town who did not always take too much notice of Cromwell and carried on singing and dancing.

Much popular culture did revive in the post-Restoration period and well into the eighteenth century with parish feasts and the observation of principal holidays such as Christmas, Shrovetide, Easter and Whitsuntide. It has been suggested that this was often the case in the more conservative, deferential and cohesive parts of the West Country, such as east and south Somerset, along with the Blackmore Vale. The very fact that so many aspects of popular culture survived for so long indicates the importance with which it was viewed by the ordinary people. The decline of popular culture in rural areas was a long-term and often gradual process, extending over several generations.

Popular entertainments and culture were to be changed out of all recognition, however, by the Victorian middle class in Bruton. Committed as they were to industriousness, labour discipline and inspired by the appropriate aspects of religion, they were contemptuous of the culture of earlier generations. By the second half of the nineteenth century many observers of working class culture nationally recorded that there was a very limited range of recreational activities available for the labouring poor. It is very noticeable that a number of the pursuits of the middle class and of the lower classes were in fact very similar, both participated, for example in singing, reading, and games. The great difference was that for the middle class these took place inside the home and not outside of it for they were in many respects much more family-orientated.

Slowly but surely the Victorians transformed the attitudes of the working class through education in their Sunday and Church Schools, through Friendly Societies, the Temperance Movement, Working Men's Clubs, and practical schemes such as allotments. The days of the dominance of the alehouse and the beerhouse in popular culture were truly numbered. On the other hand drunkenness still occurred, often in company, as did gambling and the tendency to be attracted to and to be mesmerized by the unusual or the strange.

While it has been possible to consider entertainment, customs and leisure pursuits over four hundred years, it represents just a glimpse particularly of popular culture. So much went unrecorded, either through social snobbery when it was not deemed worthy enough to merit a mention, or because it was so commonplace it was unremarkable. Women and children still went out into the countryside as they had done for generations to collect nuts and berries, men continued to hunt small birds and animals, although here the thin line between legal activities and poaching remained blurred. Beliefs and superstitions which were centuries old lingered, as a few allegations that certain women were witches indicate. 'The Green Man' continued to make an appearance and may still be seen in a carving on the screen at the west end of the parish church and in another representation, possibly made several centuries later on the Priory in the High Street.

It is also clear that there was not always the same rigid division between leisure and work which developed in the twentieth century. When a farmer or landowner was out walking alone or with his family, often on a Sunday, the opportunity was taken to examine what was being achieved on neighbouring farms or property in relation to areas such as ploughing, crop management and later drainage. While the middle class might see all or part of their garden as a leisure area, for the working man it, and any allotment he might have, was a unit of production, a place where he had to work to help maintain his family. Many labouring men knew of no other existence than work and so when education developed in the latter part of the nineteenth century, it was a constant struggle for the attendance authorities to ensure that these families complied with the law and sent their children to day school. While some labouring men saw education as a way to improve the prospects of their children, others considered that it had no value whatsoever.

Even when the Victorians believed that they had made so much progress, what was going on below the surface continued to alarm them, if only because of fears that there was within the masses a criminal class which through its activities could threaten their way of life. In some respects therefore it is possible to argue that for all their efforts and their changes they merely contained popular culture, but did not eradicate it.

Green Man on Priory House in High Street.

APPENDICES.

Appendix 1.   St Matthias Eve

1642

> All Praise and thanks to god still give:
> ffor our deliverance Mathias Eve,
> By his great power wee put to flight,
> Our rageing foes that Thursday night,
> Who came to Plunder, Burne and Slay
> And quite consume us ere the day.
> Thus he our feeble force supplied:
> In weaknes most he's magnified
> Serve god w'th fear, on him depend
> As then, soe ever, he will defend.

At some later stage the last three words of line four were crossed out and 'the Batcombeites" substituted.

(D.L. Hayward, ed., The Registers of Bruton, Co. Somerset, vol. I, 1554-1680, p. 100.)

Appendix 2   An incident at Bruton Fair.

One man who was present at a large fair in Bruton in the 1730s was Bampfylde Moore Carew, (1693-1759), the notorious 'King of the Beggars'. He was the son of the Revd. Theodore

Carew, the rector of Bickleigh, near Tiverton in Devon. In 1745 a book entitled, "The Surprising Adventures of Bampfylde Moore Carew" was published. It suggested that he indulged in many minor crimes but a number of the stories appeared rather fanciful and perhaps the book was designed to appeal to the market for mild 'rogue' literature of the period.

He seems to have arrived in Bruton disguised as a seaman and managed to convince a local important and influential sea captain that he was genuine and he was entertained at his house and given "a considerable piece of money". He also approached Lord Berkeley as he came out of the Church and claimed that he was on board the 'Antelope' when his son died and was buried at sea in 1737, for which information he received in total twenty-six shillings. He was then, however, recognised by a local apothecary who knew that he was an imposter but who wanted to get rid of "an Irish quack-doctor…who had gathered the whole market around him, and who, with more strength of lungs than sense of argument, most loudly harangued, entertaining them in a very florid manner with the sovereign virtues of his pills, plasters and self." Carew agreed to help him if he kept his secret.

"Accordingly he got a little phial, and filled it up with spirits of turpentine; he then mixed in with the gaping auditiory of this Irish itinerant physician, who was in the midst of them, mounted on his steed adorned with a pompous curb-bridle, with a large parcel of all-curing medicines in his bags behind him, and was with a great deal of confidence and success distributing health around him; we must observe, that our physician had taken his stand among the stalls of orange and gingerbread merchants, shoemakers, glovers, and other such retailers.

"Mr Carew, therefore, approached him, planted himself close by the horse, and, wetting his fingers with the spirits, rested his hand upon the rump of the steed, as an unconcerned person might have done. At the same time putting aside the hair, he rubbed the turpentine upon his bare flesh, which immediately beginning to burn and smart, the afflicted quadruped began to express his sense of pain, by flinging his hinder legs, gently shaking himself, and other restless motions, which made the poor Mountebank wonder what had befallen his horse. But the pain increasing, the disorderly behaviour of the steed increased proportionally, who now began to kick, prance, stand on end, neigh immoderately shake himself, utterly disregarding both his bridle and rider, and running a tilt against the stalls of oranges, gingerbread, shoes, gloves, breeches, etc., which he overthrew, and trampled under foot. This occasioned a scramble among the boys for the eatables, and there were some who were but too unmerciful to the scattered goods of the poor shoemakers and glovers, who, enraged by their several losses, began to curse the doctor and his Rosinate, who was all this while in a very irregular manner capering, roaring and dancing, among the oranges, panniers of eggs etc., to the entire ruin of the hucksters, who now began to deal with very heavy blows, both on the unfortunate horse and his distressed master. This odd spectacle and adventure attracted the eyes and attention of the whole Fair, which was all in an uproar, some laughing, some crying, (particularily the poor suffering pedlars) some fighting, and others most unmercifully cursing and swearing. To make short of the story, the doctor rode about the fair, without either hat or wig, at the pleasure and discretion of his horse, among the ruined and overturned stalls and the dissipated mob, who concluded both the quack and the steed to be either mad or bewitched, and enjoyed their frolicsome situation.

The doctor, being no longer able to keep his seat, fell headlong into the miry street; the horse ran into the river, and rolled himself over several times, to the entire confusion and ruin of the inestimable pills and plasters; the doctor employed a good farrier, and after some time the horse came to himself again. The reader may very easily judge what glorious diversion this was for the apothecary and Mr Carew, who were spectators to the whole scene. He was treated handsomely upon this account, not only by the apothecary, but all others of the same profession in the town, and several other gentlemen."

(The Surprising Adventures of Bampfylde Moore Carew, Anon., 1745, pp. 91-92)

Appendix 3   Bruton Town.

> In Bruton Town there lived a farmer,
> Who had two sons and one daughter dear.
> By day and night they were a-contriving
> To fill their parents' heart with fear.
> One told his secret to none other,
> But unto his brother this he said:
> I think our servant courts our sister,
> I think they have a mind to wed.
>
> If he our servant courts our sister,
> That maid from such a shame I'll save.
> I'll put an end to all their courtship,
> And send him silent to his grave.
> A day of hunting was prepare-ed,
> In thorny woods where briars grew,
> And there they did that young man murder,
> And in the brook his fair body threw.

Now welcome home, my dear young brothers,
Our servant man is he behind?
We've left him where we've been a-hunting,
We've left him where no man can find.
She went to bed crying and lamenting,
Lamenting for her heart's delight.
She slept. She dreamed. She saw him by her
All bloody red in gory plight.

His lovely curls were wet with water;
His body all agape with blows.
O Love, for thee I've suffered murder:
I'm lying now where no man knows.
Then she rose early the very next morning,
Unto the yonder brook she sped,
There she beheld her own dear jewel
In gory plight, all bloody red.

She took her kerchief from her pocket,
She took his head upon her knee;
And then she wiped his dear eyes softly:
She wiped those eyes that could not see.
And since my brothers have been so cruel
To take your tender sweet life away,
One grave shall hold us both together,
Along with you in death I'll stay.

The basic story seems to have been taken from Boccaccio's *Decameron*, c.1350 and many versions of it were common through medieval England and on the Continent which possibly suggests that this type of ballad was popular with travelling minstrels. The

tune to which it was sung in the Victorian period was believed to
be at least three hundred years old.

Appendix 4   Inns, Alehouses, Beerhouses, etc.

As alehouses, inns and beerhouses played such an important
role in popular culture for so many centuries it seems appropriate
to give some indication of those in Bruton at various times. It is
clear that while some lasted for generations others were transient.
The following is not an exhaustive list but contains those for which
evidence has emerged so far. The dates specified are ones which
appear in various sources but they do not necessarily indicate the
length of time for which an alehouse was in use or the length of
time for which a tenant/landlord controlled it. Before the nineteenth
century most leases indicate the name of the tenant but he or she was
not always the landlord/landlady as there was a tendency to sublet
or employ a landlord. Men like Robert Pavy, Henry Ricketson and
Henry Albin Martin were very wealthy men and probably used the
alehouses as an investment or a source of ready cash rather than
live in them and serve the ale. Such a situation explains why more
than one name appears in particular years.

At the end of this appendix there is a list of names of men
and women who were involved in the sale of alcohol but for whom
no location was given in the source.

THE ANGEL.

Date	Tenant/Landlord	Information

Site: north side of hill leading to West End from High Street, possibly No.85, later to be the site of the Prince of Wales

----

THE BARBER'S ARMS

Date	Tenant/Landlord	Information
1750-1758	Thomas Vigar, senior	Paid Poor Rates

Site: High Street(?)

THE BEAR.

Date	Tenant/Landlord	Information
1748		In April a Bull sold there.
1749	John Cheek, junior	Signs lease in March and promises that, "Gentlemen, Ladies and Tradesmen, might depend upon good entertainment and civil `usage." Redlynch Fair moved there. Bowls and bull-baiting took place.
1784-1813		The Earl of Ilchester paid the Church Rates for the Dropping Lane Inn, which may have been the same

premises or possibly may
have been the Fox

Site: Dropping Lane Farm

THE BELL INN. (1)

Date	Tenant/Landlord	Information
1725		Lease signed
1725-1751	Samuel Darby	1751 Darby renewed lease
1765	Mrs Darby	Revd. Woodforde had breakfast there for 6d and paid 2d to feed his horse.
1768		"Tenemt or Inn formerly in possession of Samuel Darby"
1768-1809	John Bull d. 1809	1780s Courts Baron held there. 12 Sept. 1793 Bull sent "a Haunch of Venison" to Mr Pouncett of Cole, brother-in-law of Revd. James Woodforde.
1809		June. Edward Dyne, a solicitor, Leased and later purchased a "Messuage or Dwelling house then used as an Inn called the Bell Inn" and converted it to a private residence and offices. His Accounts show that he spent over £300 on building work.

Site: South side of High Street, now Berkeley House.

Formerly the Red Lion

Date	Tenant/Landlord	Information
1819-1858	Thomas Clarke	
1840	Richard Rideout	
1841	John Cross	
1859	William Parsons	
1861	Frederick Davidge	
1864-1866	Edward Ashford	1864 fined for selling beer during prohibited times.
1871		"Old & dilapidated but now under repair"
1873	Edward Dober	until September of that year and then
1873-1878	George Day	
1876		July death of mother-in-law of landlord.
1879		Use of old clubroom by new Working Mens' Club "at what was the Bell Inn."
1881		Insurance Policy refers to it as a private dwelling "lately known as the Bell Inn."
1898		"a very dilapidated Building, formerly a Public House known as the 'Bell Inn' but now unlicenced and for very many years let as a Tenement." Visitors of Sexey's Hospital propose to demolish and build new houses.

Site: Sexey Villas, opposite Sexey's Hospital.

Date	Tenant/Landlord	Information
		Two leases in 1728 and 1733 refer to a tenement and "that decay'd Tenement adjoining……..now thrown together known by the sign of the Blue Ball."
1768-1785	Thomas Penny	Premises insured with Sun Fire Office from 1775 1769 Court Baron reported 'the backhouse…to be much out of repair.' In December 1785 it was described as "A commodious and well accustomed Inn", when it was advertised to be Let as Thomas Penny was leaving, "whose ill state of health occasions his quitting the business."
1785-1798	Martha Penny	August 1793 referred to as a widow when she hired out Chaises to Revd. Woodforde. February 1798 Martha Penny now Bennett.
1798- 1827	Thomas Bennett	The Overseers of the Poor paid Mr Hannam "for taking care of a man that was Insane at the Blue Ball."
1827-1834	George Thrush	Formerly landlord of the Wellington Inn
1840-1853	Daniel Morgan	Invoice for June 1850 called it the 'Blue Ball

		Commercial Inn and Posting House' and advertized, "Flys, Gigs and Saddle Horses Let on Hire. Good old Wines, Foreign Spirits, Home Brewed Beer, Bottled & Draught, Porter, Cider, &c." In 1852 Morgan took out an Insurance Policy for the Inn with the Phoenix Fire Office, valued at £1,000.
1853-1866	Susan Morgan, widow	In 1853 Susan Morgan took out an Insurance Policy to cover both the Blue Ball and the Wellington Inn, each of which was described as having Stables and a Coachhouse. The total value was £720. She is described as the occupier of both.
1872	Robert Joseph Martin	
1878	Harry Rees Jones	
1879-1882	Miss Foster	
1887		21st January sold at auction to Messrs Jones & Sons of Bruton Brewery for £970.
1888-1889	Mr Bullons	
1894-1898	Tom Carbart	
1902-1911	Arthur George Hill	

Site: West side of Coombe Street, present location.

YE BOAR'S HEAD.

| Date | Tenant/Landlord | Information |

At some stage before 1704
became the Coach and
Horses.

Site: Silver Street, see site of Coach and Horses.

THE BULL AND BUTCHER.

Date	Tenant/Landlord	Information
1840	John Balch	

Site: West End

THE BULL'S HEAD ALEHOUSE.

Date	Tenant/Landlord	Information
1625-1627	John Colles	On 2nd November 1625 John Coles called an "Inhoulder" and buried on 23 December 1627, of "ye Bulles Hed."
1669	Margaret Mullens.	
1705-1713	Thomas Gane, junior.	Referred to as 'ye Bull's Head' in Copyhold dated 1689. In 1705 a Thomas Gane is called a beer-maker.
1734	John Bennett	Lease of 1726 calls it 'late Ganes'.
1768	John Darby	Tenement and Malthouse.
1769		Court Baron reported tenement 'late the Bull's head….to be much out of repair'.

| 1777 | William Hoare | A Tenement in Coombe Street late the Bull's Head Alehouse |

Site: Coombe Street.

THE CASTLE ALEHOUSE (1).

Date	Tenant/Landlord	Information
1680		Copyhold for the Castle Alehouse
1713	Matthew Gibbs	Copyhold dated 1707 for 'ye Castle Alehouse'
1734-1748	Arthur Thomas	
1748-1798	Robert Pavy	1794 referred to as 'late Castle'.

Site: South side of High Street, now 40 High Street.

THE CASTLE (2).

Date	Tenant/Landlord	Information
1840-1861	James Elliott	
1861	James Pearce	1858 James Pearce, fined for selling beer during prohibited hours.
1866	William Elliott	
1870-1906	George Mitchell	referred to as a beerhouse when in September 1870 Mitchell applied successfully for a spirit licence

Site: North side of High Street, present location.

THE COACH AND HORSES INN.

Formerly the Boar's Head.

Date	Tenant/Landlord	Information
1704-1713	William Coward	Lease 1704 referred to "ye Boars head, now ye Coach & Horses"
1713-1734	Martha Coward, widow.	
1768-1777	John Vigar	Lease may date back to 1737.
1798	Benjamin Ellis	'formerly the Coach and horses Inn'

Site: North side of Silver Street between the Car Park and the lane leading to the ford. When demolished became the location of the National School, and was later taken over by King's School.

THE SIGN OF THE COCK INN (1).

Date	Tenant/Landlord	Information
1745		Mentioned in lease

Site: West End, on the north side of the road, adjacent to the path to Mill

----

THE COCK INN (2).

Date	Tenant/Landlord	Information
	Edward King	
1768-1777	William Burge	In 1768 referred to as 'late Edward Kings'
1798	William Cozens	Late the Cock Inn.

246

Site: on the corner of Patwell Street and Church Bridge, opposite
Patwell. Became the Crown Inn.

THE CROOKED FISH.

Date	Tenant/Landlord	Information
1768-1777	John Vigar	Lease of tenement may date from 1717. 1768 Court Baron found it 'to be much out of repair.'
1798	Peter Oram	'late the Crooked Fish'
1810		Visitors of Sexey's Hospital paid 7s 8 ½d "half yrs Land Tax for late the Crooked Fish and Window Tax."

Site: South side of High Street, just to the west of the entrance to St
Katherine's Hill but on the opposite side of the road. Demolished by the
Visitors of Sexey's Hospital in 1882 to make way for their new Girls'
School which subsequently became the Master's House before the new
one was built.

THE CROWN INN (1)

Date	Tenant/Landlord	Information
	William Parker	
1734	William Vigar	Lease 1712 called it 'formerly the Sign of the Crown', and was late William Parker's.
1768-1777	Parker Davis	In 1777 'late the Crown Inn'.
1800		Court Baron reported that tenement 'formerly known by the name of the Crown Inn to be out of repair' and

ordered the tenant John Flagg to undertake repairs. He and his wife, Anne, failed to do so and were repeatedly warned. The result was that in October 1809 the tenement was forfeited to the Lord of the Manor.

Site: South side of High Street on the west side of the alley which leads from the High Street to Lower Back Way and now known as Crown Barton.

THE CROWN ALEHOUSE (2)

Date	Tenant/Landlord	Information
1768-1777	Clark & Martin	
1784-1789	Richard Stock	Paid Church Rate
1798	John Young	'formerly the Crown Alehouse'

Site: Quaperlake Street, north side, possibly including archway to east of Quaperlake House.

THE CROWN INN (3)

Formerly the Cock Inn

Date	Tenant/Landlord	Information
1798	William Cozens	
1841	Samuel Barnes	
1859	Sarah Barnes, widow	28 September 1859 married John Dobel, widower, Silversmith

1860-1861	John Dobel	Called a beerhouse when Dobel successfully applied for spirit licence in September 1860.
1861-1878	Hugh Hurden	
1894	Mrs Emma Sophia Bowring	
1897-1902	Thomas James	

Site: Corner of Patwell Street and Church Bridge. Closed in 1961 and demolished in 1964 to form part of the open space to the north of Church Bridge and to allow the road to be widened and the corner made less sharp.

THE FLEUR DE LIS INN.

Date	Tenant/Landlord	Information
1784-1798	John Melhuish	In 1798 'late the Fleur delis'.

Site: on the west side of Coombe Street, opposite the entrance to St David's Place.

THE FOX INN.

Formerly the Cock Inn.

Date	Tenant/Landlord	Information
1789		By 1789 renamed the Fox.
1790		Stabling for 16 horses.
1792-9	Burdock Roberts	"with four Rooms on a Floor, a Brewhouse, a four stalled Stable, another Stable in size for twelve Horses, a Wainhouse, a Calves' House, Pigscotes &c. Homestead,

Yard and Garden. Here is
an Inn, Licenced to sell
Ale and Liquors."

1803

Site: Redlynch.

THE GEORGE INN.

Date	Tenant/Landlord	Information
1576	Edmond Ansley	When buried on 30th September 1576 he was described as "gent" and in his Will he left to his 2 sons for their lives "a common inne or hostelry in Brewton called the signe of the George." Ansley's widow married Charles Pagett who, as guardian of the young boys, leased the Inn to William Purdewe, bellfounder, for four years. Shortly afterwards it reverted to the two sons, the eldest of whom, Henry baptised on 6 January 1563 was already in trouble "being a wilde youth, having carelessly and unthriftily spent his time in ill companie."
1669	Elizabeth White, widow.	Lease 26 July 1654 "neere the Crosse." In 1669 William Parker the younger had a Shambles in front of "the Signe of the George."

250

1715	William Plumer	In February refused to serve soldiers.
1717-1725	Charles Ricketson	In 1725 he paid for the Penthouse.
1765		Court Baron reported a side wall had fallen against adjacent property
1768		Court Baron reported Inn and outhouses 'to be greatly out of repair.'
1768-1777	John Gibbs	Lease dated 1727. In 1768 Frances Loaden paid for the Penthouse in the Market Place.
1784	George Prince	'late the George Inn.'

Site: on the north side of the High Street, number 5 (immediately to the west of the present Pharmacy)

THE GREEN DRAGON.

Date	Tenant/Landlord	Information
C17th		cited in Victoria County History, vol. VII, p. 22.

THE HALF MOON INN.

Date	Tenant/Landlord	Information
1750-1759		Paid Poor Rates
1768	Harry Albin Martin	"lately known by the name of the half Moon."
1794		Name still used for rating purposes in this year.

Site: north side of the High Street.

THE HOLE IN THE WALL ALEHOUSE.

Date	Tenant/Landlord	Information
1734	John Gibbs	Lease 1720, renewed 1754
1745	Elizabeth Cantelow, widow.	Moved to the White Hart
1759	Sarah Gibbs, widow	paid the poor rates
1761-1777	William Godfrey	described as a 'freestone Mason'.
1768		Court Baron reported stables 'to be in a ruinous condition.'
1786/7	Thomas Goldesbrough	'Late the hole in the Wall'.

Site: Coombe Street.

THE KINGS ARMS INN.

Date	Tenant/Landlord	Information
1669	John Sampson	Reversion granted to Matthew Druce.
1713-1734	James Druce	Copyhold 1703. Wife Elizabeth Premises insured with Sun Fire Office from 1723.
1743		September "to be let or sold...an ancient and accustomed Inn with about 20 acres of meadow and Pasture Ground."
1761		14 March. Sold by Auction along with a large Brewhouse, Stables and Garden.
1768	Dampier & Lloyd	Lease 1763.
1784-1813	John Cox	Lease 1769.

1813	John Vigar	'late the King's Arms'
1818	Mrs Theophilia Vigar	Licence obtained by the occupant, Revd. William Cotton, "that a certain House formerly the Kings Arms situate in the High Street.... is intended to be used for a place of religious Worship by Protestant dissenters from the Church of England commonly call'd Independents."

Site: north side of the High Street, now known as Stockwell House, No 13. Converted into two shops, one on either side of the passage way which ran through the middle to the yard at the back. Dr. Stockwell in the late nineteenth century converted it into a house and added the bow windows and the doorway with the shell over it.

THE LAMB.

Date	Tenant/Landlord	Information
1705		Constable paid 10s to the Lamb for drink for those who helped with the fire in Quaperlake Street.
1710-1716	Thomas Martin	1710-11 fined £3 for obstructing officers raising men for the armed forces. 1715-6 "at the Lambe", fined 50s for "hunting not being qualified."
1713-1727	John Martin	1713 at 'ye sign of ye Lamb' and 1727 Paid "John Martin for Beer."

Site: Quaperlake Street.

THE MAY POLE INN.

Date	Tenant/Landlord	Information
1734	Wilton Phipps	
1758-1759	William Hoar	Paid the Poor Rates
1777	Christopher Chaffin	
1784-1798	Richard Chaffin	1798 'late the May-pole Inn'.

Site: on the corner of Coombe Street and Quaperlake Street, opposite the Blue Ball Inn

----

OLD BULL INN.

Formerly the Bull Inn and the Six Bells.

Date	Tenant/Landlord	Information
1681		28 February burial of "Mr Ridout at the Bull".
1713	Hugh Ash, deceased.	Ye Bull Inn
1713	Sarah Bolton	'Tenemt called ye Bull Inn'.
	Now ye wife of Robert Buffett	
1733	Joseph Melhuish	Lease 1733, 'formerly the Bull Inn'. In 1731 a Joseph Melhuish had been fined £1 for "keeping a Common Alehouse" without a licence.
See Six Bells.		
1766-1777	John Beaumont	Lease 29 April 1766 refers to 'the Bull Inn'
1784	John Andrews	In 1784 called "The Old Bull, late the Six Bells."

1788-1808	William Meacham	In 1794 Meacham paid rates to the Churchwardens of 2 ½d for the Old Bull Inn and 3 ½d for the Six Bells. May suggest premises were on either side of the archway. William Meacham made his Will on 29th October 1805 and died in 1808, being buried on 10th April aged 76. He left the Old Bull to his wife and then his son John.
1808	John Meacham	Seems to have taken over the running of the Inn immediately as his mother was elderly. Ruth Meacham, aged 83 was buried on 15th April 1811.
1819	John Coles	
1840-1841	William White	
1844-1850	George Davis	
1858-1878	Joseph Huntley	
1881-1910	Frederick Steeds	

Site: west side of Patwell Street, near the top. No. 3

OLD DARBY AND JOAN.

Date	Tenant/Landlord	Information
1796	John Vigar	"the whole premises in very bad repair." Probably occupied as 2 tenements by this time.

Site:

THE PRINCE OF WALES BEER HOUSE.

Date	Tenant/Landlord	Information
1851	Susan Kittle	

Site: on north side of the hill leading to West End from the High Street, in a yard about half way down, possibly No. 85.

THE QUEEN'S HEAD.

Date	Tenant/Landlord	Information
1840-1841	Robert Dunn	
1850-1853	Stephen Lilley	
1856	Mrs Lilly	
1859-1878	Christopher Williams	December 1878 fined 1s for selling adulterated gin
1894-1898	George Vigar	

Site: West End at the corner of Shute Lane and Trendle Hill Lane.

THE RED LION.

Date	Tenant/Landlord	Information
1754	Thomas Viggar	Lease surrendered by Thomas Viggar for a Messuage or Tenement "now converted to a publick House with ye appurts lately now Erected situate opposite the Hospital."
1776	John Ford	Fined 10s "for Suffering Tipling in his house on Sunday the 15th Day of

Dec 1776 in time of Devine Services."

1784-1807	John Vigar	
1850	Thomas Clark	Lease by Visitors to Thomas Clark 1841, "lately known by the name or sign of the Red Lion now called the Bell Inn." He had probably held the lease from at least 1819.

Site: north side of High Street, opposite Sexey's Hospital, now occupied by Sexey Villas.

THE ROYAL OAK.

Date	Tenant/Landlord	Information
1840	Nicholas Lovett	Name does not appear in subsequent Trade Directories, so may have been regarded in the nineteenth century as a beerhouse rather than an inn.
1854	Isaac Golledge	Died in an apoplectic fit in December
1861	James Parsons	
1876	Mr. Evans	

Site: east side of Coombe Street in property still bearing the name.

SIGN OF THE HORSE SHOE.

Date	Tenant/Landlord	Information
1713	John Martin	Lease dated 1699

Site: Quaperlake Street.

THE SIX BELLS.

Formerly the Bull Inn

Date	Tenant/Landlord	Information
1758-9	James Penny	Paid Poor Rates in these years.
1765	John Beaumont	Lease 14 October 1765, "formerly the Bull Inn but now the Six Bells." Following year reverted to original name.

Site: west side of Patwell Street – see Old Bull Inn.

THE SUN INN.

Date	Tenant/Landlord	Information
1734	Nicholas Everet	Copyholds of 1705 and 1724 refer to 'the Signe of ye Sun.'
1753		Overseers of the Poor paid 3d "for the sick man brought from the Sun."
1756-1759	Robert Everett	In September 1756 fined 10s for allowing Tippling during the time of Divine Service.
1768		Court Baron reported the Sun's Stable 'to be much out of repair.'
1784-1807	John Sims	1780s Court Leets held there
1808-1840	William Sims	
1840	Samuel Pitman	
1841	John Down	

1850-1859	Joseph Huntley	
1859	Edward Thomas	
1861	Thomas Riddick	
1861-1878	James Pearce	
1894-1895	Harry Smith	
1897	Henry Oscar Smith	

Site: on the north side of High Street, present position although may have expanded in size.

THE SWAN BEERHOUSE.

Date	Tenant/Landlord	Information
1852-1892	Benjamin Hobbs	1852 Insurance Policy "assured as a Beerhouse and Shop Sixty Pounds." 1862 Benjamin Hobbs fined when sold beer during prohibited hours.
1898	Thomas and Benjamin Hobbs	In 1892 Frank Coward was the landlord and he handed over to John Jeffery in 1898.

Site: on the south side of the hill leading to West End from the High Street, in a yard called the Square.

THE SWAN INN.

Date	Tenant/Landlord	Information
1669		Thomas Guy held a Shamble on the "east parte of the Swan."
1725		Mrs Norman paid rent for the Swan Penthouse.

1746		Advertizement to let on Lady Day with 3 or 4 acres of ground, "situate in the middle of the Market, with good Stables for 20 horses to lodge, and a good Brewhouse and a good Malthouse...... with everything convenient for a House of entertainment."
1758		"Occupiers" paid the poor rates
1768		Reference to "New Building where the Swan stood."

Site: south side of the High Street, No. 30 and Chapel.

THE THREE BUTCHERS.

Date	Tenant/Landlord	Information
1738		cited in Victoria County History, vol. VII, p. 22

Site: Redlynch Common.

THE THREE GOATS HEADS.

Date	Tenant/Landlord	Information
1669	Daniel Wilton	

Site: Quaperlake Street.

THE UNICORN INN.

Date	Tenant/Landlord	Information
1596	Edward Chicke	"The Signe of the Unicorne".
1610		"an inn at Brewton called the Unicorne…where many lewd and suspicious persons gathered in April."
1623-1630	Edward Cheeke	
1656	Mr Cheeke	
1713-1717	John Cheeke	
1724	Thomas Cheeke	
1734	Mary Cheeke, widow.	
1736	John Oliver	Licence for Quakers to meet in "The Dwelling house & Backside of John Oliver in Bruton commonly called the Unicorn being a publick Inn."
1740s		Governors of King's School held their Meetings there.
1762	George Cox	late Mr Yetman.
1769-1787	J. Willcox	In 1769 Revd. Woodforde commented, "The Unicorn is not near so good as Ansford Inn. The Dinner was tolerably good – we had venison there" for which he paid 3s 9d and 10d for servants' dinner.
1792-1794	John Sims	In 1794 referred to in the Churchwardens' Accounts as 'void'.
1795	Thomas Sampson	'late the Unicorn Inn'.
1798	Edward Michell	'late the Unicorn Inn'.

Site: on the north side of the High Street, No. 15.

THE WELLINGTON INN.

Date	Tenant/Landlord	Information
1813	H.J. Wallace	
1823	Robert Candy	
1826-7	George Thrush	Moved to the Blue Ball Inn.
1840	William Jason Jones Hole	
1841	Edward Holton	
1850	Daniel Morgan and then Susan Morgan – see Blue Ball Inn	
1851-1866	Ann Styles	11 June 1860 Ann Styles married Harry Herrington, yeoman, by Licence.
1872-1878	Mary Ann Holton	
1881	Joseph Taylor	
1884	Albert Featherstone	alleged fraudulent bankruptcy in February 1884
1889	William Henry Banting	
1894-1898	Mrs Amanda Smith	
1902	George Eastwood	

Site: corner of Patwell Street and Quaperlake Street. When demolished it was replaced by the building known as the Ward Library.

THE WHITE BULL INN.

Date	Tenant/Landlord	Information
1713	Eleanor Francis now wife of John Viggar, junior	Lease 1708 'ye White Bull'
1734-1777	John Vigar	Leases renewed in at least 1730 and 1740. The length of time involved may suggest more than one

		generation of John Vigar, for example, a John Vigar senior was buried on 10th January 1758.
1758-9	Martha Ellis, widow,	paid the poor rates
1774	William Oliver	Named as 'Innholder' when he took out an insurance policy with the Sun Fire Office.
1784	Robert Harris	
1794	Mrs Harris	In the Churchwardens' Accounts referred to as 'void'.
1795	James James	'late the White Bull'

Site: north side of the High Street, in the position now occupied by the Castle.

THE WHITE HART INN.

Date	Tenant/Landlord	Information
1588		December 9th Parish Registers record that "George Bathrin, gent, died at the Hart."
1603	John Illing	"the signe of the Harte".
1669	John Iling	
1691-1705	William Gibbs	Constables and Churchwardens paid for "drink at Wm Gibbs" in 1691, 1702 and 1705. William Gibbs, senior died in 1712.
1713-1723	John Gibbs	Lease 1712 and in 1723

		takes out an Insurance Policy with the Sun Fire Office.
		October 1714 disturbance at "The White heart"
1725-1734	Matthew Gibbs	
1731		Serious fire.
1742		September. Sale of "Household Goods of the late Mr Matthew Gibbs." Date of burial not recorded in Parish Registers
1745	Elizabeth Cantelow	1745 advertized for sale having "been shut for upwards of Two years last past," but "now kept by Elizabeth Cantelow of the same place, widow, removed from the 'Hole in the Wall' to the said Inn."
1750	Mrs Gibbs	
1751		Governors of King's School hold Meeting there.
1768-1777	Matthew Gibbs	Described in 1768 as "A Tenemt or Inn Stables & Curtilage."
1775	John Rawlins	Rawlins referred to as 'Innholder' when he took out an insurance policy in that year with the Sun Fire Office.
1784-1798	William James	In the Churchwardens' Accounts for 1794 referred to as 'void' and in 1795-6 as 'late the White Hart'.

Site: on the corner of the High Street and Coombe Street, in the position now occupied by the Blue Ball Hotel and No 1 High Street. As there is an overlap in time with the name of the two inns and as the White Hart was originally so large, it is possible that about 1768 it was reduced to just No 1 High Street and the Blue Ball became a separate Inn.

THE WHITE HORSE.

Date	Tenant/Landlord	Information
1750	James Thomas	.
1758	Widow Thomas	paid the poor rates
1798	Emanuel White	'formerly the White Horse'.

Site: the east side of Coombe Street, just above the property called the Royal Oak.

THE WHITE LION.

Date	Tenant/Landlord	Information
1734-1777	Henry Ricketson	Lease 1717, renewed in 1741. Probably more than one generation as a Henry Ricketson was buried on 26th April 1742. 1769 Court Baron reported 'The tenement late the White Lyon…to be much out of repair.'
1796		"the house late the White Lion, to be greatly out of repair."
1798	John Sims	'late the White Lion Inn."

Site: at West End on the corner of Shute Lane and West End, No. 95

Names of men and women involved in the sale of alcohol but premises not identified.

1555	Licence for 10 years to Henry Hussey to keep a tavern or taverns and sell wines.
1576	payment "for drinking at Haywardes."
1604	John Alvyn als Dollyn, innholder, leased Combe Close or Combe Allers.
1612	Cecilia Parker, Richard and Joanna Tabor excommunicated "for tipling and keeping ill rule upon Sundaies and holie dayies."
1623	Richard Coles obtains a malting licence.
1627	Thomas Hoskins "doth keepe drinking and playing in his howse on Sabbath dayes"
1629	Sidney Pomfrey, an innkeeper.
1629	John Stacey charged at Quarter Sessions with tipling and selling ale without a licence.
1641	"Dakes beere."
1653	Richard Wayte "who keepes an Ale howse." In 1657 Richard Waight, innholder, sent a petition to the Quarter Sessions.
1655	Richard Maby, "Alehowse keeper."
1661	Thomas Coppen, beer seller
1705	Richard Lumber, an alehouse keeper.
1715	John Bisby fined 10s "for Suffering Tipling in his House in the time of Divine Service."
1731	William Chafyn, fined £1 for "keeping a Common Alehouse" without a licence Rose Berryman ditto
1738	Mary Martin, sent to Ilchester Gaol for selling "Spiritous Liquors."
1743	Anne Hill, fined 10s for "keeping a disorderly House" on a Sunday.
1746	Mrs Anne Clarke, a widow, fined £4 "for denying entertainment to Soldiers Quartered in her House."
1759	James Andrew, an innkeeper.
1789	William Oliver, fined £2 for selling beer without a licence.

1841	Thomas Martin, Beer Seller in High Street
	Richard Day, Beer Seller at West End
1851	Anne Elliott, Beer Seller in High Street
1857	John Elliott, beer-house keeper
1859	William Parsons, fined for selling beer during prohibited hours.
1866	Elizabeth Ellicott, a beerhouse keeper, appeared before Wincanton Magistrates for infringing the Beerhouse Acts. Case dismissed.
1868	Daniel Vigar, beerhouse keeper

Queen's Head at West End.

Carving above door of Queen's Head

Notes and References.

DRO   Dorset Record Office

PRO   National Archives formerly Public Record Office

SANHSP   Somerset Archaeological and Natural History Society Proceedings

SDNQ   Somerset and Dorset Notes and Queries

SRO   Somerset Record Office/Heritage Centre

SRS   Somerset Record Society

WRO   Wiltshire Record Office/Heritage Centre

1.   E.P. Thompson, 'Eighteenth Century English Society: Class Struggle without Class?', in Social History, vol. III, 1978, pp.157-8; WRO Hoare Papers 383/327, A Survey of the Mannor of Brewton 1669; J. Beresford, ed., The Diary of a Country Parson, the Reverend James Woodforde, vol. I, 1758-1781, Oxford, 1968, p. 103. The Reverend James Woodforde was born in 1740, the second son the Rev. Samuel Woodforde the Rector of Ansford and Vicar of Castle Cary. After an education which included Oxford, he was ordained and then between 1763 and 1773 returned to Ansford to serve several curacies. In 1774 he moved to Weston in Norfolk as its Vicar and remained there until his death on 1st January 1803. During that period, however, he visited family and friends in Somerset on many occasions, usually staying with his sister, Jane who had married John Pouncett and lived at Cole. These visits often lasted up to three months and so he was well placed to observe the activities and social scene in the Bruton area.   .

DRO Ilchester Papers D/FSI/218, Household Accounts (Redlynch) 1732-1762; J. Beresford, Diary, op.cit., vol. I, p. 83.

For details of the philanthropy of individuals in Bruton, see P.W. Randell, Stones We Cannot Eat: Poverty, the Poor Law, Philanthropy and Self Help in Bruton, Somerset, c1500-c1900, Brighton, 2009, esp. pp. 359-367.

Oak Apple Day was widely celebrated in the Castle Cary area in the mid-nineteenth century when boys and men wore one or two oak leaves or an oak-apple in their buttonholes. Horses would have their heads decorated with small twigs from oak trees and public houses and also some private dwellings would have whole branches from oak trees outside of their premises. It was also known as Shig-shag Day, a term which was often seen as abuse and was shouted by boys at others who were not wearing an oak leaf. In some instances the unfortunate victim was chased by the other boys who were armed with stinging nettles. At noon all the oak leaves were thrown away and any one who had the term shouted at them after that could reply:

> Shig-shag's gone past
> You're the biggest fool at last;
> When Shig-shag comes again
> You'll be the biggest fool then.

For more details see Castle Cary Visitor, vol. X, 1914-5, p. 118.
For a fuller account of the rural year and its celebrations see R. Hutton, The Rise and Fall of Merry England: The Rural Year 1400-1700, Oxford, 2001, especially pp. 5-45.
2. J. Leland, Itinerary, vol. II, London, 1710, p. 74; PRO PROB 11/29, 133, Last Will and Testament of Robert Chyk 1542; Report of the Select Committee on the State of Children Employed in Manufacturers 1816, PP 1816

XIII, Evidence of John Sharrer Ward, pp. 74-6; Report of the Select Committee on the Silk Trade 1832, PP 1831-2 XIX, Minutes of Evidence of John S. Ward, p. 209; The Universal British Directory, vol. II, 1794, pp. 390-1; E. K. Kelly, ed., The Post Office Directory for Somersetshire, London, 1875, pp. 341-2.

3. Some indication of the level of gifts to Bruton Priory may be found in Bruton and Montacute Cartulary, SRS, vol. 8, 1894; Somerset Medieval Wills 1383-1500, SRS, vol. 16, 1901, pp. 220-1, 348; Somerset Medieval Wills 1501-1530, SRS, vol. 19, 1903, pp. 98-9, 251; PRO PROB 11/19, Will of Alice Brymmore, 1517; Revd. F. Brown, 'The Family of Fitzjames', in SANHSP, vols. 24-5, 1878-9, p. 36; SRO DD/WR/2, Will of Sir Henry Berkeley, 1600; D. L. Hayward, ed., The Registers of Bruton, Co. Somerset, 1554-1813; SRS, vol. 16, op.cit., pp. 87, 348; Somerset Medieval Wills 1531-1558, SRS, vol. 21, 1905, pp. 86-7.
   For a fuller account of the role of the Church Courts in Bruton, see P.W. Randell, Crime, Law and Order in a Somersetshire Market Town: Bruton c1500-c1900, Brighton, 2011, pp. 80-114.
   SRO Q/SR Sacramental Certificates, 315/268, 318/3/60, 322/2/70, 330/2/54, 335/3/67; Quarter Session Records, James I, SRS, vol. 23, 1907, p. 357; SRO D/P/brut 9/1/1, Bruton Select Vestry Minute Book for the Administration of the Poor 1790-1806.

4. H. de Misson, 'Memoirs and Observations', cited in R.W. Malcolmson, Popular Recreations in English Society, 1700-1850, Cambridge, 1973, p. 44; Calendar of the Manuscripts of the Dean and Chapter of Wells, vol. II, London, 1914, Letter from Edward VI, pp. 264-5; SRO D/D/cta, Inventories W36 and A18; SRO D/P/brut, 13/2/2 and 13/2/10, Bruton Overseers' Accounts; SRO D/P/brut

4/1/1 and 4/1/2, Bruton Churchwardens' Accounts; Castle Cary Visitor, vol. IV, 1902-3, p. 49; 'Sherborne Journal', 25 March 1831; Castle Cary Visitor, vol. VI, 1906-7, p. 28; SRO D/P/brut 9/1/3, Bruton Church Minute Book: loose sheet headed 'St Mary the Virgin Bruton, Belfry Rules, 1901'; J. Beresford, Diary, op.cit., vol. I, p. 35; 'Shepton Mallet Journal', 28 May 1858.

5. John Gay, The Shepherd's Week, Oxford, 1950, p.102; J. Beresford, Diary, op.cit., vol. IV, pp. 222-3; Gentleman's Magazine, vol. LXXV, 1805, part I, p. 202; Calendar of Letters and Papers, Domestic and Foreign, Henry VIII, vol. V, 1531-1532, London, 1880, p. 456; Calendar of Letters and Papers, Domestic and Foreign, Henry VIII, vol. VI, 1533, London, 1882, p. 189; WRO Hoare Papers 383/142, Reply to the Society of Antiquaries, undated but c1757, No. 44; M. St. Clare Bryne, ed., The Lisle Letters, vol. I, Chicago, 1981, p. 336; E. Robinson, et al. ed., Cottage Tales, John Clare, Ashington, 1993, p. 55; 'Western Flying Post', 17 August 1752. For a discussion of the dates of fairs in Somerset, see Somerset and Dorset Notes and Queries, vol. XXXVI, pp. 124-33, 308-13, 361-4; DRO Ilchester Papers FSI Box 189, General Day Book, 1735-54; WRO Hoare Papers 383/326, A Survey of the Manour of Brewton, 1734; WRO 383/427, Leases 1717-1784; WRO 383/160, Survey of Bruton c1816; WRO 383/159, Leasehold Property at Bruton, undated but probably pre 1820; 'Western Flying Post', 29 April 1843, 26 September 1846, 21 September 1852; 'Western Gazette', 30 April 1864, 27 April 1873; 'Shepton Mallet Journal', 25 April 1873; W.G. Willis Watson, Calendar of Customs, Superstitions, etc. , Somerset County Herald, 1920, pp. 323-4; SRO DD/HY 16/2/3, Account Book of James Twyford, 1679-1727, p. 195; G. Sweetman, Stavordale Priory, Wincanton, Wincanton, 1900, pp. 13-15; 'Salisbury Journal', 1 July 1793; DRO Ilchester

Papers D/FSI Box 167A: Redlynch Manor, Abstract of Leases; Box 170A, A Survey of the Manor of Redlinch, September 1712; 'Western Flying Post', 19 June 1749; SDNQ, vol. XXXVI, op.cit., p. 363; W. Howitt, The Rural Life of England, London, 1838, p. 497. A narrative version of the dispute between Sir Henry Berkeley and the Earl of Pembroke may be found in L. Hotson, I, William Shakespeare, London, 1937, pp. 71-92; SRO Quarter Sessions Records Q/SR 59/15-17, Examination and Information April and June 1627; SRO Q/SR/64/97, Information 27 April 1631; SRO Q/SR 38/60-1, Examination and Information 1621.

6. 'Western Flying Post', 17 August 1752, 15 September 1755; WRO Hoare Papers 383/157, Accounts with Mr Dyne 1807-1810; Gentleman's Magazine, vol. VIII, 1738, p. 465; W. Borlase, The Natural History of Cornwall, Oxford, 1758, p. 301; 'Western Flying Post', 20 September 1756; John Clare, Village Minstrel; R.L. Winstanley, ed., The Ansford Diary of James Woodforde, vol. 4, 1769-1771, published privately by the Parson Woodforde Society, 1986, p. 63; ibid., vol. 3, p, 108; 'Western Flying Post', 12 September 1791, 27 August 1750. For the recollection of Bruton Feast about 1818 see C. Clark, Tales from Old Bruton, Charledon Publications, 1998, pp. 15-6. A Donnybrook fight was a free-for-all, a public brawl which took its name from the village in Ireland where their annual fair, which could last up to fifteen days, was accompanied by extensive fighting. By the eighteenth century it was a term widely used for any public brawl. Maiden Hill may be a misunderstanding and could be Marydown. Pitcombe also seems to have staged a Feast as there is a passing reference to it by Woodforde on 8 November 1773 when he recorded "Pitcombe Feast today – Brother John at it." vol. 5, p.181.

7. A. Everitt, 'Farm Labourers', in J. Thirsk, ed., The

Agrarian History of England and Wales, vol. IV, 1500-1640, Cambridge, 1967, p. 451; W. Savage, 'Somerset Towns', in SANHSP, vol. 99, 1954-5, p. 54; R.W. Dunning, Victoria History of the Counties of England: Somerset, vol. IX, 2006, p. 142; SRO Q/SR 11/34, 1611; Calendar of Patent Rolls, Elizabeth, vol. III, 1563-1566, London, 1960, pp. 322-3.

8. J. Leland, op.cit., vol. II, p.45; Replies, op.cit., No. 32; WRO Hoare Papers 383/327, A Survey of the Mannor of Brewton in the Countie of Somersett, 1669.
    There are two further points which need to be made concerning the Market Cross. Although traditionally viewed as being built by the Abbot, a small number of surviving Wills from that period do suggest that other inhabitants were involved as well, for example that of Robert Chyk previously cited. Secondly, and probably more significant, there is some disagreement about the description of the Cross. Leland refers to six arches but the respondent to the Society of Antiquaries in the 1750s, at a time when the Cross was still standing, calls it "a Pentagon, it is supported by five Pillars on the outside." That would create five arches and not six. As all other accounts date from the time after the Cross was taken down it is impossible to determine which was correct. The only other almost contemporary account was from Collinson, writing in 1791, just after its demolition, and he refers to it as "a curious old hexagonal market Cross", but he may not have actually seen it and was using Leland as his source. J. Collinson, The History and Antiquities of the County of Somerset, Bath, 1791, p. 211. 'Old Barton' was the area immediately at the top of St. Catherine's Hill before Tolbury House and on the eastern side.

9. WRO Hoare Papers 865/588, Letter from Fitzharding, 25 June 1684; SRO DD/SE 58/1, Survey of Tenements of Sexey's Hospital, 1716; SRO DD/ CTN Box 8,

Bruton Hospital Leases, 1803; SRO Q/RRW, Meeting House Licences 1736 and 1752; Replies, op.cit., No. 44; 'Sherborne Mercury', 23 January 1749; G.V. Harrison, 'The South West', in J. Thirsk, ed., The Agrarian History of England and Wales, vol. V, 1640-1750, Cambridge, 1984, p. 376; Howitt, op.cit., p. 87; Castle Cary Visitor, vol. X, 1914-5, Bruton Market 1788, p. 146; 'Western Flying Post', 22 February 1808; Castle Cary Visitor, vol. X, op.cit., Bruton Market, 1818 p. 162; Pigot, London and Provincial Commercial Directory: Somerset 1822-3, p. 438; 'Yeovil Times', 5 November 1850; 'Somerset and Wilts Journal', 25 August 1855; 'Western Flying Post', 25 September 1855; 'Somerset and Wilts Journal', 12 January 1856; Post Office Directory: Somerset 1861, p. 300; C. Clark, ed., Diary of a Wessex Farmer, Josiah Jackson 1882-1904, Charldon Publications, 1996, see for example 16 June 1896 p. 177, 8 July 1896 p. 178; SRO D/D/ca 196, Ex Officio 1615; SRO Q/SR 38/20, Information March 1621; SRO Q/SR 86/49-50, Information and Examination 19 and 21 September 1653.

10. H. Fielding, An Enquiry into the Causes of the late Increase of Robbers, London, 1751, p. 7; PRO PROB 11/19, Will of Alice Brymmore, 1517; Somerset Medieval Wills, SRS, vol. 19, 1903, p. 207; Somerset Wills from Wells, SRS, vol. 40, 1925, p. 23; Somerset Medieval Wills, SRS, vol. 21, 1905, pp. 48-50; PRO PROB 11/163/535, Will of Agnes Morris 1632/3; Replies, op.cit., No. 38; SRO DD/BT 27/8, Surveyor's Note Book 1831-2, 6th September 1831; 'Western Flying Post', notice of Auction, 23 January 1855; Gentleman's Magazine, 1789, pt. II, pp. 800-1; 'The Travels through England of Dr Richard Pococke', Camden Society, New Series, vol. 44, 1889, p. 150; H. Walpole's description of Redlynch House cited in J. Martin, Wives and Daughters: Women and Children in a Georgian Country House, London,

2004, p. 89; C. Clay, Public Finance and Private Wealth: The Career of Sir Stephen Fox, 1627-1716, Oxford, 1978, pp. 209-10.

11. For some account of violence in the Bruton area see, P.W. Randell, Crime, Law and Order, op.cit., esp. for violence pp. 48-72 and for poaching pp. 15-23; J. Beresford, Diary, op.cit., vol. I, p. 12; Winstanley, Diary, op.cit., vol. 4, p. 130; Bishop Beckynton's Register, SRS., vol. 49, 1934, p. 181; Earl of Ilchester, The Home of the Hollands 1605-1820, privately printed, 1937, p. 46; 'Shepton Mallet Journal', 20 December 1872, 3 December 1875; WRO Hoare Papers 383/13, Notebook of Sir R.C. Hoare; Howitt, op.cit., pp. 30, 32; J. Beresford, Diary, op.cit., vol. II, p.267, vol. IV, pp. 55-6; 'Western Flying Post', 12 September 1791; J. Beresford, Diary, op.cit., vol. I, p. 33, also pp. 78-9, vol. II, p. 272; 'Shepton Mallet Journal', 9 April 1869, 11 February 1870; WRO Hoare Papers, 383/114, Letter from W. Philip to Sir R.C. Hoare, n.d. but early nineteenth century; C. Clark, Diary, op. cit., 23 November 1897 p. 204, 22 November 1895 p. 165, 10 March 1897 p. 191, 2 November 1897 p. 203, 12 December 1898 p. 223; 'Western Gazette', 28 February 1863.

12. SRO DD/BT 25/1, Letter Book of T.O. Bennett, 1873: Letter to Sir Henry Hoare 26 September; C. Clark, Diary, op.cit., 24 January 1899 p. 225, 10 March 1899 p. 227, 16-17 November 1899 p. 236; 'Western Gazette', 31 March 1876; ibid. 5 July 1889; J. Beresford, Diary, op.cit, vol. IV, p. 232; Winstanley, Diary, op.cit., vol. 2, 11 January 1764; 'Shepton Mallet Journal', 15 January 1875, 23 May 1879; 'Western Flying Post', 30 December 1856; 'Western Gazette', 22 December 1876; J. Beresford, Diary, op.cit., vol. I, p. 79, vol. II, p. 257, vol. III, p. 119; Gentleman's Magazine, 1789, pt. II, p. 801; 'Western Flying Post', 30 December 1856; 'Shepton Mallet

Journal', 6 January 1876; SRO DD/BT 25/97, Sexey's Hospital Letter Book 1893-1896: Letter 16 December 1895; The Lisle Letters, op.cit., p. 334; J. Beresford, Diary, op.cit., vol. IV, pp. 224 and 227; WRO Hoare Papers, 383/114, Game List, 1807; C. Clark, Diary, op.cit., see for example 31 December 1894 p. 148, 20 December 1895 p. 166, 1 December 1899 p. 237.

13. SRO D/D/ ca 289, Comperta 12 November 1633; Howitt, op.cit., p. 31 J. Beresford, Diary, op.cit., vol. III, pp. 131-2, vol. IV, p. 229; 'Western Flying Post', 31 July 1749; Winstanley, Diary, op.cit., vol. 4, pp. 52,134-5; 'Western Flying Post', 13 February and 13 August 1832, 28 July, 1 September and 15 September 1834; ibid., 21 September 1772; 'Shepton Mallet Journal', 21 June 1867; B. Wright, ed., King's School Bruton Remembered, Castle Cary, 1991, pp. 25 and 30; ibid., p. 15.

14. Replies, op.cit., No. 15; SRO DD/BRU 2/1/1, Governors' Account Book 1679-1757; SRO DD/BT 7/2, Bruton Hospital Small Account Book, vol. I, 1791-1798; R. Winstanley, Diary, op.cit., vol. 4, pp. 51 and 111; SRO DD/BRU 1/2/1, Governors' Register 1554-1700; 'Western Flying Post', 9 April 1770; ibid 7 March 1808; J. Beresford, Diary, op.cit., vol. I, p. 254, vol. II, pp. 35, 258; DRO D/FSI/Box 189, General Day Book 1735-1754 and Box 218, Housekeeping Expences 1747-1752; SRO D/D/Ca 267, 9 September 1626; SRO D/D/Ca 310, October 1636; J. Beresford Diary, op. cit., vol. I, pp. 63, 93, 107, 87, 108 and 254.

15. R. Winstanley, Diary, op.cit., vol. 1, p. 183, vol. 4, p. 225; J. Beresford, Diary, op.cit., vol. I, pp. 56, 100; ibid., p., 57; 'Shepton Mallet Journal', 20 April 1866; 'Western Gazette', 13 January 1888; J. Beresford, Diary, op.cit., vol. I, p. 52; J. Martin, ed., A Governess in the Age of Jane Austen: The Journals and Letters of Agnes Porter, London, 1998, p. 324; J. Beresford, Diary, op.cit., vol.

I, pp. 61-2; 'Shepton Mallet Journal', 20 March 1863; SRO DD/ BRU 10/6, Report of Celebrations June 1850; J. Beresford, Diary, op.cit., vol. I, p. 62; 'Western Flying Post', 12 September 1791; ibid., 9 May 1836.
For accounts of Subscription Balls, see for example, 'Western Flying Post', 17 January 1842, 10 January 1846, and 'Somerset and Wilts Journal', 11 February 1860.
For other Balls, see for example, 'Shepton Mallet Journal', 22 February 1867, 3 January 1868, 8 January 1869 and 'Western Gazette', 13 May 1881.

16. R. Winstanley, Diary, op.cit., vol. 5, p. 41; J. Beresford, Diary, op.cit., vol. IV, pp. 57, 45, 49, vol. I, pp. 88 and 100; J. Martin, op.cit., p. 118.
For Woodforde's card playing, see for example, ibid., vol. I, p. 81, vol. II, pp. 38 and 269, vol. III, p. 135, vol. IV, pp. 228 and 230.
'Western Flying Post', 12 September 1791; J. Martin op.cit., pp. 27-8, 324; SRO DD/X/KR, Pocket Ledger of J. Goldesbrough 19 August 1816; PRO PROB 11/149, Will of Dame Elizabeth Berkeley, 1626; PRO PROB 11/662, Will of Lucy Temple, 1733; J. Beresford, Diary, op.cit., vol. I, p. 78; Earl of Ilchester, op.cit., pp. 45-6.

17. 'Somerset and Wilts Journal', 6 August, 26 February 1859; 'Shepton Mallet Journal', 20 October 1871; 'Western Flying Post', 19 February 1856; 'Western Gazette', 23 January 1891; ibid., 6 February 1891; ibid., 3 February, 10 February 1888, 4 April 1890; 'Somerset and Wilts Journal', 6 August 1859; F. Kelly, ed., Directory for Somerset, 1861, London, p. 300; F. Kelly, ed., County Topographies: Somersetshire, London, 1875, p. 120; C. Clark, Diary, op.cit., 6 October 1893 p. 129, 2, 18 and 20 November, 14 December 1893, 30 March 1894, p. 130; 'Western Gazette', 20 March 1891; 'Shepton Mallet Journal', 8 December 1865.
For an account of education for the poor in Bruton, see

P.W. Randell, Stones etc. op.cit., esp. pp. 325-350. 'Western Gazette', 18 March 1898; 'Shepton Mallet Journal', 15 July 1859, 'Western Gazette', 3 November 1882, 24 February 1888.

18. 'Somerset and Wilts Journal', 21 July 1855; 'Shepton Mallet Journal', 4 April 1879; 'Western Gazette', 13 March 1891; Castle Cary Visitor, vol. VI, 1906-7, p. 103; 'Shepton Mallet Journal', 5 March 1886, ibid. 16 April 1858, ibid. 3 December 1875; 'Western Gazette', 10 May 1889, 9 May 1890; 'Shepton Mallet Journal', 30 December 1859, 11 May 1860; 'Shepton Mallet Journal', 1 May 1863; 'Western Gazette', 26 December 1879; Castle Cary Visitor, vol. V, 1904-5, p. 47; 'Shepton Mallet Journal', 4 February 1859; 'Western Flying Post', 2 January 1855; 'Western Gazette', 20 May 1881; 'Somerset and Wilts Journal', 9 July 1859; ibid. 19 November 1880; 'Shepton Mallet Journal', 24 March 1876.

19. The majority of the examples of entertainments cited in this section in the period up to 1880 are taken from the 'Shepton Mallet Journal' and those in the 1880s and 1890s from the 'Western Gazette'.
For handbell ringers see C. Clark, Diary, op.cit., 23 October 1889 p. 69, 9 February 1893 p. 119 and 8 February 1894 p. 134.
For ad hoc celebrations in detail, see P.W. Randell, Stones etc. op.cit., pp. 379-384. 'Somerset and Wilts Journal', 22 September 1855; 'Shepton Mallet Journal', 8 July 1864; Castle Cary Visitor, vol. I, 1896-7, p. 152.

20. C. Dukes, Health at School, London, 1894, p. 284; H.B. Philpott, London at School: the Story of the School Board, London, 1904, p. 127; 'Shepton Mallet Journal', 20 July, 6 August, 3 September 1858, 6 July 1877; Castle Cary Visitor, Vol. IX, 1912-1913, Hadspen Cricket Club: Recollections of W.E. Cooper, pp. 22 and 26; C. Clark,

Diary, op.cit., for cricket 31 March and 2 April 1891 p. 86, 6 June 1892 p. 105, for football 13 September 1893 p. 127, 17 February 1894 p. 134, 23 and 24 August 1895 p. 160, 8 and 9 September 1897 p. 200; Castle Cary Visitor, vol. IV, 1902-3, p. 131; Sweetman's Monthly Illustrated Journal, April 1874; B. Wright, op.cit., p. 11; 'The Dolphin', Christmas 1925, p. 5, where it was also recorded that the boys played hockey "with ordinary walking stick crooks or hedge sticks with bent ends." C. Clark, Diary, op.cit., 26 August 1893 p. 127; B. Wright, op.cit., p. 16; H. Scott, Your Obedient Servant, London, 1959, p. 14; B. Wright, op.cit., pp. 30-1; 'Western Gazette', 24 June and 21 October 1898; ibid., 17 July 1891.

21. SRO DD/LW/31, Extract of Minutes; 'Shepton Mallet Journal', 15 January 1886, 29 October 1858; 'Western Gazette', 6 October 1882; C. Clark, Diary, op.cit., see for example 27 November 1896 p. 185, 18 and 26 March 1897 p. 192.

22. 'Western Flying Post', 15 December 1834; 'Shepton Mallet Journal', 22 October 1858; 'Western Flying Post', 13 December 1841, 10 December 1842; 'Shepton Mallet Journal', 23 December 1859; 'Western Flying Post', 11 December 1847, 19 December 1863; ibid. 25 July, 15 August, 12 October 1854; 'Shepton Mallet Journal', 19 November 1880; Willis Watson, Calendar, op.cit., pp. 387-390 details particularly the importance of the Ploughing Matches; 'Shepton Mallet Journal', 30 November 1860; 'Western Flying Post', 18 December 1866.

The *Alabama* was a ship built at Birkenhead, purchased by the Southern States of America which managed to beat the embargo on such ships being sent to America as it was on sea trials. As a warship it was extremely successful and sank a large number of vessels of the Northern States.

After the Civil War the U.S.A. launched a successful
bid for compensation against the British Government,
although the amount it received was just a fraction of the
sum originally demanded.
'Western Flying Post', 13 December 1853; 'Western
Gazette', 14 October 1892; C. Clark, Diary, op.cit., 10,
11, 15, October 1892 p. 111;
A. Partridge, 'Bruton, a Town in a Dilemma' in Somerset
and Wessex Life, vol. 7, January 1973, p. 28 contains
a reminiscence that Blondin was in Bruton in 1896
and Castle Cary Visitor, vol. IV, 1902-3 records that,
"'Blondin' gave a tight-rope performance at 3.30" in
1902.
'Shepton Mallet Journal', 23 December 1859; SRO DD/
BT 25/1. Letter Book of T.O. Bennett, April-November
1873: Letter to R.H. Paget, M.P., 8 November 1873;
'Shepton Mallet Journal, 27 January 1871, 18 December
1863.

23. R.K.R. Thornton, ed., The Rural Muse: Poems by John
Clare, 1835, Ashington, 1982, p. 106. For a discussion
of crime and violence in the Bruton area see P.W.
Randell, Crime, op.cit., esp. pp. 8-80. For more details
of Sword and Dagger through time see J. Clements, 'Get
Thee a Waster' published by Arma: the Association for
Renaissance Martial Arts, **www.thearma.org**. 'Western
Flying Post', 27 August 1750, 10 September 1768, 19
September 1774, 12 September 1791, 1 May 1749, 14
September 1772, 9 September 1751; 'Salisbury Journal',
13 September 1790; SRO Q/AGi 15/2 and 15/3, Ilchester
Description Books 1824-1827, 1828-1838; 'Western
Flying Post', 13 October 1806; 'Salisbury and Winchester
Journal', 3 June 1811; 'Shepton Mallet Journal', 11
September 1863; Replies, op.cit., No. 30; 'Western Flying
Post', 9 September 1754; J. Beresford, Diary, op.cit., vol.
I, pp. 89-90, 110, 86. Crocker was the tenant of the Royal

Oak in Castle Cary/Ansford. Winstanley, Diary, op.cit., vol 5, p. 73; Winstanley, Diary, op.cit., vol. 4, pp. 130, 112-113; John Clare, Village Minstrel, 83.

24. G. Sandys, ed., English Worthies in Church and State, London, 1684, p. 740, an abridged version of Fuller's Worthies. 'Sherborne Mercury', 4 April 1748; SRO DD/SE/58/2, A Survey of Lands lying in & near Brewton, belonging to the Hospital of Hugh Sexey, Esq., June 1717.

Bull Plott or Bull Pit was a name used for this field within living memory. There used to be a depression in the field which was probably an old quarry. It was filled in when part of the field was used as a football pitch for Bruton Town Football Club with the old Nissan Hut serving as the changing rooms and from which tea was served at half time.

DRO Ilchester Papers, D/FSI, Box 218, Accounts; J. Beresford, Diary, op.cit., vol. I, p. 12; the case of Swallow v. Finch cited in Castle Cary Visitor, vol. X, 1914-15, p. 188; SRO Q/SR 222/8 and 10, and 230/5, Examinations June 1703; 'Sherborne Mercury', 5 February 1740, 10 May 1747; J. Beresford, Diary, op.cit., vol. I, pp. 86, 108; Thynne Papers, Longleat House, TH. vol. XII 1665-1711, Letter from Viscount Fitzharding, 13 March 1686; 'Western Flying Post', 23 February 1784.

25. D. Hay et. al., Albion's Fatal Tree: Crime and Society in Eighteenth Century England, London, 1975, pp. 66-7. For more details on punishments used in Bruton see P.W. Randell, Crime, op.cit. pp. 220-234. Although penance in a church was medieval in origin, it clearly continued for several centuries as on 3rd February 1768 Revd. Woodforde noted in his Diary, "One Sarah Gore, came to me this morning and brought me an instrument from the Court of Wells, to perform publick Pennance next Sunday at C. Cary Church for having a child, which

I am to administer to her publickly next Sunday after Divine Service." He was able to report that he duly did so after the sermon on Sunday February 7th. See J. Beresford, op.cit., vol. I, p. 69. Skimmington Riding was often called in the late nineteenth century 'Skimmerton Riding', see for example Castle Cary Visitor, vol. X, 1914-15, p. 122. SRO Q/SR 86/2/55, Evidence 1653; H. Williams, ed., The Poems of Jonathan Swift, Oxford, 1937, vol. I, p. 221.

26. PRO MH12/10573, 21327/72, Report of Dr. Homes on Fever in the Union of Wincanton, 12-16 February 1872; The Brewers Plea, London, 1647, p. 3; H.F.B. Brett-Smith, ed., 'Gammer Gurtons Nedle', by W. Stevenson, Oxford, 1920, p. 18; Register of Bishop Bekynton, SRS, vol. 49, 1934, p. 182; Collectanea, vol. I, Visitation of Religious Houses and Hospitals, 1526, SRS, vol. 39, 1924, pp. 217-8; SRO D/P/brut 13/2/1, Bruton Overseers' Accounts 1653-1678; SRO D/D/cta, Administrators' Accounts W36 and A18; SRO D/P/brut, Bruton Overseers' Accounts 13/2/1 1653-1678, 13/2/2 1678-1687, 13/2/8 1779-1789; D/P/brut 12/2/1, Bruton Constables' Accounts; SRO D/P/brut 4/1/1, 4/1/2, 4/1/3 Churchwardens' Accounts 1735-1874; J. Beresford, Diary, op.cit., vol. I, pp. 174-5; 'Sherborne, Dorchester and Taunton Journal', 22 September 1831; 'Western Flying Post', 30 October 1809; 'Western Gazette', 21 March 1863; 'Western Flying Post', 30 September 1856; Stephen Duck, 'The Thresher's Labour', in Poems on Several Subjects, London, 1730, pp. 24-5.

27. Register of Bishop Bekynton, op.cit., p. 182; SRO Q/ SR 93/143, Evidence 16 May 1658;. For presentments in the Church Courts, see P.W. Randell, Crime, op.cit., esp. pp. 82-104; SRO D/PS/winc 1/1-13, Magistrates' Entry Books; 'Shepton Mallet Journal', 25 July 1862; SRO Q/ SR 234/11, Information 20 November 1704 and Q/SR

236/2-4, Examinations 14 and 27 July 1705; SRO Q/SR 332/2/34, Information 10 April 1764; J. Beresford, Diary, op.cit., vol. I, p. 101.

28. J. Vanes, ed., The Ledger of John Smythe 1538-1550, Historical Manuscripts Commission, J.P. 19, London, 1974, pp. 54, 268; SRO DD/SAS C795 PR 40, Hayward Papers, Churchwarden Accounts of Mere, 1587; J. Beresford, op.cit., vol. I, pp. 62; E.C. Pulbrook, English Country Life and Work, London, 1922, p. 174; SRO Q/SR/63/235, Order of Discharge 1629; 'The Industrious Smith', in Roxburgh Ballads, vol. I, pp. 470-1; R. Jefferies, The Toilers of the Field, London, 1898, p. 101; SRO Q/SR 92/77, Information 14 May 1655; SRO Q/SR 93/216, Information 25 January 1656; SRO DD/ca 97, Ex Officio 31 July 1593; 'Western Flying Post', 16 June 1800. The reference to 'October' is to beer brewed in that month and 'Old Ally Crocker' was a song which had been popular from at least the middle of the eighteenth century. J. Beresford, Diary, op.cit., vol. II, p. 271; D. Macmillan, 'Songs of Somerset', in The Somerset Year-Book, 1922, p. 82-88; Dialect story by Dan'l Grainger in Castle Cary Visitor, vol. VIII, 1910-11, p. 189. For details of Friendly Societies in Bruton, see P.W. Randell, Stones, op.cit., pp. 396-411. 'Shepton Mallet Journal', 25 March 1859; SRO DD/SE 45/1, Petition to the ffeoffees of Sexey's Hospital, Nos. 13 and 29; 'Shepton Mallet Journal', 9 August 1861, 6 January and 21 July1876, 16 April 1869, 27 May 1870, 20 December 1872, 4 January 1884, 30 October 1862; 'Western Flying Post', 2 July 1842; Calendar of State Papers, Domestic, Charles I, 1635, London, 1865, p. 33; Calendar of State Papers, Domestic, 1665-1666, London, 1864, p. 539; Kirkby's Quest for Somerset, SRS, vol. 3, 1889, p. 103; Calendar of Patent Rolls, Philip and Mary, vol. III, 1555-1557, London,

1938, p. 104; Howitt, op.cit., p. 491; SRO Q/SR 11/65-6, Information 1610; SRO D/D/Cd 35, Depositions 1603-1605; Anon., A Dissertation upon Drunkenness, London, 1727, pp. 8-9; Quarter Sessions Records, Charles I, SRS, vol. XXIV, 1908, p. 144; SRO Q/SR 43/138 Licence 15th February 1624.

29. For the role of the Church Ales see M. Moisa and J.M. Bennett, 'Conviviality and Charity', in Past and Present, vol. 154, 1999, pp. 221-242, and J.M. Bennett, 'Conviviality and Charity in Medieval and Early Modern England', in Past and Present, vol.134, 1992, pp. 20-38. For examples of Somerset Church Ales see D. Underwood, Revel, Riot and Rebellion: Popular Politics and Culture in England 1603-1660, Oxford, 1985, pp. 97-8. A.R. Wright, British Calendar Customs, London, 1936, p. 153; SRO D/D/ca 191, Comperta 6 October 1615; Calendar of the Manuscripts of the Dean and Chapter of Wells, vol. II, London, 1914, pp. 264-5, Lettre from the king's Majestie's Commissioners, 1 November 1547.

30. SRO Q/SR 86/107, Examinations 24 February 1653; 'Shepton Mallet Journal', 22 April 1870; SRO D/PS/winc 1/12, Magistrates' Entry Book 1880-1882; 'Western Gazette', 10 July 1881; J. Beresford, Diary, op.cit., vol. I, p. 81; WRO Hoare Papers 383/321, Manor Courts, p. 147; 'Shepton Mallet Journal', 8 November 1867; 'Western Gazette', 12 November 1875; 'Shepton Mallet Journal', 12 November 1880, 11 November 1870, 12 November 1869; 'Western Gazette', 10 November 1876, 12 November 1875, 11 November 1881, 24 October 1890; 'Shepton Mallet Journal', 7 November 1873, 10 November 1876; J. Beresford, Diary, op.cit., vol. I, p. 81; SRO D/PS/winc 1/3, Magistrates' Entry Book 1859-1863; Castle Cary Visitor, vol. III, 1900-1, p. 85; C. Clark, Diary, op.cit., 3 October 1899 p. 234 and 6 November 1899 p. 236 as 5 November was a Sunday.

31. The Diurnal of Thomas Rugg, 1659-1661, Camden Society, Third Series, vol. 91, 1961, p. 179; J. Beresford, Diary, op.cit., vol. I, p. 86; 'Western Flying Post', 13 May 1856; 'Sherborne, Dorchester and Taunton Journal', 22 September 1831; 'Sherborne Journal', 5 July 1838; Castle Cary Visitor, vol. IV, 1902-3, p. 69; J. Beresford, Diary, op.cit., vol. I, p. 89; 'Western Gazette', 17 June 1887; C. Clark, Diary, op.cit., entries for 19, 21, 22 June 1897, p.197; Castle Cary Visitor, vol. I, 1896-7, p. 152; 'Shepton Mallet Journal', 20 March 1863; Sweetman's Monthly Illustrated Journal, vol. 2, July 1872; 1699 reference cited in Castle Cary Visitor, vol. VI, 1906-7, p. 138; 'Somerset and Wilts Journal', 13 September 1856; 'Shepton Mallet Journal', 2 August 1867.

32. SRO Q/SR 196/15-16, Information 25 July 1694; SRO DD/JO/26, Parish Accounts, pp.70-1, 212, 73; The Register of Bishop Bekynton, op.cit., vol. 49, p. 180; for Apprenticeship Indentures, see for example, SRO DD/SE/46; F.W. Weaver, 'Foundation Deed of Bruton School', in SDNQ, vol. 3, 1892-3, p. 245; T.D. Tremlett, 'The Sixteenth Century Articles of King's School, Bruton', in SANHSP, 1948-9, vol. 94, p. 90; SRO DD/BRU 2/1/1, Governors' Account Book 1679-1750; B. Wright, op.cit., pp. 7, 10, 11; J. Beresford, Diary, op.cit., vol. I, pp. 37, 48, 76; Parish Accounts, op.cit., pp. 209 and 212; Magistrates' Entry Book, op.cit., 28 March 1881; Winstanley, Diary, op.cit., vol. 3, p. 108, vol. 5, p. 142; H. Phillips, Journey to Nowhere, London, 1960, p. 58; J. Lello, Centenary History of Sexey's School Bruton, Shaftesbury, undated but 1991, p. 10; 'Shepton Mallet Journal', 20 March 1863; Castle Cary Visitor, vol. VI, 1906-7, p. 177; Parish Accounts, op.cit., p. 201; 'Western Flying Post', 30 May 1814; 'Shepton Mallet Journal', 2 November 1860; C. Clark, Dairy, op.cit., 15, 25 December 1890 p. 82; 'Western Gazette', 6 January

1888; C. Clark, Diary, op.cit., 5 February 1894 p. 134, 28 February 1894 p. 135, 28 February 1896 p.171; Winstanley, Diary, op.cit., vol. 4, p. 208.

33. SRO D/D/Ca 140, Metropolitan Visitation, 1605; SRO D/D/Ca 85, Ex officio 1588-90; Register of Bishop John de Drokensford, SRS, vol. I, 1887, p. 45; T. Hall, Funebria Florae, the Downfall of the May Games, London, 1661, p. 13; Gentleman's Magazine, vol. LXVIII, 1797, pt. II, p. 125; Howitt, op.cit., p. 414; I. Watts, 'Against Idleness and Mischief', in D.N. Smith, The Oxford Book of Eighteenth Century Verse, Oxford, 1926, p. 57; Hannah Moore cited in R.W. Malcolmson, Popular Recreations in English Society 1700-1850, Cambridge, 1973, p. 103; W. Booth, In Darkest England and the Way Out, London, 1890, p. 47; Report of the Select Committee on Drunkenness, PP 1834 VIII, p. viii; K. Wrightson, 'Alehouses, Order and Reformation in Rural England 1590-1660', in E. and S. Yeo, ed., Popular Culture and Class Conflict 1590-1914, Brighton, 1981, p. 21; SRO Q/SR 299/17-19, 7 and 11 May 1731; 'Sherborne Mercury', 12 September 1738; SRO Q/SR 332/4/30, Conviction 10 January 1789; SRO D/P/brut 13/2/5, Bruton Overseers' Accounts 1726-1748; 'Somerset and Wiltshire Journal', 8 September 1860; 'Shepton Mallet Journal', 26 February 1864; Sweetman's Monthly Illustrated Journal, vol. I, January 1871; 'Western Gazette, 15 December 1882; Sweetman's Monthly, op.cit., vol. 2, April 1872, and vol. 3 July 1873 gives an account of the principles behind Good Templarism and its activities. Somerset Visitor: A Monthly Temperance Magazine, No. 18, January 1889; 'Western Gazette', 25 February, 13 May, 17 June 1887.

34. For an account of Friendly Societies in Bruton, see P.W. Randell, Stones, op.cit., pp. 396-410; SRO A/DBR/10, Rules of Bruton Friendly Society, p. 8; 'Western Gazette',

14 June 1889; C. Clark, Diary, op.cit., 20 December 1894 p. 148; 'Shepton Mallet Journal', 29 May 1863; 'Western Gazette', 14 June 1878; C. Clark, Diary, op.cit., 19 May 1891 p. 88; 'Shepton Mallet Journal', 28 October 1864; 'Western Gazette', 30 September 1881, 6 October 1882, 22 October 1864; C. Clark, Diary, op.cit., 22 October 1894 p. 145; 'Shepton Mallet Journal', 15 October 1886, 22 June 1859; 'Western Flying Post, 13 March 1866; Castle Cary Visitor, vol. IV, 1902-3, p. 50; Report from the Select Committee on the Labouring Poor (Allotments of Land),1843, PP 1843 VII, p. 18: Evidence of Captain George Scobell, R.N.; SRO DD/ BT/27/6, Surveyor's Note Book 1823; Report of the Poor Law Commissioners, 1834, PP 1834 XXX, Appendix BI, Answers to Rural Queries, pt. I, p. 399; 'Western Flying Post', 28 December 1840, 27 December 1841; Report from the Select Committee on Small Holdings, 1890, PP 1890 XVII, pp. 354-376; 'Western Gazette', 16 October 1870.

35. 'Shepton Mallet Journal', 9 and 23 September 1859, 28 February and 7 March 1879; 'Western Gazette', 6 May 1881; P. Bailey, Leisure and Class in Victorian England, London, 1978, p. 121; 'Shepton Mallet Journal', 31 July 1863; ibid. 18 June 1875, 20 June 1862. For more details on the 1861 Choir Trip to Weymouth, see C. Clark, Tales from Old Bruton, Charldon Publications, 1998, p. 42. 'Western Gazette', 21 August 1891; ibid., 29 August 1890; ibid., 19 June 1891; 'Somerset and Wilts Journal', 13 September 1856; 'Shepton Mallet Journal', 2 August 1867; 'Western Gazette', 18 October 1889; PRO Ed.7/104, Preliminary Statement of Income and Expenditure, 1853; The Wincanton, Castle Cary and Bruton Monthly Review, November 1893; Somerset Education Committee Reports, 1898-9, pp. 7, 13, 24 and 1899-1900, pp. 7-9; Howitt, op.cit., p. 510; 'Western

Gazette', 14 and 28 October 1898; J.M.Golby and A.W. Purdue, The Civilization of the Crowd: Popular Culture in England 1750-1900, London, 1984, p. 190; Rowntree and Kendall, How the Labourer Lives, London, 1913, p. 313; Western Flying Post', 21 April 1800; 'Sherborne and Yeovil Mercury', 29 April 1843; C. Clark, Dairy, op.cit., 22 June 1897 p. 197, 14 October 1897, p. 202, 29 July 1898 p. 216.